POWER and INEQUALITY
in Interpersonal Relations

POWER and INEQUALITY in Interpersonal Relations

Vladimir Shlapentokh
Eric Beasley

Transaction Publishers

New Brunswick (U.S.A.) and London (U.K.)

Library of Congress Catalog Number: 2014024592
ISBN: 978-1-4128-5566-2
Printed in the United States of America

Library of Congress Cataloging-in-Publication Data

Shlapentokh, Vladimir.
    Power and inequality in interpersonal relations / Vladimir Shlapentokh, Eric Beasley.
        pages cm
    Includes bibliographical references and index.
    ISBN 978-1-4128-5566-2
 1. Interpersonal relations. 2. Power (Social sciences) 3. Equality. I. Beasley, Eric. II. Title.
HM1106.S537 2015
303.3--dc23
                                                          2014024592

Contents

Preface

This book explicates the interpersonal situations in which weak or vulnerable people find themselves and the ways in which others help create, sustain, and eradicate such social dynamics. It is not a book about relations between people with different social positions, races, genders, ages, places of residences, etc. confronting each other in political, macro-economic, and cultural battles. It is not a book about people who oppress and exploit "others" from long distances—conceptual and actual—without seeing them, such as heads of government agencies or big corporations. It is a book about the people who become the victims of those whom they know personally, who are their relatives, friends, and even lovers; who are their colleagues and neighbors; who stay in the same ward in a hospital and sit together in the same class or play sports on the same teams. It is about those who bring harm—to use the terminology of Lois Presser—to the people whom they supposedly have to love and help. As numerous data show, people are often victimized by those familiar to them (DeKeseredy 2011).

People cannot live without "others"—human beings are social animals—but these "others," while often helpful, are sometimes the source of great suffering. Ultimately, we will try to prove that people can gain power over each other and then abuse this power because of an initial condition of inequality of resources among them—wealth or physical strength, intellectual capacity and information, sexual attractiveness, etc. We will pay particular attention to the role of the relative availability of resources vis-à-vis weak and vulnerable people. It is important to note that those who are powerful in one or another respect in interpersonal relations are also able to skirt surveillance and in this way add another layer to their victims' helplessness.

The origin and plight of the weak and vulnerable people who suffer for various reasons is one of the most important contemporary problems. It is as dramatic and, at times, as tragic in rich democratic nations as it is in poorer and/or nondemocratic societies. The fate of these people was at the center of political discourse during the 2000s in the United States and Europe, and during the 2012 American presidential campaign. The case of weak and vulnerable people has serious political, economic, and social implications for society.

To use Pierre Bourdieu's terminology, there are two "fields," each of which contains their own categories of weak and vulnerable people (Grenfell 2012).

In macro space, individuals with a relative deprivation of resources interact with societal institutions and their representatives; these can help, pester, and/or exploit them. This category of weak people includes the unemployed, illegal immigrants or undocumented workers, sick people, victims of crime, people who are discriminated against in society for racial, ethnic, cultural or political reasons, people without medical insurance, and homeless people, among many others. Of course, weak people need not only be victims of circumstance. They can also, at times, be seen as responsible for their lack of necessary resources (e.g., chronic drunkards or addicted people).

In micro space, which exists inside social units (e.g., in a family, office, college, army unit, romantic relationship, sports team, or psychiatric ward), people can be the object of an abuse of power by another. The abusers possess a relatively large amount of key resources compared to those whom they abuse: more social prestige, a bigger social network, more money, better health, more physical strength and sex appeal, etc. In some cases, an individual, for example an unemployed person, can be abused by society at the macro level as well as by his or her family on the micro level.[1]

The interactions of "weak" and "vulnerable" people with larger society have been well documented (see, for example, Bromley 2012 or Shi and Stevens 2010). For the purposes of this book, we will focus on the less-studied dynamics surrounding the resources of poor people in micro space. We will identify the uneven distribution of resources such as physical strength, wealth, and status, which leads to the abuse of power within various social institutions. The role of resources in the lives of weak and vulnerable people is clearly seen in the case of a woman and her children seeking safety and a type of asylum in shelters. Women and their children come to shelters deprived of all sorts of resources, including financial, nutritional, and educational. They are also, as a rule, socially isolated.

The dependence of weak, resource-poor people on stronger, resource-rich people is pivotal. We believe that inequality in the distribution of resources among the members of social units is the main cause of conflict inside all types of social units, and ultimately produces situations where members of a social unit can abuse other members of the same unit. We have realized that the distribution of resources inside social units is a neglected theme in contemporary social science. It is rather amazing that while many illustrious authors have engaged in so-called group dynamics, intra-group conflicts, and interpersonal relations, they almost completely skirt the issue of the distribution of resources inside groups or units. Among other things, they do not understand that almost all socially valuable resources (e.g., wealth or prestige) are limited or scarce. Emotional resources such as cooperativeness or friendship should also be treated as scarce (Anderson and Kilduff 2009).

Even those scholars who deal with the study of status in social groups have avoided analyzing the "objective" distribution of resources within a group as a crucial factor in determining the relative places of the individuals comprising the group (Berger, Cohen, and Zelditch 1972). They have also ignored the idea that each characteristic of each member of the group has meaning only in relation to the characteristics of other members (e.g., someone is only rich relative to some other person being poor). It is meaningless to talk about the leadership skills of a member of an organization without comparing his or her skills with those of others. This means it is necessary to consider the proportion of the possession of the sum of a given resource held by each individual within a social unit. Being the person with all of the money comes with more power than being the person with half of the money, even if the latter half is larger than the former whole.

Remarkably, in his well-known book *Violence*, prominent sociologist Randall Collins's (2009) explanation of why weak people are vulnerable does not mention the difference in the amount of resources possessed by perpetrators and victims. Instead, he focuses on the "fear" that emerges in certain moments of interpersonal socialization. He asserts that "the victim cannot defend him or herself . . . chiefly because it allows the aggressor to take the initiative and control over the process and direction of mutual estrangement seminal." Ignoring the crucial factor resources play in determining violence, Collins (2009) focuses on the immediate idiosyncratic sociospatial environment.

The key mistake of many human relations studies is their dogmatic belief that the control of resources, and the subsequent power such possession yields, is only concentrated in the upper echelons of the macro-social hierarchy. Thus, we hear about the upper class, the 1 percent, the working class, the 99 percent, the disparity between CEO salaries and that of the average workers in their companies, the increasing polarization of wealth, etc. Magazines publish stories rating the world's richest people, the world's most powerful people, and the world's sexiest people. While macro space is ripe for this analysis of the disparity of resources, so is the less-studied uneven distribution of resources and power found within individual social units. A college roommate may have had a preponderance of resources at his disposal throughout his life, and be a bearer of power who possesses the ability to abuse his relatively resource-depleted roommates, even if the overarching demographic variables and past history of the individuals place them in a very similar position in larger society. Proletarians abuse other proletarians, black people who have been discriminated against by larger society abuse other blacks (e.g., for acting "too white"), Jewish victims of anti-Semitism abuse other Jews, the victims of an earthquake abuse other earthquake victims (e.g., by looting their homes). Being a victim in one realm does not prevent a person from being cruel to others in different realms.

Within families, there are two categories of people who generally depend on others due to a lack of resources at their disposal, which puts them at risk of being abused: women and children. Of course, any and all types of individuals may be susceptible to abuse if they draw the short end of the resource stick. Many men and adults are abused within the family structure; however, the abuse of women and children in this setting occurs much more frequently. Although there is a deeply heated debate as to the cause of women's physical weakness in comparison to men—cultural, biological, both, or other—the fact remains that 85 percent of the victims of domestic violence are women.

Perpetrators of domestic violence in families, whether rich or poor, educated or not, take advantage of their physical power resources and exploit their (usually female) partner's comparative lack of strength. The uneven distribution of physical strength, as well as material resources, such as income, allows men to exploit—using direct or indirect intimidation or the threat of it—weaker women for status within the family in order to receive personal services (food, laundry, sexual favors, etc.)

and gain psychological benefits, including the fulfillment of sadomasochistic sexual desire.

The character of the relations—the intensity and frequency of abuse and/or mutual help found inside social units—is an important ingredient in estimating one's quality of life. In *Mismeasuring Our Lives,* Stiglitz, Sen, and Foutossi (2010) strongly argue against the overestimation of the role of economic indicators in determining life satisfaction. In fact, these authors implicitly call for a resurgence of interest in the "quality of life" concept, which was born in the late '60s and was popular in the '70s before falling mostly out of fashion in the sociological literature (most publications on the quality of life in the '80s and '90s were devoted to subgroups, such as old and/or sick people), only to surge again in the early 2000s (Nussnaum and Sen 1993[2]; Parsons 1977[3]).

While our main focus here is on illuminating the relationship between disparate resource possession and the potential for abuses of power within social units, another goal of this project is to investigate how society and its institutions—nationally, regionally, and locally—protect weak, vulnerable people. People who are relatively weak in macro and/or micro space get help from various sources: private individuals (e.g., a wealthy grandparent), local groups (e.g., LGBT advocacy groups), and governmental agencies (e.g., Medicaid), among others. We try to offer the readers an illustration of the inclusionary mechanisms people and society use to help the weak and vulnerable.

There are many informative issues that are tangential to our focus. For example, has the number of people being deprived of necessary resources been growing, declining, or remaining steady over the last several years in the United States? While we will mention statistics related to this question in context, our major focus is not to explicate the specific relationships among these variables. So, while it is helpful to know how many battered women take refuge in shelters—this gives us an idea of the scope, frequency, and severity of some of the dynamics we examine—we will not delve into what these numbers say about the total number of women battered in society, the percentage who seek asylum in homes, or cross-sections of these based on race, age, location, etc.

Ultimately, we will not take up the task of determining if our increased awareness of weak people in society is due to better monitoring, increased chances for people to speak out, an actual increase in the total number of weak people, some combination of these, or none of these (a similar problem faces those who study the dynamics of autistic children: is the increase in the number of children diagnosed with autism due to more vigilance, more inclusive definitions, actual increases, or something else?).

The first part of the book is devoted to the theoretical issues that are raised by the study of weak people inside social units. The second part is devoted to specific resources whose unequal distribution inside social units leads to the abuse of power by one of its members over another. In the third part, we will discuss how society tries to protect weak people inside social units.

Notes

1. The *British Office of the Public Guardian* defines abuse as "a violation of an individual's human and civil rights by another person or persons. Abuse may consist of a single act or repeated acts. It may be physical, verbal or psychological, it may be an act of neglect or an omission to act, or it may occur when a vulnerable person is persuaded to enter into a financial or sexual transaction to which he or she has not consented, or cannot consent. Abuse can occur in any relationship and may result in significant harm to, or exploitation of, the person subjected to it.

2. This book was an exception in the early 1990s.

3. Regarding the differences between Hobbes and Locke, see, among numerous other publications, Melossi 1990, Burger 1997, and Shlapentokh 2003.

References

DeKeseredy, Walter S. 2011. "Feminist Contributions to Understanding Woman Abuse: Myths, Controversies, and Realities." *Aggression and Violent Behavior,* 16:297–302.

Anderson, Cameron and Gavin J. Kilduff. 2009. "The Pursuit of Status in Social Groups." *Current Directions in Psychological Science,* 18(5):295–8.

Berger, Joseph, Bernard P. Cohen and Morris Zelditch, Jr. 1972. "Status Characteristics and Social Interaction." *American Sociological Review,* 37(3):241–55.

Burger, Thomas. 1997. "Talcott Parsons, the Problem of Order in Society, and the Program of an Analytical Sociology." *American Journal of Sociology,* 83(2):320–39.

Bromley, David. 2012. *Vulnerable People, Vulnerable States: Redefining the Development Challenge.*

Collins, Randal. 2009. *Violence: A Micro-Sociological Theory.* Princeton, NJ: Princeton University Press, 135–6.

Grenfell, Michael, ed. 2012. *Pierre Bourdieu: Key Concepts.* Durham, UK: Acumen, 65–80.

Melossi, Dario.1990. *The State of Social Control: A Sociological Study of Concepts of State and Social Control in the Making of Democracy.* New York: St. Martin Press, 17–21.

Nussbaum, Martha, and Amartya Sen, eds. 1993. *Quality of Life (Wider Studies in Development Economics)*. New York: Oxford University Press.

Parsons, Talcott. 1977. *Social Systems and the Evolution of Action Theory*. New York: Free Press.

Shlapentokh, Vladmir. 2003. "Hobbes and Locke at Odds in Putin's Russia." *Europe-Asia Studies*, 55(7):981–1007.

Shlapentokh, Vladimir. 2006. *Fear in Contemporary Society: Its Negative and Positive Effects*. New York: Palgrave Macmillan.

Shi, Leiyu and Gregory D. Stevens. 2010. *Vulnerable Populations in the United States*. San Francisco, CA: Jossey-Bass.

Stiglitz, Joseph, Amartya Sen and Jean-Paul Fitoussi. 2010. *Mismeasuring Our Lives: Why GDP Doesn't Add Up*. New York: The New Press, 62.

Acknowledgment

We would like to express our gratitude to Larry Busch, who was immensely helpful to our forming of the major arguments of this book. We are also very thankful to Natalia Shushkova who helped us with her Russian perspective on the main perspectives of the book. Additionally, we want to express our gratitude to Craig Harris, who organized a very useful debate on this project at a seminar at Michigan State University. We also want to send our thanks to the anonymous reviewer of our text whose sharp and witty comments helped us improve the book.

Along with their dedicated work on their coauthored chapters, Shikha Bista, Shelby Bierwagen, and Jeff Oliver also helped in doing a lot of the little things that are needed in a book project. Sierra Johnson helped in this regard as well. We deeply appreciate all of their work.

Last, our special gratitude goes to Judy Spanogle, whose editing and various comments greatly improved the quality of the manuscript.

Vladimir Shlapentokh and Eric Beasley

1

Weak People and Dependence on Others

BELLUM OMNIUM CONTRA OMNES INSIDE EACH SOCIAL UNIT[1]

Since the eighteenth century, the enduring struggle between the Hobbesian and Lockean perspectives has taken place in the arena of political and economic development, through a lens calibrated to see society at the macro level (see Parsons 1977; Burger 1997).

The debates between the two theoretical perspectives mostly deal with the interactions between the government and its subjects, between rivals of social, economic, and/or political actors—such as the barons of the Middle Ages—or between contemporary multinational mega-corporations and their competitors and naysayers. In fact, Hobbes applied his famous formula *"homo hominem lupus est,"* which charac-terizes the menacing relationship between men in their most natural state almost exclusively to big politics. The conflicts among ordinary people inside social and political units—in the family, inside the feu-dal estate, in the city, and in the peasant community—were outside of Hobbes's interests. Hobbes wrote nothing on either the issue of people's security inside social units or the abuse of power between people who essentially belonged to the same social or political class.

Weak People as a Concept

In this project, we take on the task of analyzing the social condition of the special class of people whom we will name "weak people"—those who lack the resources to defend themselves against others within social units. Social scientists such as Zygmunt Bauman (2001) or Johnatan Litelle were inclined to use the term *weakness* in the same sense we do, whereas the American media and mainstream society opt for political correctness, using the label *vulnerable people*.

There are two radically different approaches to the definition of weak, or vulnerable, people. One of them, the "genetic" or "anthropological" approach, describes weak people as those who were born (or became) unable to survive in this world without the help of "strong" people who are entitled to command over these not-so-fortunate members of society. Another approach—we call it the "resource" view (this view most closely approximates the authors' viewpoint)—sees weak people as the product of various circumstances that deprive them of certain resources, without which they become dependent on others and exposed to abuses of power in both the macro and micro worlds. The most renowned theorist of the first approach was, of course, Friedrich Nietzsche.

Nietzsche and his followers never gave a sociologically clear definition of "weak people," using several other terms including the masses, slaves, crowds, or herds. These were all terms they used to delineate the object of their contempt. Nietzsche described them as making up the majority of the population. He asserted that they were pessimistic and cynical, and that, using their numerical majority, "the slaves" were able to convince "the masters" that their weakness was not chosen by them but imposed on them from the outside by "evil." Nietzsche (2003) demanded the segregation of "healthy people," the masters, from "sick people" because the healthy can confound themselves with the sick if they observed their morals. According to Nietzsche (1973), weak people used Christian morality, which was also invented by them, in order to impose the importance of humility, charity, pity, and equality on society. Nietzsche hated the state mostly because it usually became the instrument of the slaves. For the same reason, much of Nietzsche's hatred of democracy lays in his conviction that, because of their numerical majority, weak people could force society and the state to serve their interests—so close to the heart of today's Tea Party activists. Nietzsche (1999) preached the creation of a new aristocracy, consisting of supermen who would be totally different from "the crowd."

The deeply antidemocratic and antiegalitarian spirit of Nietzsche was accepted by Josè Ortega y Gasset in his book *The Rebellion of the Masses* (1929). Ortega y Gasset insisted on illuminating the imposition of the values of the barbaric masses on everybody who tried to be excellent, individual, and original. Ortega y Gasset's (1994) "mass man" took his convenient life for granted without being grateful to the creative people who provided it. Ortega y Gasset called these men who took without gratitude "spoilt children." The masses, affirmed Ortega y

Gasset (1994), imagined "their role [was] limited to demanding these benefits peremptorily, as if they were natural rights." The author continued writing about "the sovereignty of the unqualified individual, the idea that democratic procedures [were] put at the service of the masses, who can satisfy their needs without thinking about the future" (13–14).

The famous hater of "weak people," Ayn Rand, essentially repeated Ortega y Gasset. Rand (1966) argued that weak people can survive (temporarily) only by looting the goods created by others. In fact, the main pathos of Rand's major books is an echo of this slogan in the form of the uncompromising condemnation of "unearned income," one of the most frequently used terms in *Atlas Shrugged* and in many of the publications created in the iconic novel's wake. Still, for the first time in the history of law, it was the Bolsheviks who introduced the concept of a societal "parasite"—much earlier than Ayn Rand, who was likely influenced by them (she was born in Russia and left the country in 1926)—and who severely persecuted those who did not earn their income.

Rand (1961) described everybody who did not have their own income, and/or who was not engaged in production, as the "bums, the loafers, the moochers we saw all around us" (119). This phrase was widely used by Rand's heroes. Her supermen did not want to make the distinction between those who were unwilling and those who were unable to work ("what difference did that make to us?" exclaimed one of Rand's heroes) (Rand 1961). The famous character John Galt, whom Rand assigned to express her views on the world, used speech that scared readers into believing that helping others would degrade society, destroy its moral compass, and make people vicious and envious. Galt proclaimed, with great pomposity, that it was highly immoral to enjoy anything that you did not earn. Cursing "sacrifices," Galt made no distinction between healthy and sick people, between adults and children, between unemployed and employed (Rand 1961, 156, 161).

Contrary to the views described above, we do not equate "weak people" with the materially poor or only with those holding subordinate positions in a hierarchy. The main objects of this book are those weak people who reside inside social units: family, the office, school, the hospital, and the army. The typology of people as "weak" and "non-weak" does not coincide with traditional stratifications-based social criteria such as wealth, public status, or education, and is not based on ethnic, racial and cultural principles, even if it does overlap with them in some ways. While the traditional stratifications can be considered vertical, we will treat the stratifications based on weakness as horizontal.

As a matter of fact, there is a legion of weak people among the members of the highest strata of population. We find weak people among the very rich, among those with the highest social standing, and among those with the highest educations, as well as among people belonging to the dominant racial, ethnic, and cultural groups. But, of course, whatever criterion of stratification is used, weak people are a higher proportion of those who belong to the lowest strata of the population. The weak are found among abused spouses and children, in both rich and poor families; humiliated employees, CEOs, and rank and file workers; abused residents in hospitals; younger siblings; and the elite's servants and employees, even if their salary is high relative to the macro norms of their area.

Class and Humanistic Morals

Interest in the inequality that stems from belonging to different large classifications, and the lack of interest in the inequality inside social units, reflect two different moral positions: one based on class, whatever the interpretation of that term may be, and another on humanistic values.

In some ways, Nietzsche and his followers' attitudes toward strong and weak people turned out to be similar to the Marxist view on the division of society. Unsurprisingly, before the revolution, Nietzsche was very popular in Russia among socialists such as writer Maxim Gorky. Nietzsche, Marx, and particularly Lenin, talked about leaders who possessed truth and acted ethically as well as those who were blind and moved by petty, everyday interests. Nietzsche and Marx held so-called humanistic morals and religion in contempt and were deeply indifferent to bourgeois or existential issues such as death and sickness and relations between children and parents. Remarkably, as soon as the ideological pressure weakened following Stalin's death, the Soviet liberal intelligentsia were deeply hostile to Nietzsche's cult of "masters" (it reminded them of the cult of their leaders) and to Marx's class approach, with its hostility to other human problems.

Advancing humanistic values at the fore of public interests, the Russian intellectuals of the 1960s not only published poetry and novels about life inside their families or offices but also offered high praise for Western authors for describing the feelings of ordinary people in ordinary situations. Of the Americans, they liked Hemingway, Faulkner, and Salinger; of the Russians, they liked Dostoyevsky and Bunin, both of whom had not previously enjoyed the sympathy of Soviet ideologues (Shlapentokh 1990).

With their focus on classic social inequality, American liberal authors, except for some feminists, have followed Soviet patterns, concentrating their attention on the suffering of people deprived of material resources relative to society at large, and have not been explicitly interested in the tribulations of people suffering from the various inequalities that exist inside materially secure families or in prestigious schools and colleges.

Modernist Sociology and Vulnerable People: Individualization

Postmodernist sociology is another theoretical school that shifts society's responsibility for the existence of weak or vulnerable people and contributes to the neglect of this issue in modern social science. It downgrades the role of the material basis of social relations and upgrades the power and importance of mental processes in society. This theme is particularly clear in the writings of such European sociologists as Habermas, Luchmann, and Ulrich Beck. They focus on information and communication as the major bricks of society, and on the individual who creates—and does not merely obey, as was the popular notion of past paradigms—the rules of the social game (Beck and Beck-Gernsheim 2002). This shift relegates the role of the distribution of resources to the bin of social theory history. As Zygmunt Bauman (2001), a great enthusiast of the "individualization" concept, suggested, people today are responsible for all their problems.[2] Rejecting solidarity in social life as an outmoded phenomenon and expressing high skepticism for the family and other humanities, Ulrich Beck places the individual fully in command of all the troubles in his or her life.

We, of course, operate with weak or vulnerable people as relative terms. It is meaningless to talk about the absolutely vulnerable or weak person apart from context. Weakness is only defined as such when it is compared to, and interacting with, strength. A single person need not be weak or strong in every attribute in every context. Still, the fluidity of these variables, and the ontological necessity of their entanglement, does not negate their importance. As discussed, these dynamics, no doubt, influence quality of life.

Sociological literature, particularly in its liberal and radical leftist-leaning manifestations of theory, focuses on a different, yet very important, issue: how the dominant class or ruling elite, in general, not only exploits its "legal status" to enjoy power over others but often abuses its power to get illegal benefits (or to make its nefarious actions legal). But this literature pays much less attention to the plight of a considerable part of the population, who suffer inside social units despite their normally dominant wealth, race, and social status in macro space. The people who suffer abuse within the social unit may even be among the people who dole out abuse outside of the social unit. Thus, the poorest member of the country club might regularly be on the receiving end of other members' taunts and jeers but may also wield the same tactics against his own family, where he is the wealthiest one (Smith and Hurley-Smith 2009).[3]

Fear in Interpersonal Relations

The disregard shown for the issue of weak people as a product of the relations inside social units is deeply connected with the neglect of another issue: fear (Shlapentokh 2006). In fact, the members of most social units live in a state of fear that varies in degrees of intensity. Even the few who do not deny the extreme influence of Hobbessian fear on public life tend to ignore its importance in interpersonal relations, focusing instead on its role in macro space. Such authors as Joseph Stiglitz, Amartya Sen, and Jean-Paul Fitoussi (2010)—all of whom have paid more attention than others to the role of human relations in determining people's quality of life—omitted the micro world of fear and unbalanced resources creating friction in everyday life. So, in talking of "personal security" as a factor of quality of life, they only discussed the danger of being victimized in macro space and did not utter a single word about personal security and abuse inside social units (Stiglitz, Sen, and Fitoussi 2010).

Meanwhile, it is well known that most rapes and murders are not performed by strangers to the victim and/or by people of different socioeconomic status but rather by acquaintances of the victims, very often family members (Sanchez 2012). In fact, a person in the United States is more than three times as likely to be murdered by a family member, friend, or acquaintance as by a stranger, and about three times more likely to be raped by someone familiar to them than by someone they don't know (Ruane and Cerulo 2012).

Some social units can be considered protective institutions against the fear people encounter in "big society." The family is a good example. In a totalitarian society, the family can be considered as a single shield against the various state agencies working to supervise the minds and bodies of the people (e.g., the police, schools, colleges, or assemblies of people in residential areas). While not without merit, ascribing to the family to serve this function too much is problematic, as the family is also fertile ground for inner power differentials, fear (even fear of being ratted on to a totalitarian regime by family members), abuse, and dependency. These dynamics are also present in life inside an office or college. We are not only referring to "the collective" in a totalitarian society here, which was and is a faithful watcher of the state. Even in a democratic society, the fear of being atheist, or pro-Communist, or a critic of political correctness or political policy—the subject of fear varies but is always present—permeates in the office or school setting and makes people afraid of being cast in the role of outcast and victim (Shlapentokh and Beasley 2013).

Abuse of Power in Interpersonal Relations

The great role fear plays in the lives of members of a social unit ultimately lies in the unequal distribution of resources and power within the unit. Again, the mainstream typically deals with power only in the study of macro society. The most obvious repositories of power in this sphere are governments, corporations, and various political and religious institutions. Thus, the conflicts generated by power relations inside smaller social units are, as a rule, ignored.

Referring to the theory of power advanced by Lukes (2005) (and earlier by Bachrach and Baratz [1970]), we can describe abuse of power in interpersonal relations as conveying a "covert" dimension of power. Indeed, only rarely do those who use power for the exploitation of people in their social unit explicitly proclaim their right to do it, as is done by people who represent state agencies or corporations. Consider some of the comments we have heard of husbands, after inflicting physical abuse, telling their wives: "you deserve this," "look at what you made me do," "this is for your own good," "I'm only doing this because I love you," etc.; the same dynamic occurs during child abuse.

Those who are involved in the use of the leftist concept of "empowering"—the process of getting power by minorities—are somewhat close to shedding light on the dynamics involved in the dependence of one person on another inside a social unit and the abuse of power it allows (Blanchard, Carlos, and Randolph 2001; Sadan 1997; Smith and Hurley-Smith 2009). Oftentimes, empowering is a way for a marginalized person within a social unit to attach to other similarly marginalized people in other social units and, together, encourage/help each other to fight the coerced acceptance of the hegemonic ideology purported by the resource-rich and powerful.

The work of Pierre Bourdieu, a sort of neo-Marxist scholar, provides a good example of the way a meaningful and insightful analysis on human relations can avoid the issue of power and subjugation within social groups. Using the concept of social space, he supposes that only economic and cultural capital separate people from each other. For Bourdieu (1998), members of the same group who possess similar economic and cultural capital tend to have the same habitus: "dispositions, values, tastes" (6). He makes no distinction between disparately positioned people inside social units within the same chunk of macro social space (Bourdieu 2000). Amusingly, Bourdieu cites the pension Vauquer in Balzac's *Le Pere Goriot* as an example in which "the settings" (cultural capital) make all of the members of this place similar, forgetting that the novel is full of conflicts among "agents," to use Bourdieu's terms, inside the institution, albeit with the same style of life and language. The immense volume edited by Bourdieu—*The Weight of the World: Social Suffering in Contemporary Society* (1993)—almost completely ignores those "sufferings" born inside of social or ethnic groups. The authors of the volume, like many other social scientists who have written about weak and vulnerable people, assume that these people only have troubles because of injustices in the big world (Bourdieu 2000).

However, even this traditional approach, with its focus on differences between people identified within macro society, obscures the conflicts inside of social units. Take the concept of the middle class, for example. With such broad and ambiguous coverage, this concept denigrates social analysis by cloaking many of the differences and conflicts in society.

The ultimate origin of all problems generating unequal distributions of resources inside social units lies in the need for people to cooperate with each other within the framework of organizations, and not strictly through the market mechanism—the libertarian dream. People with different amounts of individual resources have to coexist with one another, and the dependence of one person on another is an unavoidable necessity, which is an anarchist's nightmare.

Dependence—A Way to Vulnerability?

In many cases, the dependence of one individual on others, which often leads to an abuse of power, brings the dependent person material and psychological benefits, including security (Bauman 2001, 41–42).

Throughout history, people have given up their independence and freedom for personal and familial security. In the Middle Ages, particularly between the seventh and ninth centuries, commendation was a key institution. It supposed the voluntary submission of small land owners to the feudal lord in exchange for protection. Commendation was one of the factors that accounted for the emergence of the serf class. Those who fell under the protection of the lord paid him regularly in the form of goods, work on the lord's land (the famous corvée), or military service. Dependence, with its security- and stability-enhancing benefits, was so appreciated by slaves and serfs that some of them protested against their liberation amid fears of independence bringing great insecurity and unwanted decision-making responsibilities.

In contemporary society, whether in post-Soviet Russia (Shlapentokh and Woods 2007) or even in America (Shlapentokh and Woods 2011), many people view their dependence on somebody who will protect them as being beneficial, and they are ready to pay a price for this by taking humiliation and many other manifestations of abuses of power (Eisenstadt and Roniger 1984). People's dependence on others, which facilitates abuses of power, cannot be reduced to dependence based solely on wealth, race, and/or gender. The unequal possession of factors, such as a person's physical strength and health, access to information and intellect, sexual attraction, and networks of friends, divides people. Those with a lot of these resources are depended on by those with less, the weak and vulnerable people. In this book, we are only dealing with a person's dependence on his or her personal relationships, leaving aside all other forms of human dependence: on culture and traditions; on ideology; on civil society, government, and its institutions; on substances; on the geographical milieu, etc.

The American who proudly thinks of himself as a free person is limited in his behavior by innumerable regulations of government and society (Shlapentokh and Beasley 2013). However, this individual is also constrained in his interpersonal conduct with others through power dynamics. Additionally, he can be dependent on such substances as drugs, alcohol, nicotine, caffeine, Big Macs, and pornography. These substances can be treated as a sort of anonymous "other" that regularly abuses addicted/dependent persons.

Some categories of dependency that are accompanied by maltreatment have been relatively well studied in social science. Among them are children who suffer at the hands of their parents (i.e., child abuse) as well as the elderly; both of these groups have been heavily studied in psychology and medicine (Williamson 2012). However, in personal relations, dependence on substances has generally drawn more attention than dependence on other people (Peabody 2006).[4]

Studying the interactions and interdependence of people is fundamental to social science. However, scholars have viewed the dependence of "others" in micro interactions (especially those within the same social strata) in a positive way for centuries; with good reason, they have seen these relationships as necessary and fundamental characteristics in creating and sustaining a functional society—one full of social progress and "win–win" relationships, as opposed to zero-sum games.

Liberal thinkers since the times of John Locke and Jeremy Bentham have been particularly adamant in their condemnation of Robinson Crusoe's life prior to Friday's arrival and eulogize human interaction, within which, according to Homan's exchange theory, everybody gains. Advocates of interdependence also greet this type of relationship glowingly. A famous author of the WWII era, Will Durant, even published a special "Declaration of Interdependence" in 1944.

Contemporary Libertarians also herald individual freedoms and the productive character of interpersonal interactions that are devoid of outside, especially governmental, oversight. They believe that a free-market, bottom-up system can cure most of society's ills. Most Libertarians, along with most theorists concentrating on social capital and networks, also implicitly suppose that each participant can benefit through his or her interactions with others, even when—or perhaps especially when—the interacting individuals possess approximately the same amount of summed resources. Some authors, including Zygmunt Bauman (2001), have continued to extend the Libertarian line, suggesting that people's dependence on one another has diminished radically in the contemporary world and that we have now entered "the individualized society," where the interactions of people have diminished to being a very small part of everyday life.

Meanwhile, even with all the changes that have occurred in society in the last few decades, interactions among individuals continue to be the core of social life. Personal interactions, unavoidable in various collectives and teams, are a necessary condition for the functioning of most institutions in society. However, the growing role of robots in contemporary society has made it necessary to also study the interactions of robots with each other as well as with humans. These interactions have become the main topic of various disciplines, such as automation, artificial intelligence, and robotics, as well as, of course, science fiction tales (Stanley Kubrik's famous film *2001: A Space Odyssey* (1968) was the first to describe the dramatic conflict between robots and humans, who were on the spaceship together. This did not end in the humans' favor).

Whatever future perspectives on interactions between robots and between robots and humans will bring, interactions between human beings continue to be an essential element of today's society. However, contemporary social science is far from understanding the complexity of these interactions, particularly those involving the dependency of certain people on certain other people.

Only a minority of scholars have recognized the necessity of using a cost–benefit calculus for analyzing dependency. This is vitally important, as interactions have a dark side, mostly because people interact with each other while possessing different amounts and types of resources, all of varying quality. These resources can be material, but they can also be intellectual or informational. Alasdair MacIntyre is among the rare authors who write about this. In *Dependent Rational Animals: Why Human Beings Need the Virtues* (2001), he writes:

> Dependence on others is of course often recognized in a general way, usually as something that we need in order to achieve our positive goals. But an acknowledgement of anything like the full extent of that dependence and of the ways in which it stems from our vulnerability and our afflictions is generally absent. (2–3)

The pessimistic, or misanthropic, view of the dependence of people on each other is supported by those who assume that people loathe one another and harbor destructive intentions toward others, as formulated by a famous Sartre expression in his play *No Exit*: "Hell is other people" (in French "L'enfer, c'est les autres"). A more modern spin on the concept is offered by Catherine Hakim (2011), who shows her pessimistic view of a particular kind of human relationship: intersexual.

The misanthropic view of mankind is not very constructive because, despite the many problems that emerge in the interactions of human beings, these interactions are absolutely necessary for society. At the same time, we cannot ignore that, in the assemblage of internal relations among members of the team—despite the existence of a supposedly common goal and the necessity of close cooperation—internal tensions are unavoidable. Tensions arose in such collectives as the Manhattan Project or the Beatles. These dissensions happened mostly because the distribution of resources, intellectual or musical, was not equal and therefore was bound to breed conflict, hidden or open.

Many authors who study human interdependence and the interactions that fuel the phenomenon, such as network theorists, crowd-sourcing advocates, or game theorists, assume the equality of the participants involved in the interaction and their independence from each other as individual consumers in the market. Meanwhile, life inside all strata of society, and inside all ethnic and cultural groups, is replenished with problems arising out of the dependency of people on those with whom they interact outside of their social, ethnic, or cultural unit.

If, as several authors, including Bourdieu and Bauman, contend, it is true that the composition of single social units—whether the family or the collective in an office or factory—is precarious and capricious in the contemporary world, then the probability of abuse by people who possess more/better resources than others will increase. This is because the chances of long-lasting friendship or simply cordial relations are lower than they were in the permanent social collectives that dominated during the industrial era and before. There is a great deal of research showing that the abuses of power in temporary teams are much greater than those in stable teams.[5]

We could also talk about "group selection" in the Darwinian sense, where some people will sacrifice some of their evolutionary fitness, say by offering a mating opportunity to someone else, if they think it will make the collective more likely to prosper. So, people who do this may survive and make babies more than others will because they are part of stronger groups and not just because they are stronger individually. However, this principle supposes that the group is more than transient.

Of great importance is the ability of people to predict what they can expect from their spouses, colleagues, roommates, or children—how much they trust the readiness of others to help them in cases of emergency or "rainy days." Failed expectations about the willingness and ability of others to help an individual often lead to feelings of ingratitude, great frustration, and even suicide. The ingratitude of King Lear's daughters and their refusal to be of help and consolation for him in his "retirement" is an example of failed beliefs in the nobility of Goneril and Regan.

The epic tales of big families, such as the *Forsyte Saga* by Galsworthy, Thomas Mann's *Budenbrocken*, Maxim Gorky's *Artamonovs*, or Roger Du Garre's *Tibault Family*, vividly describe how members of a family can abuse their power over other family members who are dependent on them.[6] Although a husband depends on the whims of his wife, parents depend on their mischievous children, a wealthy tycoon depends on his servant or mistress, and old people often depend on those who take care of them, all of these people (the wife, the kids, the servant, the old people) in general, and in the specific context of their relations, are usually weak.

Yearning for Power and Influence

Meanwhile, most of social science disregards the important psychological feature of the propensity for one to yearn for power over others, and to derive pleasure from exercising this power once obtained, even if illicit means are used to acquire and apply the power. Of course, some scholars (Bargh and Lee-Chai 2001) highlight this notion. Exerting power and, in some cases, even the abuse of power can be the basis of one's identity and highly related to his or her self-esteem. Others, Nietzsche and Adler among them, suggest the importance of the pleasure of power as the motivation for behavior in interpersonal relations (Bargh and Lee-Chai 2001). Lynn Chancer is probably right when she writes in *Sadomasochism in Everyday Life: The Dynamics of Power and Powerlessness* (1992), "Sex is not sought for its own sake, perhaps for variety and novelty, or for a merely libidinal satisfaction: instead, both sadist and masochist are searching for some kind of recognition and acknowledgement that goes beyond and likely originated outside, the realm of erotic—even as it somehow became married to it."

Unfortunately, sadistic elements in the human psyche cannot be treated as simply pathologies belonging to the disturbed few.[7] People from all walks of life might derive joy from exerting their dominion over others, even going so far as to get egoistic and sexual pleasure in torturing others. Again, Lynn Chancer: "Sadomasochistic interaction, then, may be a thread that subtly weaves its way through a number of otherwise dissimilar relationships in which we are frequently entwined: at the work place, at school, in love, or with friends, family members, or significant or insignificant others to whom we are intimately related at home or in bed" (Chancer 1992; see also Buss 2006).

David Buss, in his book *The Murderer Next Door: Why the Mind is Designed to Kill* (2006) and other academic work, shows that most people have thought about killing someone. Popular media also points to hedonistic pleasure related to torture and/or killing someone: seven out of one hundred characters on TV are murdered; the acclaimed show

Dexter has a serial killer protagonist; and the S&M-heavy novel *Fifty Shades of Gray* has sold incredibly well. David McClelland (1988) says that the yearning for power is one of the three most influential human motives (see also Winter 1967).

Perceptions of Abuse of Power in the Context of Accommodation

People tend to downplay the harm brought on by dependency on others and the ensuing mistreatment. Even slaves and serfs did not often consider their fate tragic. It was Etienne Boetie, a friend of Michelle Montaigne, who expressed amazement at the ease with which people tolerate their dependence on others in his mid-sixteenth-century work *The Discours sur la Servitude Volontaire*. The mechanism of accommodation makes people less susceptible to mistreatment, and even less frustrated when they are the object of mistreatment by their spouses, bosses, colleagues, or classmates. For millennia, people have been amazed by the tolerance of beaten wives, humiliated relatives, and discriminated minorities in cases when they had opportunities to resist abuses of power, either individually or collectively. John Gaventa (1982), in his famous study *Power and Powerlessness: Quiescence and Rebellion in an Appalachian Valley* and *Radical Power* (1982 with Steven Lukes), was one of the few scholars who paid special attention to this pervasive quiescence by those dependent on others, even if he, like other power theorists (Clegg 1989; Foucault 1995; Giddens 1982; Mann 1986), did not substantially expand his theory on interpersonal relations (Gaventa 1982).

Those who are personally dependent on others internalize ideologies that justify not only their dependence on others within a social unit but also the abuse of power that occurs at their expense. Most of these ideologies are rooted in the notion that unequal resource and power distributions are created outside the social unit. The paternalistic ideology, which posits the leading role of the man in the family, also presupposes a vulnerable position for the other members of the family. This ideology, with its Darwinistic overtones praising the special role of brute physical strength, tries to persuade weak children and weak adults of the right of the strongest people to use their advantages in a variety of ways, from imposing additional chores all the way up to rape.

Dependence and Self-Respect

No matter how effectively weak people accommodate dependent people, psychologically and otherwise, they remain weak and vulnerable people;

they are victims. This does tremendous damage to their mentality. These people lose their self-respect, the ability to defend themselves, and their rights even outside of their dependent relationship.

The impact of an authoritarian father or mother on his or her children—referred to as "hostile aggressive parenting" in some places—has been discussed frequently in social literature as well as in novels (Iova 2012). Additionally, both short- and long-term consequences of school bullying have been magnified, especially lately. Somewhere between 10 and 15 percent of American children are the victims of regular bullying (Bully Statistics 2009). Catherine Bradshaw, an expert on bullying, found that victims of bullying in childhood were 4.3 times more likely to have an anxiety disorder as adults, compared to those with no history of being bullied (Saint Louis 2013).

Jobs that Facilitate Power Abuse and the Opportunity to Torture

Not surprisingly, many people look for a job that will provide them with power over others. A 2007 survey of one thousand American workers, released by the San Francisco–based *Employment Law Alliance*, found that 45 percent of respondents had been bullied at the office—verbal abuse, job sabotage, misuse of authority, deliberate destruction of relationships (Drexler 2013). It has been suggested that an aspiration to work as a teacher or a nurse is determined, at least partially, by the desire to command others, even if another reason, perhaps bigger and certainly more manifest, is so they can help people.

The naturally occurring human characteristic of pining for power over others has been vastly exploited by authoritarian regimes quite easily able to recruit members to employ physical and psychological coercion and domination toward millions of people, particularly the young. After the October Revolution in 1917, the Bolsheviks almost immediately created the political police, whose members, without any visible reluctance, started to harass the population; they busted into the apartments of "alien people," humiliating them, confiscating their property, and executing hundreds of thousands during the Red Terror. Similarly, in the 1930s, the Nazis—once again with no ostensible resistance from hundreds of thousands of Germans, supposedly very civilized people—allowed the *SchutzStaffel* (SS) and *Sturmabteilung* (SA) to commit atrocities. Mao's experience during the revolution was very similar in this regard; it was not hard to recruit people to carry out nefarious plans that required interpersonal abuses of power.

Hatred of Dependence and Yearning for Dependence

People are aware of the vulnerability that emerges with any dependence. In many cases, though not always, people have a choice between dependence and independence in relations with another. The attitudes toward being self-employed or depending on a boss or company for a job and pay strongly divide society. Facing the choice between two alternatives (and, of course, alternatives that combine both types of work), people have to weigh various pluses and minuses.

For many people, the downside of working under the control of a superior is compensated by the release of responsibility for making important business decisions and taking big risks, with the added pleasure of a social life in an office and/or the opportunity of learning various skills from colleagues.

Many people even love to live and work under command, free of the necessity to be responsible for their family or office, their social and professional work. Adorno and colleagues (1950) call the people who yearn to be under the umbrella of someone else's authority "authoritarian personalities." To some degree, Riesman's other-directed individuals, with their tendency to conform to people around them, are individuals who take their obedience to another as a palatable norm. When they have a choice, many people on the playground, in the family, and in the office, choose the dependent position.

While many people like, or at least tolerate, working under supervision, other people detest being dependent on a superior, though they still work for someone else. These people like to work for a company at "home." In 2012, 24 percent of employed Americans worked from home at least some hours each week (Miller and Rampell 2013). The longing of Americans to reduce the control of bosses over their work manifests in other ways as well. Some employers yield to the pressure of the labor force and offer their employees more opportunities to choose their best ways of working. In 2004, 27.5 percent of all employees worked on a flexible schedule (US Bureau of the Census 2012c). In 2008, 37 percent of employers permitted their employees to "periodically change starting and quitting times within some range of hours," 55 percent could "have control over when to take breaks," and 45 percent could take "family or personal time off without loss of pay" (US Bureau of the Census 2012b).

Another chunk of people go a step further, by wanting to have their own small business. In 2008, ten million Americans were self-employed, about 7 percent of the labor force (US Bureau of the Census 2012a).

If you add independent contractors to this number, it reaches 14 percent (US Bureau of the Census 2012d). 16 percent of Americans (Pew Research Center 2003) prefer to have a small and/or family business and to be their own boss rather than work in a hierarchical organization, even if they can garner higher wages at the latter. In 2006, 92 percent of small business owners felt they were successful in their business (Jacobe 2006). In 2005, 67 percent of small business owners were satisfied with the balance between their work and personal lives (Jacobe 2005). Gallup summarized the attitudes about the personal-life satisfaction of small business owners: "Being a small business owner clearly has many rewards. Even during challenging times, most small business owners would do it again. Still, this survey and previous Wells Fargo/Gallup Small Business Index surveys suggest small business owners must have a passion for what they do. They find themselves working many hours and discover working hard becomes an essential part of their work-life balance" (Jacobe 2006).

We can speculate that one of the reasons Americans consider the importance of small business to be almost as high as that of corporations is because of the autonomy of the small business owner. The yearning for autonomy is also, at least partially, behind the popularity of the work.

Yearning for Solitude

The deep dialectical character of the dependence of people on each other is evidenced in the longing of many people for solitude. Robert Putnam (2000) describes this asocial tendency in his book *Bowling Alone*. In some cases, this phenomenon is caused by people's growing mistrust, as Putnam suggests. But the pining for alone-time also has a biological explanation and can be caused by an illness such as autism, whose major characteristics include the avoidance of social contacts and the inability to cooperate with others. These general characteristics of those on the autism spectrum have been vividly described in two famous novels: Mark Haddon's *The Curious Incident of the Dog in the Night-Time* (2004) and Paolo Giordano's *The Solitude of Prime Numbers* (2009). Of course, we can also point to various religious movements that have encouraged people to have only minimal communication with others, such as the Catholic Church, which was started by hermits, as well as pieces of Buddhism, Hinduism, Taoism, and Islam including Sufism.

However, the desire to live alone is not found only among people hit by various forms of autism or by religious devotion. We observe this phenomenon among the most ordinary people. The urge to avoid contact is typical of many people who, being concerned about their self-esteem, try to avoid personal contact with those who can undermine it. The addiction to various devices, including the opportunities to watch the world through the Internet or play innumerable games alone, and the opportunity to communicate with people without having direct, face-to- face contact through social networks also explains the growing tendency to play alone.

The apprehension of becoming dependent prevents many people from indulging in full-scale love, which, as stated in Ian McEwan's novel *Sweet Tooth* (2012), is "always burden." This is one reason why a considerable number of people avoid marriage and even avoid having a boyfriend or girlfriend. A typical explanation might be, "I don't want to depend on anyone but myself," "I'm just working on me at the moment," or "I'm just looking out for number one."

Conclusion

The origin and plight of weak and vulnerable people is one of the most important contemporary problems, which is as dramatic and, at times, as tragic in rich democratic nations as it is in poorer and/or nondemocratic societies. The division of people into weak and strong can be detected in the richest families as well as in the dominant racial and cultural groups.

The fate of weak and vulnerable people was at the center of political discourse during the 2000s in the United States and Europe as well as during the 2012 American presidential campaign. The case of weak and vulnerable people has serious political, economic, and social implications for society. This book concentrates mostly on those people who are members of the micro world, or small social units—school, family, hospital, office. In the process of interaction, people become dependent on others, and this often generates abuses of power. In fact, the elements of Hobbesian perceptions of the world should also be applied to life inside social units. The people within these are very different in their attitudes toward dependence. Those who tend to like to be dependent on others coexist with those who try to minimize any contact with others. The character of the relations, the intensity and frequency of abuse and/or mutual help inside social units, is an important ingredient in estimating one's quality of life.

Notes

1. This phrase, which loosely translates to "the war of everyone versus everyone," was introduced by Hobbes and later became a part of the intellectual vernacular as more scholars adopted it.
2. Bauman, Zygmunt. 2001. *The Individualized Society.* Cambridge, UK: Polity Press; his foreword in Beck, Ulrich and Elisabeth Beck-Gernsheim. 2002. *Individualization: Institutionalized Individualism and Its Social and Political Consequences.* London: Sage, 47.
3. Soviet ideology gives a rather amusing example of hatred for the so-called universal, humanistic values and the belief that these values threaten class values. It states that human suffering can only have class origins and can only be created by the conflicts generated by different social positions in society.
4. Amusingly, the dependence in romantic love is one of the rare issues that has drawn widespread attention.
5. The factor of the duration of a relationship has a great impact on its character. So, in the iterated prisoner's dilemma game that economists and psychologists use, where people have different payouts for "snitching" on their partner (or not), people are more likely to snitch, given the traditional payout structure, when they know that the game will be over after, say, three rounds. When the game is of unknown length, both parties usually reach an equilibrium point, where they do what is best for the collective; both usually deny the crime. So, in an era of bouncing around from job to job and from city to city, the chance that a person will know when his interaction with another will end is higher than it was before, when people had one job in one city all of their life. Thus, even stripping away the psychology of emotions, attachment, and mere exposure, people in short-term groups are less cooperative than their counterparts in long-term groups.
6. Interestingly, the actions of a person in a position to abuse power may inform his future chances of power abuse. This is perhaps especially true in a family. Some resources may only be used once (e.g., disclosure of a secret; however, the threat of disclosing the secret may be used repeatedly, although probably not forever). If one does not abuse his power, he may lose legitimacy in the minds of those he might have abused, which would lessen his chances for doling out abuse in the future.
7. Dr. Nikolay Vorobiev, a prominent doctor from Kiev suggested in the 1940s to one of the authors that people often confuse the variation of normality with pathology.

References

Adorno, T. W., Else Frenkel-Brunswik, Daniel J. Levinson, and R. Nevitt Sanford. 1950. *The Authoritarian Personality: A Volume in Studies in Prejudice Series.* 1st edition. Harper & Brothers.

Bachrach, Peter and Morton S. Baratz. 1970. *Power and Poverty: Theory and Practice.* New York: Oxford University Press.

Bargh, John A. and Annette Y. Lee-Chai. 2001. *The Use and Abuse of Power: Multiple Perspectives on the Causes of Corruption.* Philadelphia: Psychology Press, 44.

Bauman, Zygmunt. 2001. *The Individualized Society*. Cambridge, UK: Polity Press.

Beck, Ulrich and Elisabeth Beck-Gernsheim. 2002. *Individualization: Institutionalized Individualism and Its Social and Political Consequences*. London: Sage.

Blanchard, Kenneth H., John P. Carlos, and Alan Randolph. 2001. *Empowerment Takes More Than a Minute*. San Francisco, CA: Berret-Koehler Publishers.

Bourdieu, Pierre. 1998. *Practical Reason: On the Theory of Action*. Stanford, CA: Stanford University Press, 6.

Bourdieu, Pierre. 2000. *The Weight of the World: Social Suffering in Contemporary Society*, trans. Priscilla Parkhurst Ferguson. Stanford, CA: Stanford University Press.

Bully Statistics. 2009. "Welcome to Bullying Statistics." http://www.bullyingstatistics.org (accessed August 14, 2013).

Burger, Thomas. 1997. "Talcott Parsons, the Problem of Order in Society, and the Program of an Analytical Sociology." *American Journal of Sociology*, 83(2):320–39.

Buss, David. 2006. *The Murderer Next Door: Why the Mind Is Designed to Kill*. New York: Penguin Books.

Chancer, Lynn. 1992. *Sadomasochism in Everyday Life: The Dynamics of Power and Powerlessness*. New Brunswick, NJ: Rutgers University.

Clegg, Stewart R. 1989. *Frameworks of Power*. London: Sage Publications.

Drexler, Peggy. 2013. "The Tyranny of the Queen Bee." *The Wall Street Journal*, March 6.

Eisenstadt, Shmuel Noah and Luis Roniger. 1984. *Patrons, Clients, and Friends: Interpersonal Relations and Structure*. Cambridge, MA: Cambridge University Press.

Foucault, Michel. 1995. *Discipline & Punishment: The Birth of the Prison*. New York: Random House.

Gaventa, John. 1982. *Power and Powerlessness: Quiescence & Rebellion in an Appalachian Valley*. University of Illinois Press.

Giddens, Anthony. 1982. *Profiles and Critiques in Social Theory*. University of California Press.

Giordano, Paolo. 2009. *The Solitude of Prime Numbers*. New York: Random House.

Haddon, Mark. 2004. *The Curious Incident of the Dog in the Night-Time*. New York: Random House.

Hakim, Catherine. 2011. *Honey Money: The Power of Erotic Capital*. London: Penguin Books.

Iova, Ica. 2012. *My Children, His Victims*. Bloomington, IN: Xlibris.

Jacobe, Dennis. 2005. "Work Is Labor of Love for Small-Business Owners." Gallup, August 23. http://www.gallup.com/poll/18088/Work-Labor-Love-SmallBusiness-Owners.aspx (accessed August 13, 2013).

Jacobe, Dennis. 2006. "Most Small Business Owners Feel Successful." Gallup, August 14. http://www.gallup.com/poll/24103/Most-Small-Business-Owners-Feel-Successful.aspx (accessed August 13, 2013).

Lukes, Steven. 2005. *Power: A Radical View*. Basingstoke, Hampshire: Palgrave Macmillan.

Mann, Michael. 1986. *The Sources of Social Power: Volume 1: A History of Power from the Beginning to AD 1760*. New York: Cambridge University Press.

MacIntyre, Alasdair C. 2001. *Dependent Rational Animals: Why Human Beings Need the Virtues*. Chicago: Open Court Publishing, 2–3.

McClelland, David C. 1988. *Human Motivation*. New York: Cambridge University Press.

McEwan, Ian. 2012. *Sweet Tooth*. New York: Doubleday.

Miller, Claire and Catherine Rampell. 2013. "Yahoo Orders Its Home Workers to Report to the Office." *New York Times*, February 25.

Nietzsche, Friedrich. 1973. *Beyond Good and Evil: Prelude to a Philosophy of the Future*, trans. R. J. Hollingdale. London: Penguin Books, 63.

Nietzsche, Friedrich. 1999. *Thus Spake Zarathustra*, trans. Thomas Common. New York: Dover Publications.

Nietzsche, Friedrich. 2003. *The Genealogy of Morals*. New York: Dover Publications.

Ortega y Gasset, Josè. 1994. *The Revolt of the Masses*. New York: W. W. Norton & Company, 39–40.

Rand, Ayn. 1961. *For the New Intellectual: The Philosophy of Ayn Rand*. New York: Random House, 119, 146, 161.

Rand, Ayn. 1966. *Capitalism: The Unknown Ideal*. New York: Signet, 8.

Ruane, Janet M. and Karen A. Cerulo. 2012. *Second Thoughts: Sociology Challenges Conventional Wisdom*. Thousand Oaks, CA: Sage Publications.

Parsons, Talcott. 1977. *Social Systems and the Evolution of Action Theory*. New York: Free Press.

Peabody, Susan. 2006. *Addiction to Love: Overcoming Obsession and Dependency in Relationships*. Berkeley, CA: Celestial Arts.

Pew Research Center. 2003. "The 2004 Political Landscape Evenly Divided and Increasingly Polarized." http://peoplepress.org/2003/11/05/the-2004-political-landscape (accessed August 26, 2011).

Putnam, Robert D. 2000. *Bowling Alone*. New York: Simon and Schuster.

Sadan, Elisheva. 1997. *Empowerment and Community Planning: Theory and Practice of People-Focused Social Solutions*. Tel Aviv: Hakibbutz Hameuchad Publishers.

Saint Louis, Catherine. 2013. "Effect of Bullying Last into Adulthood Study Finds." *New York Times*, February 21.

Sanchez, Mary. 2012. "What the Homicide Numbers Don't Tell." *Chicago Tribune*, January 27.

Shlapentokh, Vladimir. 1990. *Soviet Intellectuals and Political Power: The Post-Stalin Era*. London: I. B. Tauris & Co. Ltd.

Shlapentokh, Vladimir. 2006. *Fear in Contemporary Society: Its Negative and Positive Effects*. New York: Palgrave Macmillan.

Shlapentokh, Vladimir and Eric Beasley. 2013. *Restricting Freedoms: Limitations on the Individual in Contemporary Society*. Piscataway, NJ: Transaction Publishers.

Shlapentokh, Vladimir and Joshua Woods. 2007. *Contemporary Russia as a Feudal Society: A New Perspective on the Post-Soviet Era*. New York: Palgrave Macmillan.

Shlapentokh, Vladimir and Joshua Woods. 2011. *Feudal America: Elements of the Middle Ages in Contemporary Society*. University Park, PA: Pennsylvania State University Press.

Smith, Charles P. 1992. *Motivation and Personality: Handbook of Thematic Content Analysis*. New York: Cambridge University Press.

Smith, Jerry E. and Kimm C. Hurley-Smith. 2009. *Strength-Based Empowerment Theory: A Model for Lifting the Spirit, Reprogramming the Mind, Instilling Self-Love, and Developing Self-Reliance in African American Male Offenders.* Charleston, SC: BookSurge Publishing.

Stiglitz, Joseph, Amartya Sen and Jean-Paul Fitoussi. 2010. *Mismeasuring Our Lives: Why GDP Doesn't Add Up.* New York: The New Press.

US Census Bureau, Statistical Abstract of the United States. 2012a. "Table 592. Civilian Labor Force—Percent Distribution by Sex and Age: 1980 to 2010." http://www.census.gov/compendia/statab/2012/tables/12s0592.pdf (accessed August 14, 2013).

US Census Bureau, Statistical Abstract of the United States. 2012b. "Table 593. Civilian Labor Force and Participation Rates by Educational Attainment, Sex, Race, and Hispanic Origin: 2000 to 2010." http://www.census.gov/compendia/statab/2012/tables/12s0593.pdf (accessed August 14, 2013).

US Census Bureau, Statistical Abstract of the United States. 2012c. "Table 594. Characteristics of the Civilian Labor Force by State: 2010." http://www.census.gov/compendia/statab/2012/tables/12s0594.pdf (accessed August 14, 2013).

US Census Bureau, Statistical Abstract of the United States. 2012d. "Table 595. Civilian Labor Force Status by Selected Metropolitan Areas: 2010." http://www.census.gov/compendia/statab/2012/tables/12s0595.pdf (accessed August 14, 2013).

Williamson, Kevin D. 2012. *The Dependency Agenda.* New York: Encounter Books.

Winter, David. 1967. *Power Motivation in Thought and Action.* Cambridge, MA: Harvard University.

2

The Distribution of Resources and Dependence on "Others"

Ascribing great importance to the human relations occurring inside social units and their influence on quality of life, we argue that the unequal distribution of individual resources among the members of the social unit ultimately causes the nature of these relations, and the social inequality and abuses of power that simmer within them.

The Concept of Individual Resources

Let us now define the concept of resources: the means necessary for the satisfaction (or achievement) of needs (or goals). Note that mathematical models describing any sort of activity usually use the term *goal function* or *utility function*. Since the eighteenth century, mostly under the impact of economics, social scientists have tended to use the term *capital* as a synonym for *resource*. It was, of course, Marx who made capital a leading concept in economics and social science in general. Marx's capital, however, focused only on material resources such as "capital goods" or "financial capital"—things necessary for production. Contrary to Marx, it was Weber who concentrated on the means for the achievement of not only material goals but also power and prestige.

Some outstanding sociologists in the second half of the twentieth century, such as Mancur Olson (1971) and, to some degree, Talcott Parsons and Neil Smelser, aligned more closely with economists than they did with Weber; they used capital in the same spirit as Marx. However, the majority followed the Weberian way of thinking about capital. Under Weber's impact, the evolution of the concept of capital went in three directions in social science: cultural, social, and economic.

The cultural direction is connected with members of the Frankfurt School (Theodore Adorno, Max Horkhheimer and Herbert Marcuse, among others) who introduced the concept of "the cultural industry" in the 1940s. This special branch of the economy—comprising the merchants of cultural industry—possesses the capacity to impose its products on the minds of the population. In this way, this sector of the economy has homogenized individuals, helping the dominant class to keep power in society by stifling innovative resistance. In the 1960s, Jurgen Habermas (1984) continued this line of thinking by focusing on the decisive role of information and media, not economic capital, in controlling the political order in society.

The social capital direction started in 1916, when L. J. Hanifan (1916) first used this concept straightforwardly, shifting some focus from land ownership, personal property, and money to such resources as "goodwill, fellowship, mutual sympathy and social intercourse among a group of individuals and families who make up a social unit" (130–8). Afterwards, a few authors (Jane Jacobs, Robert Salisbury, and James Coleman, among others) also started to use this concept, and it became a fixture in the sociological literature (Castiglione, Van Deth, and Wolleb 2008).[1] The modern concept of social networks, with its "friends" and its ability to grant individuals easy access to others, can be considered a further development of the concept of social capital. However, past and present authors working with the concept of social capital, even those who treated social capital as a resource, were not in a hurry to talk about other "non-material" resources.

It was Pierre Bourdieu, in the 1970s, who declared it necessary to broaden the concept of capital beyond its initial linkage to economics and even social capital (Grenfell 2012, 98). To some degree, Bourdieu followed Nietzsche, who included strength, beauty, and intelligence in his list of resources at the disposal of the individual. Bourdieu (1998) proposed that we operate with at least five types of capital as sources of power: economic, social, political, cultural, and symbolic. He was strongly engaged in the debate about the relations between economics and social science, applying economic concepts such as production, (e.g., production of ideas), capital (e.g., cultural and symbolic), investment (e.g., in institutions), profit (e.g., material and symbolic), and monopoly (e.g., of professionals) and economic methodology to many social and linguistic issues (see Bourdieu and Wacquant 1992; Bourdieu 2003; Swartz 1997).

It is particularly remarkable how Bourdieu inserted economics into the study of culture by withdrawing culture from Marx's superstructure, where it was lingering with religion, politics, and the economy. Some of Bourdieu's colleagues even accused him of "economism" (Swartz 1997, 67–8). (The emergence and development of economic sociology is a different matter because this branch of sociology or economics has little interest in the theoretical issues of both sciences; it deals mostly with consumer behavior.)

Several other scholars joined the trend of broadly interpreting the term *capital* (Hakim 2011; Verba, Schlozman, and Brady 1995). Characteristically, some economists, in their turn, moved toward traditionally sociological objects, trying to use their own methodology in the studies of new subjects. Noble Prize winner Gary Becker (1974) received a lot of publicity for his study of marriage; he was trying to prove that this institution followed market laws.

As a result of these developments in social science, the initial concept of capital as an economic category almost lost its old meaning. It is only natural that the next step was to replace the concept of capital with a broader concept, resource. The resource concept, in the way we define it, has already been used by a few sociologists. It was Bourdieu (2008) who first operated with the concept of valued resources as a synonym to capital. Zygmunt Bauman (2001) worked with the concept of resources even more than Bourdieu did. Then the authors of the book edited by John Bargh and Annette Lee-Chai, *The Use and Abuse of Power* (2001), widely used the concept of resources in their analysis of the role of power in interpersonal relations.

Individuals' Resources and Special Types of Weak People

Our approach to the concept of individual resources, which is so crucial to explaining human relations inside social units, is close to Amartya Sen's (1993; 2006) theory of capabilities. Sen viewed capabilities—he included various resources under this umbrella term, from economic to education—as the opportunities necessary for making human beings happy. The quality of people's lives was evaluated by the availability of the resources that provide them with freedoms to do what they want—"to choose the lives that they have reason to value" (Sen 1992, 81).[2]

The list of resources at the disposal of the individual can be aggregated into a few categories. The unequal distribution of all of these resources among the members of a social unit—within a family, a school, an office, etc.—largely accounts for the character of the human relations inside the unit and for the precipitation of interpersonal abuse.

The Mostly Biological Resources: Physical Strength and Health

Biological resources are, of course, among the individual resources whose distributions shape human relations. Their role is, of course, less significant today than it was in the early stages of human evolution, as described in the famous 1911 novel *Quest for Fire* (French: *La Guerre du Feu*) by Belgian novelist J. H. Rosny (the movie with the same name was made in 1981). Hardly any pure, individual biological resources exist that have not been affected by social factors. Nature and nurture are interwoven entities in people's lives. Still, we can talk about a few primarily biological resources, whose roles in interpersonal relations are very significant and which, when disproportionately possessed, can be used to abuse others.

Physical strength is one of these resources. As will be shown in chapter 3 in this book, this resource influences human relations inside families, at school, in the army, and even in nursing homes. Sociologists who study violence seem to ignore such an evident factor in human relations as physical strength. For example, a well-known sociologist, Randall Collins (2009), described the features that make children prone to bullying. Amazingly, however, he did not pay any mind to the role of physical advantages in bullying. He does not even ascribe this quality to those whom he names as aggressive and dominant.

The same is true about health. People with poor health often become dependent on those who can help them. Sick people can be dependent on their relatives, domestic assistants, neighbors, even colleagues, as well as nurses and other personnel in hospitals or nursing homes, all of whom can abuse their position of power.

A special category of people who suffer from a deficiency of physical strength are elderly people, whose diminishing physical health is often associated with the decline of mental skills, rendering them particularly vulnerable. Additionally, the deficiency of physical and cognitive resources is often accompanied by a lack of adequate financial means.

Elderly people with weak cognitive resources can and do make decisions against their own interests, a subject of many judiciary cases (e.g., Hefler 2013). Related to this, with their weakening mental capacity, some old people may not even be aware of their own exploitation by others. Even an ailment as simple as hearing loss, an issue that ranges from moderate to severe in almost half (46 percent) of all elderly persons, can be an exploitable flaw (Pirkl 1995).

The elderly often lack the physical or cognitive ability or knowledge to proficiently deal with computers and the computer-automated reality in which most modern businesses and government services run. So, these people may have difficulty dealing with welfare agencies (e.g., securing social security benefits after the death of a spouse), utility companies, pharmacies, etc. Even the use of the telephone in communicating with various companies (pharmacies or doctor's offices among them) demands that the user have the ability to operate the complicated, tree-like ("if not, dial 3 followed by your PIN number and the # key . . .") systems of automatic, nonhuman sources of information. As a result, this group belongs to the most weak and vulnerable people in society (Lyon, Kinney, and Colquhon 2002).

Physical strength is also a major issue for children, especially sick and/or disabled children (including those with mental abnormalities) who are already in a precarious position in the family and at school.[3]

To some degree, women, who have historically been viewed as the "weaker sex," also belong to the category of people who suffer from inequalities in the distribution of physical strength. It is certainly true that women and children within an upper socioeconomic status (SES) family who are harassed still have serious advantages over similar groups in lower SES families. They have better chances of finding some resources to protect them or at least mitigate their sufferings. Rich elderlies who are neglected or even abused in some way by their children can find some refuge in a comfortable, safe nursing home or an assisted living institution. Still, the physical abuse of children, women, elderly, and sick people is a problem for any category of family in society.

Sexual Attractiveness as a Resource

Sexual attractiveness is another example of a mostly biological resource that often has an immense impact on human relations. Catherine Hakim (2011) even went so far as to declare that women are biologically more attractive than men. Certainly, sexual attractiveness is a product of more than inherited genes; it is also the ability of women or men to adapt to the requirements of their milieu and their ability to adjust to the dominant image of what is considered beautiful and attractive. Additionally, they have to amend and master their social skills, dress, and even their skills in sexual situations.

In any case, whatever the proportion of genetic and cultural factors, the sexual resource is powerful in interpersonal relations. Catherine Hakim (2011) was right when she wrote that "attractive people draw others to them, as friends, lovers, colleagues, customers, clients, fans, followers, supporters and sponsors" (190). Applying—not without some brilliance—the economic approach, she contends that because men are always supplicants in heterosexual sex, their erotic capital has zero value, while the erotic capital of women is very large. This provides women with leverage in their conflicts with men (Hakim 2011). Catherine Hakim was also right when she accused sociologists, including Bourdieu and Giddens, of ignoring the role of "erotic capital." The role that appearance plays in discrimination in the business world has been discussed in recent years under the term *lookism* (Associated Press 2013).[4]

The sexual attractiveness of a woman or a man, when coupled with jealousy, allows the person who is the object of passion to manipulate his or her victims (those taken by the attractiveness of the potential abuser), almost without restraint. Of course, jealousy can be generated by more than the inaccessibility of the object of strong emotion. Other factors, such as anger against those who violate the one's claimed special right to the object of jealousy, can also lead to jealousy. It is only natural that a resource such as sexual attractiveness has always been a powerful instrument in the spy activities used by secret services in every nation.

Gender as a Resource

It is important to note that the possession of a gender is also a powerful resource in some contexts. Indeed, a disproportionate gender ratio in a particular context creates a power imbalance congruent with the laws of supply and demand: where there are relatively few men, they can be more discerning and demanding in courtship and beyond; where there are relatively few women, the power may flip. Consider the social relations that took place when there was a dearth of men (or a surplus of women, if you prefer) in the aftermath of WWI, WWII, and other wars. More recently, in North Dakota, the large influx of young men in the early 2000s for jobs in the prospering gas industry meant there was a shortage of women, which affected several aspects of life (e.g., there was a higher demand for sex workers and hyper use of alcohol, similar to what happened when the major railroads were first being built in different areas of the country; see John Eligon's January 16, 2013, *New York Times* article entitled "An Oil Town Where Men Are Many, and Women Are Hounded.") Due to a specific demographic policy in post-Mao China, which limited couples to having only one child, and the preference of the Chinese to have sons, the lack of women in Chinese society has entered the list of serious concerns for Chinese society (Hesketh, Lu, and Xing 2005). Many men, unable to find a spouse, turn destructive as they age, often extending adolescence deep into their twenties.

Quite often, however, it is the lack of men fit for marriage that is a highly important social problem. Catherine Hakim (2011) even wrote about the "universal male deficit" (190). This issue has dominated the Russian landscape over the last few decades, and not only because of "the echo of WWII"—the killing of young men (and a relatively few young women) in battle—but also because of the great amount of drunkenness and criminality among men.[5] Some scholars have noted that, in the past, war-torn societies have sought to accommodate their gender imbalance by allowing and promoting polygamous relationships: if there are five females for every male, then let every male marry five females.[6]

Mental Resources

An individual's mental aptitude—intellectual, moral, ideological, and religious—provides her with powerful resources that can be used toward the betterment or detriment of the other members of the unit. Having persuaded the members of the unit of her mental superiority, the "superior" member of the unit can force the others to think and behave in certain ways.

Of all the mental resources listed above, let us dwell on the ideological and religious, which are deeply interconnected. The ideological or religious member of the social unit is often able to force other members to share his views, whether sincerely or only as a way of accommodating and placating others in order to keep peace in the unit. The pressure put on members of the family by its deeply religious figurehead can reach the level of mental torture and can strongly restrain behavior. Various cults fit this mold, as do the thousands of stories that tell about religious and ideological terror in families headed by an aggressive fundamentalist.

As a matter of fact, authoritarian states have always made extensive use of individuals in families or in business offices as the conductors of their ideology. The Soviets, Nazis, and Maoists assigned the major ideological authority to youngsters, who were usually more receptive to the slogans of the new regime than older people were. These youngsters often terrorized the rest of the family or office with their militancy. Using their ideological zeal as their resource—they appeared closer to the government than did other members of the social unit—the zealous individuals could extract various benefits from others.

Education as a Resource that Can Be Used to Abuse Others

While people tend to marry others of the same educational and social background, this is not always the case. Big differences in the level of education between spouses account for some of the conflicts found inside families.

These differences, which loomed quite large in American society several decades ago, were significantly reduced by the rise in the education level of women. Women continue to constitute a higher proportion of degree recipients as the years move forward, so we are moving toward a dynamic where, in heterosexual marriages, it is becoming more common for a wife to outrank her husband in education than vice-versa. This development also generates conflict in the family—when the man cannot reconcile having a lesser role as the major breadwinner, compared to his wife.

Information as a Resource

Access to information that is vital to others can provide power to those who have the special knowledge over those who do not have it or who are afraid of its dissemination (Snyder and Kiviniemi 2001). The latter is signified by the term *blackmail*.

The opportunity to report on other members of the family is a powerful resource that can be used to help people control their family members. In a totalitarian society, any member of the family, even a child, can terrorize others with the prospect that she might report their nonorthodox views to the police or the party. The Soviet, Nazi, and Maoist societies are full of examples of this sort. In modern Western society, a person possessing information that shows the criminal or lewd activities of another serves the same function. Intra-family fear has spurred several cases where one member of a family murders another to keep a secret hidden.

The Wealth of the Member of the Social Unit

The amount of wealth controlled by a member of a social unit determines a lot of his or her potential to control others. The family serves as a good example. The possibility of a family member writing and/or changing the last will and testament provides tremendous power over other members of the family. In *Middlemarch*, George Eliot (1985) vividly described how the patriarch of a nineteenth century family manipulated family members with the threat or promise to change his will, either in their favor or against them. Contemporary society is full of factual cases that depict the fierce struggle for inheritance among members of a family (see Accetura 2011 for an analysis of these cases and the motives behind them).

An unemployed person, especially one who is unemployed by circumstance rather than choice, is, by definition, a weak person in his family and in the circle of his working friends. Meanwhile, the number of people who are temporarily unemployed, along with the great many whose employment is tenuous, has been growing in Western society.

The growth of this category of vulnerable people is the result of the increasing uncertainty in the market economy, accompanied by a trend of moving away from stable career jobs—on the part of both employers and employees. Technological progress and outsourcing are two essential causes of this process (Bauman 2012).

Status in Society

Status in society and the prestige that society bestows on the individual members of a social unit also play a powerful role within social units. If the social position of a spouse in the larger world is much higher than that of his partner, the difference in this resource creates the possibility for a serious abuse of power. It is well known that if a social position (along with income) of one partner is growing over time, while that of the other remains stagnant or decreases, the differences will quite often lead to divorce or separation.

The view that external society holds of the individual's position within it influences much of her relations with others inside the social unit, as well as the amount of resources at her disposal inside the social unit. When a member of a social unit is more discriminated against in macro society than his social unit counterparts are, this person is more likely to be abused within the social unit than he would be if society held the same attitudes toward all of the members of his social group. For instance, Jews in American colleges or offices before World War II or in the Soviet Union after the war (the rise of anti-Semitism in the United States and the USSR did not coincide) were victims of harassment—sometimes strong, sometimes mild—by other students for whom anti-Semitism was a powerful resource. This resource also allowed non-Jews to have an unfair advantage in spoiling the records and reputations of their Jewish counterparts as they competed for grades and jobs.

The enmity of society toward a category of people whom the state considers nonloyal or even enemies provides others with the resources to exploit those who fall into the maligned category. For example, people could collude to make sure the work of a person belonging to a category of people deemed nonloyal to the ruling regime never gets published. Ghost writers have often been labeled nonloyal to the government and so could not publish their work themselves. For this reason, they have borrowed another person's "good" name, who is subsequently listed as the formal author.[7]

During the McCarthy era, many hundreds of people suspected of Communist sympathies were turned into weak people who were exploited by those of their colleagues who were considered to be loyal citizens. Woody Allen's movie *Front* eloquently highlighted an example; in this film, talentless scriptwriters exploited a talented author accused of being a Communist.

Protection of Law in the Soviet Union

The state took away the most important resource of these weak people in the USSR—the protection of law, which makes all people equal before the state. Those who fell into this category varied tremendously over time; each period of Soviet existence targeted a different group. Until 1953, the regime always identified certain categories of the population as its enemies, who were immediately turned into victims and prey for others, who blackmailed them, extricated various benefits from them, and simply enjoyed the pleasure of having power over them. Over time, among the weak people—real and potential victims—were members of the former dominant classes (including members of the bureaucracy); priests; kulaks; the members of non-Bolshevik socialist parties in the same period; people excluded from the party in the 1930s and 1940s; the big and diverse group of so-called special migrants; people who were transferred against their will to the Eastern region of the country; people from the territories that were annexed in the 1930s (Western Ukraine, Belorussia, Bessarabia, and the Baltic republics); several ethnic minorities in the 1930s and 1950s; people who corroborated with Germans; prisoners of war; and even those who simply lived in the occupied territories (after Stalin's death in 1953, Jews remained the sole "legal" category of weak people in the country).

Social Capital—Networks of Relatives and Friends

The network of people who can and want to help an individual in one way or another is among an individual's most powerful resources. In conflicts inside any social unit, this resource determines most of the balance of power. It also creates the possibilities for abuse of power. Inside schools (even in kindergartens), prisons, and offices, among other places, the network that supports the individual is often more influential in his life than his other qualities are. The "gang of support" is shaped on different principles specific to particular units: race or ethnicity, common biography (e.g., alumni of the same university, a common mentor in the past, previous service in the army, the same birth place), common religious or political views, and even common hobbies, in addition to common kinship (such as the description of ethnic gangs in prison in Wolfe 2001).

Social capital belongs to categories of resources, which tend to fluctuate. Indeed, older adults are likely to be less socially integrated than younger persons. Social resources, including the support of friends, diminish rapidly between the ages of fifty and seventy due to increasing mortality and morbidity and to disengagement from the workforce, among other things. These often lead to social isolation (see http://www.icpsr.umich.edu/icpsrweb/ICPSR/studies/205 for a wealth of data on this topic).

Compassion, Love, and Indifference of Others

Love and compassion are two of the strongest psychological resources that allow individuals to control and abuse each other. The threat of losing love and/or compassion can, in fact, be a serious instrument of abuse when held over individuals for whom this threat can be realized. Begging to restore lost love can also provide an opportunity to extract various benefits from the individual in the role of supplicant.[8]

At the same time, indifference, or rather, the threat of indifference is a powerful resource in its own way for extricating various benefits—financial, sexual, or other—from weak and vulnerable people. Not delivering medicines to a patient or refusing to help him to satisfy any vital needs—whether by a nurse or relatives—and the threat of doing it again, even implicitly, is often enough to make victims do anything the person in power wishes.[9]

Leadership and Connections

While the aforementioned resources play an important role in interpersonal relations inside the social unit, the most important resource is the degree of formal power possessed by members of the social units. No matter how stupid the chairman of a department may be, or lacking in intellectual or ideological authority, or deprived of the support of a network of colleagues, etc., his position provides him with ample possibilities for abusing his power (Hogg and Reid 2001). Of course, the combination of a formal position with many attendant resources, as described above, can turn a leader, even in a democratic society, where there is no need to resort to authoritarian threats, into a formidable figure whose opportunities for abusing power become enormous.

Special Categories of Weak People

Victims of Victims

There is an enormous amount of literature from the last few decades on the abuse of power inside families, schools, corporations, nursing homes, orphanages, congregations, and the army. However, the idea of "victims" also acting as the perpetrators of various forms of abuses of power has escaped the attention of both scholars and public opinion. Social scholars' attention to the victims of victims has been minimal. The victims are often almost absolved of their pernicious behavior because they themselves suffer from the abuse of others. Political correctness, with its very laudable humanistic tendency, makes the protection of the first level of victims its primary focus, while ignoring the second level. Concerns about the solidarity of victimized groups play their own significant role in covering up the "second line of victims."

Meanwhile, various forms of abuse are perpetrated by victims, who take revenge with Schadenfreude—not against those who abuse them but on other vulnerable people who lack the means to resist such abuse. The abuse of power perpetrated on them provides them with an exemplar of behavior that may not have been known to them before. Hazing, as it happens in dormitories, schools, fraternity houses, military barracks, and prisons, is one of the rituals immersed in violence (Collins 2009). The Russian public of the 1990s and 2000s—when hazing in the army became a big national problem—was fascinated by the fact that as soon as first-year service members (the main object of torture for senior soldiers) moved to second-year status, they immediately indulged themselves in the same practices that had brought some of them to suicide just one year before.[10]

Women as Bullies

The real discoverers of the "women as bullies" phenomenon were those who coined the term *queen bee syndrome:* Graham Staines, Toby Epstein Jayaratne, and Carol Tavris. They examined promotion rates and the impact of women's mobility in the workplace. In 1974, they found that women who achieved success in male-dominated environments were likely to oppose the rise of other women. Far from nurturing the growth of younger female talent, they pushed aside possible competitors by chipping away at their self-confidence or undermining their professional standing.

A recent survey of one thousand American workers found that 45 percent of respondents (40 percent of whom were women) had been bullied at the office. When females do the bullying, their targets are other women four out of five times, whereas males are indiscriminate about what sex to torment (Drexler 2013). Psychology professor Peggy Drexler: "What makes these queen bees so effective and aggravated is that they are able to exploit female vulnerabilities that men may not see, using tactics that their male counterparts might never even notice" (Drexler 2013).

Conclusion

The concept of resources is of vital importance for sociological analysis. While the unequal distribution of resources is a central focus of those who study macro society, the same issue is mostly ignored in the study of the micro world. Meanwhile, interpersonal relations inside social units and groups—in the family, school, office, hospital, etc.—are very much determined by the number of specific resources that are at the disposal of each individual. Inequality in the distribution of resources often generates conflicts and abuses of power. Various social agencies, governmental as well as nongovernmental, that try to prevent the abuse of power in social units have to pay heed to the distribution of resources. While society can somewhat influence the distribution of resources inside the social units, such as the wealth or social networks of the individuals, it can only partially restrain the abuse of such resources as physical strength or information.

35

Notes

1. The concept is present in both the work of Robert Putnam and that of Francis Fukuyama.

2. The fact that these freedoms depend on the possession of certain resources has been somewhat obfuscated by Sen. Some of Sen's followers insist that capabilities, not resources, should be the basis for evaluating issues of justice in society.

3. Disabled children are about four times more likely to be physically abused and three times more likely to be sexually abused than other children. Despite the prevalence of disabled children, there is a lack of local and national data on disabled children who require safeguarding (see Murray and Osborne 2009).

4. The court case about a dentist firing his assistant because she was "too beautiful and too attractive" aroused debates on the role of erotic resources or about lookism in media.

5. One of the authors of this book was involved in organizing the first dating service in the USSR in the late 1960s. Reacting to an article in *Literaturnaya Gazeta*, the single female readers inundated the newspapers with their complaints about the complete lack of potential grooms around them while rejecting the idea of marrying the available drunkards, loafers, and criminals. These women were ready to take any man who was more or less feasible for a relationship as their partner.

6. For more information, see http://www.religioustolerance.org/polyprac.htm.

7. Woody Allen's movie *Front* was devoted to this exact issue. In the 1960s and 1970s, the prominent Soviet academic and political figure Alexei Rumiantsev, using his tremendous resources as vice president of the Academy of Science and member of the Central Committee, had a big stable of ghost writers in his service. These were people who could not publish under their own names because of their nationality—they were mostly Jews—or their bad political reputations. Among them were such prominent people as the economist Roman Levita, the sociologist Mikhai Loiberg, and historian Leonid Batkin.

8. According to the definition from Office of the Public Guardian (2013): "Psychological/emotional abuse includes emotional abuse, threats of harm or abandonment, deprivation of contact, humiliation, blaming, controlling, intimidation, coercion, harassment, verbal abuse, isolation or withdrawal from services or supporting networks."

9. Research has shown that neglect is the most prevalent form of abuse of elders in the United Kingdom, with financial abuse a close second (Office of the Public Guardian 2008).

10. We are grateful to Oksana Katzeneliboigen and Elena Kuzmina for their remarks about the spiral of violence among victims.

References

Accettura, P. Mark. 2011. *Blood & Money: Why Families Fight Over Inheritance and What to Do About It.* Farmington Hills, MI: Collinwood Press.

Associated Press. 2013. "Iowa: Court Reaffirms Dentist's Firing of Woman He Found Too Attractive." *New York Times*, July 12.

Bargh, John A. and Annette Y. Lee-Chai. 2001. *The Use and Abuse of Power: Multiple Perspectives on the Causes of Corruption.* Philadelphia: Psychology Press.

Bauman, Zygmunt. 2001. *The Individualized Society*. Cambridge, UK: Polity Press, 46.

Bauman, Zygmunt. 2012. *Collateral Damage. Social Inequalities in a Global Age*. Malden, MA: Polity Press, 19–27, 52.

Becker, Gary. 1974. "A Theory of Marriage." In *Economics of the Family*, ed. T. W. Schultz. Chicago: University of Chicago Press, 293–344.

Bourdieu, Pierre. 1998. *Practical Reason: On the Theory of Action*. Stanford, CA: Stanford University Press.

Bourdieu, Pierre. 2002. "The Forms of Capital." In *Readings in Economic Sociology*, ed. Nicole Biggart. Malden, MA: Blackwell.

Bourdieu, Pierre, John Thompson, ed., Gino Raymond and Mathew Adamson, trans. 2003. *Language and Symbolic Power*. Cambridge, MA: Harvard University Press.

Bourdieu, Pierre and Loïc J. D. Wacquant. 1992. *An Invitation to Reflexive Sociology*. Chicago: University of Chicago Press, 119.

Castiglione, Dario, Jan W. van Deth, and Gugliemo Wolleb, ed. 2008. *The Handbook of Social Capital*. New York: Oxford University Press, 13–22.

Collins, Randall. 2009. *Violence: A Micro-Sociological Theory*. Princeton, NJ: Princeton University Press.

Drexler, Peggy. 2013. "The Tyranny of the Queen Bee." *The Wall Street Journal*, March 6.

Eligon, John. 2013. "An Oil Town Where Men Are Many, and Women Are Hounded." *New York Times*, January 16.

Eliot, George. 1985. *Middlemarch*. New York: Bantam Dell.

Grenfell, Michael. 2012. *Pierre Bourdieu: Key Concepts*. Durham, UK: Acumen, 98.

Habermas, Jurgen. 1984. *The Theory of Communicative Action, Vol. 1: Reasons and the Rationalization of Society*. Boston, MA: Beacon Press.

Hakim, Catherine. 2011. *Honey Money: The Power of Erotic Capital*. London: Penguin.

Hanifan, L. J. 1916. "The Rural School Community Center." *Annals of the American Academy of Political and Social Science*, 67:130–8.

Hefler, Jan. 2013. "Woman with Alzheimer's Won't Be Tried in Husband's Killing." *The Inquirer*, August 21. http://articles.philly.com/2013-08-21/news/41425797_1_fredricka-rosa-rosetta-rosa-valpa-c (accessed May 6, 2014).

Hesketh, Therese, Li Lu, and Whu Wei Xing. 2005. "The Effect of China's One Child Policy After 25 Years." *New England Journal of Medicine*, 353:1171–6.

Hogg, Michael A., and Scott A. Reid. 2001. "Social Identity, Leadership, and Power." In *The Use and Abuse of Power: Multiple Perspectives on the Causes of Corruption* by John A. Bargh and Annette Y. Lee-Chai. New York: Psychology Press, 159–81.

Lyon, Phil, Dave Kinney, and Anne Colquhoun. 2002. "Experience, Change, and Vulnerability: Consumer Education for Older People Revisited." *International Journal of Consumer Studies* 26(3):178–87.

Murray, Moira and Chris Osborne. 2009. "Safeguarding Disabled Children: Practice Guidance." https://www.gov.uk/government/uploads/system/uploads/attachment_data/file/190544/00374-2009DOM-EN.pdf.

Office of the Public Guardian, 2008. "Office of the Public Guardian and Local Authorities: A Protocol for Working Together to Safeguard Vulnerable Adults." http://www.justice.gov.uk/downloads/protecting-the-vulnerable/mca/joint-working-protocol1-1208.pdf (accessed August 18, 2013).

Office of the Public Guardian. 2013. "Safeguarding Policy." http://www.justice. gov.uk/downloads/protecting-the-vulnerable/mca/safeguarding-policy.pdf (accessed August 18, 2013).

Olson, Mancur. 1971. *The Logic of Collective Action: Public Groups and the Theory of Groups.* Cambridge, MA: Harvard University Press.

Pirkl, James J. 1995. "Transgenerational Design: Prolonging the American Dream." *Generations,* 19(1):32–6.

Portes, Alejandro. 1998. "Social Capital: Its Origins and Applications in Modern Sociology." *Annual Review of Sociology,* 24:1–24.

Sen, Amartya. 1992. *Inequality Reexamined.* Cambridge, MA: Harvard University Press, 81.

Sen, Amartya. 1993. "Capabilities and Wellbeing." In *Quality of Life (Wider Studies in Development Economics),* ed. Martha Nussbaum and Amartya Sen. New York: Oxford University Press.

Sen, Amartya. 2006. *Identity and Violence: The Illusion of Destiny.* London: Penguin, 32–9.

Snyder, Mark and Marc T. Kiviniemi. 2001. "Getting What They Came For: How Power Influences the Dynamics and Outcomes of Interpersonal Interaction." In *The Use and Abuse of Power: Multiple Perspectives on the Causes of Corruption,* ed. Annette Y. Lee-Chai and John A. Bargh. Philadelphia: Psychology Press, 134–5.

Swartz, David. 1997. *Culture and Power: The Sociology of Pierre Bourdieu.* Chicago: University of Chicago Press, 66–70.

Verba, Sidney, Kay Lehman Schlozman, and Henry Brady. 1995. *Voice and Equality: Civic Voluntarism in American Politics.* Cambridge, MA: Harvard University Press, 211.

Wolfe, Tom. 2001. *Man in Full.* New York: Dial Press Trade Paperback.

I

Resources

3

Physical Strength

When one person is dependent upon another, the potential for abuse is present. Generally speaking, dependency arises out of the relative resources belonging to the participants in the relationship. This can occur at the macro level, such as when rich countries or companies provide needed capital to poor people and countries and, in doing so, set up exploitative processes. Dependency theory[1] and its postwar derivatives (all of which have many detractors) provide insidious critiques of this system.

Our main argument in this book, however, concentrates on the dependency that arises out of disparate resource possession *within* social units. Some of the same resources that play an important role at the macro level also do so at the micro level, even if the dynamics are not exactly the same. Thus, access to money influences relationships within a home and a family's neighborhood in much the same way it influences a country's relationships with others.

Other resources are not as influential at the macro scale but are powerful at the micro level. Physical strength may have been a salient predictor of human activities at the macro level in the past (e.g., with the fittest collectives dominating warfare, like the Spartan army who were sorted in infancy for physical prowess by the governing *Agoge* and then placed into daily life emphasizing physical fitness; see Cartledge 2003), but nowadays, its primary influence occurs at the micro level, even if we usually only hear about extreme feats of physicality at the society level (e.g., during the Olympics).

Although not a popular topic—and at times a despised topic—in contemporary social science, physical strength and ability, and the appearance of it, has long been an important feature in human-to-human interaction (and, of course, in solitary pursuits such as during individual hunting and farming). From Samson to Goliath, from Hercules to Zeus, from Gilgamesh to He-Man, and from gladiators at the Coliseum to Arnold Schwarzenegger on the silver screen, our cultures have prized physical strength. The type of strength most venerated in fables of the past is that of short-burst-power physical strength and fighting ability; this type of strength would also have served our evolutionary ancestors well in the Paleolithic Era.

The emphasis on physical strength, or at least the packaging of it, is also prevalent in modern media. Movie stars pump themselves full of human growth hormone (HGH) (Zeman 2012),[2] undertake rigorous physical training, meticulously diet, and get supplemented with brawn-enhancing clothing, lighting, and computer-guided editing before their images reach the sensation-saturated public.

This is not the only type of strength that acts as an individual resource, of course. Take the case of Phidippides, the Athenian soldier who was called upon to run the original "marathon." The story goes that he ran 26.2 miles at a blistering pace to communicate war news to the leadership in Athens, where he succumbed to fatigue and dropped dead shortly after finishing his run. His strength, although of a different caliber, was somewhat esteemed by his contemporaries and has certainly been memorialized as an admirable attribute. (There are 644 marathons scheduled in the United States in 2013, according to *FindMyMarathon.com*.) Today, there are cultural variations, both within the United States and cross-nationally, as to the prestige and utility of different types of physical strength. Eastern Europe, for instance, has given more social caché to the big and bulky who wield brute strength, as have the small, football-crazed communities of the US heartland. Muscular and aerobic endurance, however, holds more sway in Ethiopia, at running hotspots such as the University of Oregon (where star distance runners of all ages matriculate to work, to perform, and to be sponsored, and whose football team is known for its collective speed and endurance), or the Tarahumara people of remote Mexico, whose culture and running prowess were canonized by Christopher McDougall (2009) in the bestseller *Born to Run: A Hidden Tribe, Superathletes, and the Greatest Race the World Has Never Seen*. Some people become more popular, richer, and more respected due to their physical dominance relative to others within their social unit (e.g., the powerful middle linebacker in Dallas; the swift miler in Eugene); others become less popular, poorer, and less respected because of their "inadequate" physique.

We do not need to limit ourselves to extraordinarily high levels of physical strength, and its connected status (or its absence), when discussing strength as a useful resource in interpersonal interactions. There is a certain baseline of physicality that needs to be met if one wishes to perform the everyday tasks expected of him (e.g., bathing himself, moving up and down stairs, opening cans of food, removing garbage from his home, manipulating the controls of an automobile, and the ability to type). While the great majority of US inhabitants possess the capacity to complete these tasks, there are many millions who cannot—more than fifty million Americans have at least one disability (dosomething.org 2013)—due to genetic abnormalities, diseases (including aging), injury, malnutrition, etc. Usually, these people must rely on others to facilitate the fulfillment of their needs; they are dependent on neighbors, family members, nurses, social workers, etc. due to their relative lack of resources.

A relative lack of strength has also been shown to be influential in dividing entire classes of people. For example, during the Holocaust, strong, able-bodied captives were often routed to work camps, while their counterparts were sent to extermination camps. Similarly, many nations, including the United States, have "euthanized," run invasive experiments on, and/or quarantined those with abnormal physicality. Journalist Mike Stobbe (2011) writes, "Shocking as it may seem, US government doctors once thought it was fine to experiment on disabled people and prison inmates. Such experiments included giving hepatitis to mental patients in Connecticut, squirting a pandemic flu virus up the noses of prisoners in Maryland, and injecting cancer cells into chronically ill people at a New York hospital."

Thus, those with extreme physical strength, or a lack thereof, are afforded different opportunities and limitations in general society. Compared to individuals with physical disabilities, able-bodied people earn higher incomes—in 2006, the median income for able-bodied persons in the United States was $28,000, while it was only $17,000 for the disabled (United States Census Bureau 2006)—live longer (Thomas and Barnes 2010), and are more likely to marry and procreate (Krahn and Drum 2007).

Additionally, we know that, in general, tall men earn more money than short men (The Telegraph 2009) and are more likely to become Fortune 500 CEOs. Malcolm Gladwell, in his popular book *Blink: The Power of Thinking Without Thinking* (2005), finds that "[i]n the U.S. population, about 14.5 percent of all men are six feet or over. Among CEOs of Fortune 500 companies, that number is 58 percent." Controlling for sex, age, and weight, people find taller men and women more competent and persuasive than their shorter counterparts (Judge and Cable 2004).

Moreover, if we conflate physical ability with sexual attraction, there are a variety of studies that point toward sexually appealing and fit (it also helps if they are tall) men and women receiving a disproportionately high amount of respect, money, crime and punishment leniency, etc. The well-known Halo Effect illustrates the influence that one's physical attractiveness can have on other's opinions of him or her in other areas (e.g., see Dion, Berscheid, Walster 1972). While these effects are present in macro settings and in studies assessing macro trends, they also leave an impression on micro, interpersonal interactions. Of course, there are social components to the construction of beauty, sexiness, fitness, etc. Thus, we see variations not only across space (e.g., Ethiopia versus Alabama) but also across time (e.g., the American South of the 1900s vs. that of the 2000s).

The role of physical strength and the type of strength most heralded has changed over epochal history, even if the changes in the structure of societies preceded the tied change to the characteristics of the social perception of strength (this is an extension of Ogburn's *Cultural Lag* [1957] theory, which asserts that cultural changes lag behind technological advancements; e.g., we had online chat rooms before we established cultural beliefs about who should participate in this form of communication and how much they should disclose). The types of strength most needed in the hunter–gatherer era differed from those needed in the agrarian era (as did the associated prestige). Industrialization emphasized new physical abilities, and postindustrialized societies have eased physical activity out of the realm of necessity (even, somewhat, during warfare).

Still, in contemporary society, we have millions of images promoting a physical ideal and selling the products and know-how that can make you into what marketers posit you "need" to be. This social constructionism, no doubt, influences the way one's physicality influences her status, both in her own eyes and also in the eyes of others. Of course, these images and their influence on status assessments in our everyday lives are gender specific.

In analyzing "ideal" sexualized bodies and the relative utility of physical strength in social situations, we must pay heed to gender. Certainly, physical strength as a social good, and the related sexual and/or power attractiveness, are gendered variables (e.g., extremely muscular women do not derive the same social status from their bodies as do extremely muscular men). Age is also inextricably tied to our physical strength from a macro perspective, with the very young and the very old generally being the most physically weak. While these heavy macro variables (HMVs) are usually measured in relation to physicality at the macro level (e.g., establishing the body mass index [BMI] at which women find men the most attractive), micro-level studies, especially descriptive ones, are not very prominent.

There are social/cognitive psychological principles with tangential connections to physical strength: the halo effect, social influence (conformity, obedience, and persuasion), perceived self-efficacy (locus of control), etc. Baumeister, Vohs, and Tice (2007) even used muscular strength as an analogy to self-control: ego depletion, like muscle depletion, inhibits premium function, and you can work to make each stronger by using them. Furthermore, those who must exert more effort to complete everyday tasks such as walking up stairs will become more ego-depleted over the course of a day and be more likely to make decisions that undermine their long-term well-being, such as smoking a pack of cigarettes.

Researchers have identified handgrip strength as a marker in male college students for predicting perceived popularity (the stronger, the more popular) and frequency of intrasexual peer victimization (the stronger, the less victimization). Additionally, third party ratings of photos of male high school seniors yielded a positive correlation between hand grip strength and perceived aggressiveness, dominance, and health. Testing women on the same attributes illustrated little relationship between hand grip strength and other factors (Gallup, White, and Gallup 2007).

Scholars have also illustrated a connection between male bicep size and politico-intensity: those with larger biceps were more likely to support, and supported more intensely, the political ideology regarding wealth distribution that would most benefit them. Poor men who were muscular supported redistribution of wealth more fervently than their less muscular counterparts did, whereas rich men who were muscular opposed wealth redistribution more fervently than their weaker counterparts did (Petersen et al. 2013).

In sum, physical strength matters. It is inextricably connected to sexual and romantic attractiveness and physical size, all of which generally provide benefits to those who hold high levels of them and costs to those with low levels. Strength helps people to not get bullied and to not have to depend on others for basic daily tasks, while lack of strength makes individuals more dependent and susceptible to abuse. An abundance of strength also provides prestige to those who have the version most praised in their particular spatial and temporal contexts—prestige others cannot individually access but may have to rely on others to use to gather needed items (e.g., the young, healthy, and strong member of the family may be the only one who can earn enough money to support the family).

While the advancements of technology and science have lessened the role of strength in everyday life, they have not completely diminished its influence. Within social units, where people are often quantified based on their affiliation with larger groups by macro researchers in social science (e.g., as women, middle class, Black.), power dynamics exist that are based on disparate levels of physical strength, which creates possibilities for power to be abused. In other words, when physical strength and capability are not distributed equally (and thus, by proxy, sexual attractiveness, financial capability, and social success), and one party depends on the other to assist him with certain tasks, the potential for abuse exists.

Those people who in the macro world often appear as the victims of the structural factors (e.g., women, children, racial and ethnic minorities) often abuse their contextual, intra-social unit, micro-world advantages to abuse power over those who are dominant in the "big world." There are many cases, for instance, when women abuse men, and their behavior is in direct contrast to conventional "dependent, submissive" femininity (see Danielle Lindemann's *Dominatrix: Gender, Eroticism, and Control in the Dungeon* 2012).

Physical Strength and Its Relationship to Heavy Macro Variables

When social scientists study physical strength, it is usually as part of an index meant to measure some overarching abstract variable (e.g., "capability" as the combination of physical, emotional, and intellectual fitness, and positioning within the existing social framework; or "masculinity," whether hyper or hypo, measured by strength, appearance, attitudes, and actions), or as a latent force operating under the umbrella of gender or age (i.e., males and people of a certain age are assumed to possess the most physical strength on average). So, while physical strength is hardly ever explicitly studied as a standalone variable in social science, it is entangled and correlated with other variables that are regularly used.

Pierre Bourdieu once said that "the body is in the social world, but the social world is in the body" (Bourdieu and Wacquant 1992). He was one of the only theorists to deal with the body as an inescapable part of the social world; others preferred to speak only of people with disembodied voices, relegating a person's physicality to the realm of nearly pure constructionism. Bourdieu, seeking to tear down what he saw as false dualisms in the social sciences, tied the physical body to the mind and the objective body to its subjective counterpart. He argued that physical space—including the size, shape, and position of human bodies within it—plays an influential role in human relations (Bourdieu 2013; Bourdieu 1977).

Still, many sociologists and anthropologists working in the area of the body have sought to distance the body from the biological realm (e.g., Reischer and Koo 2004). No doubt, part of the apprehension to using the physical body (especially in its differentiated forms) and its capabilities in the delineation of social theory and during social analysis came from a fear of creeping back to biological determinism; to eugenics; to the past.[3] Bodies and their component parts could be measured, their performance could be tested, and their relative worth ranked. This was too dangerous to a progressive, postwar social science community.

Since modernity, individual strength has been disregarded by social scientists (mostly with good reason) at the macro level. Social problems, such as domestic violence and school bullying, have been analyzed through the lens of culture (e.g., Perilla, Bakeman, and Norris 1994), gender construction (e.g., Anderson 1997), social networks (e.g., Levendowsky et al. 2004), status (e.g., Koenig et al. 2003), etc. While these approaches have taught us much about the phenomena in question and helped us to create programs to minimize their occurrence and influence, physical strength still seems to have some effect in determining when, where, and how these problems occur. Sociologist Richard Felson (1996) showed that when power-neutralizing weapons are not involved, those who are physically more powerful will be more aggressive and harmful than those who are less powerful. These effects diminish, however, when weapons are present.

Micro theorists of the constructionist, pragmatist, and symbolic interaction schools (Mead, Blumer, Cooley, etc.), and others subscribing to the bottom-up, socially spurred, spontaneous creation of reality have treated physical strength as another variable whose influence lies in the definitions people apply to it. In this way, a person only has power as the

47

result of social strength if the prevailing norms and constructed power structures frame it as such; this power only has the potential to exact influence insofar as the prevailing norms and created power structures allow. This perspective has certainly enhanced our understanding of cultural and temporal variation and provided a stunning commentary on the social role of knowledge creation.

However, most would agree that humans, like other animals, have bodies and physical capabilities that exist even devoid of social experience. The relative utility of bodily strength in interpersonal relationships is, of course, dependent on the social context, although there is a tangible and varying antecedent to this construction (i.e., the biology of the body). While a large part of the utility of physical capital is in others' perceptions of its existence/quality in another, as well as in one's own feelings about one's bodily power, these layers must be piled onto the extant existence of something. Thus, physical strength is socially appraised, used, denounced, vilified, heralded, etc., and its power is mediated by perceptions that consider race, gender, class, etc.; but it cannot be completely willed away by social forces. This may be especially true within social units, where interaction is, as Erving Goffman would say, "backstage" from the most encompassing and influential social mores.

In micro interactions, with many pretenses in abatement, spouses exploit their physical dominance over their spouses (for a recent article that unpacks the social/cultural and biological influences of this phenomenon, see Kaur and Garg 2008); children procure stolen lunch money through threat of bodily harm at recess (Colvin et al. 1998); and American female military members, who are generally—though certainly not always—weaker than their male counterparts, in combat zones are "more likely to be raped by a fellow soldier than killed by the enemy" (PBS 2013). In her recent eye-opening book *For Love of Country: Confronting Rape and Sexual Harassment in the U.S. Military* (2008), Terri Nelson relayed the words of these rape victims. The following is a quote from a teenage victim who was on active duty when raped: "I was prepared to be a POW (prisoner of war) or worse for my country. I wasn't prepared to have my superiors and comrades sexually abuse me. I must admit that a chaplain I told my story to in 1996 said something I had not realized. He said, 'Your comrades were your enemy and you were in a combat zone.' I thought that was rather interesting. I was only nineteen. I just wanted to carry on the tradition of our family being in the military" (Nelson 2008, 3).

This part of the social world—the interactions that exist within a family, in a group of classmates, or in a military unit—remains largely hidden and understudied as a social science phenomenon.

Modern social scientists do pay heed to resource allocation in some micro interactions. Behavioral economics, social psychology, and game theory all detail the role of resources in close interpersonal situations, although these approaches do not generally register the influence of the micro culture in which individuals are embedded for a substantial portion of their lives. Moreover, while experimenters in the social sciences often manipulate explanatory variables to determine their influence (e.g., the relative amount of money, or a money proxy, that an individual begins with may vary in the experimental design), physical strength is rarely, if ever, used as an explanatory variable in these artificial-setting experiments.

Physical Strength in Interpersonal Relationships: In the Family, at School, and in the Military

The remaining portion of this chapter will articulate the theoretical and empirical significance of physical strength in the family, in school, and in the military. There will most certainly be overlap between the different units, and some general themes will emerge. While acknowledging that this variable, and the dynamics surrounding it, has been studied and found to be salient when measured as a static concept in correlative macro studies, we will mostly concentrate on the interpersonal dynamics related to a disparity in strength within a particular social unit.

Physical Strength in the Family

In the family, the division of household tasks relies somewhat on assessments of, as well as actual, physical strength and ability, even if tradition plays a larger role. Some members of the household (e.g., children, the disabled, and elderly members) rely on others to get their basic needs met by having them open jars, drive cars, remove barriers, reach shelves, remind them of tasks they need to perform (e.g., taking pills), etc. People, society, and technology all strive toward providing people at the mercy of others with autonomy over their own lives and well-being. Nevertheless, even in modern families, there are individuals who possess physical capabilities needed by another who does not have this same ability at his disposal.

Even though the line between the physical and the mental—the biological and the psychological—is messy at best and nonexistent at worst, we still categorize disabilities using these terms. So, there are physically disabled people, mentally disabled people, and people who are both physically and mentally disabled (we could further classify disabilities by distinguishing the emotional from the mental, and the sensory from the physical). As brain science has become more sophisticated, we have uncovered physical correlates to mental processes, personality, and behaviors, among other things (Kennis, Rademaker, and Geuze 2013). So, in many ways, those that have traditionally been known as mental, psychological, and/or cognitive abilities are also physical abilities, and their "sub-optimal" functioning can be considered a physical disability (or, at least, a sign of physical variation). Regardless of the semantics concerning classification, disabled people, when living within a family unit, are likely to depend on others for the fulfillment of basic needs.

Abuse of Disabled Family Members

The health care industry uses an index called the Activities of Daily Living (ADLs) to denote a person's inability/ability to care for him- or herself. The index usually includes such tasks as being able to bathe oneself, successfully void oneself in the bathroom, move, eat, feed, take one's medications, and operate one's medical devices. A related, broader index is the Instrumental Activities of Daily Living (IADLs). This list includes activities that help one live a happy and integrated life within the community: the ability to manage finances, take care of a pet, communicate via a computer or phone, successfully manage the role of one's caregiver, etc.

In 2006, the *National Health Interview Survey* asked a multistage probability sample of over 75,000 noninstitutionalized members from the United States about the capabilities of those who live in their dwelling (Center for Disease Control 2008). This means that the sample excluded people who were in hospitals, nursing homes, and other long-term health facilities (including those for the severely disabled). However, due to the myriad living arrangements of disabled people, it is hard to know exactly who/what met the criteria for exclusion.

Based on this survey, the Center for Disease Control (CDC) estimated that 2 percent (3.9 million adults in 2006) of American adults required assistance in completing ADLs, while 4 percent (7.8 million adults in 2006) did so with IADLs. Older and poorer individuals were more likely than their counterparts to have an ADL and/or an IADL limitation (CDC 2008).

With our ever-increasing life expectancy, not only are people staying alive for extended periods of time while also needing help with basic daily tasks, but many are also, in their older years, being directly cared for by family members, as opposed to receiving more institutionalized care. Thus, it has become common for many middle-aged adults to be directly responsible for the care of their elderly parents (Pedrick-Cornell and Gelles 1982). As the number and percentage of de-institutionalized disabled people rises, it becomes even more likely that these individuals will be classified under umbrella HMVs and that the dynamics of the power-imbalanced interpersonal relations in their homes will be missed by social scientists.

So, there are millions of adults unable to perform all tasks related to daily living, who may live with their families, or by themselves with a daily assistant, or in private residential group homes, etc. These people depend on others to provide them with what they cannot provide for themselves. This resource imbalance creates a power dynamic ripe for doling out abuse (physical, sexual, mental, emotional, etc.). Additionally, there is evidence that the more care one needs (for physical or mental impairments), the more likely that person is to be abused. Arling and Williams (2003) documented the not-so-surprising phenomenon that the more time, emotional work, physical effort, etc. caretakers spent in assisting one individual, the lower the caretaker's tolerance, self-control, and energy became. This leads to anger and higher occurrences of poor judgment and abuse on behalf of the caretakers.

Still, disability is not an HMV usually used by social scientists, although the concept may be gaining traction (Shuttleworth and Meekosha 2013). Disabled people are likely to live with others (family, friends, and/or hired staff) from the same community, of the same race, and often of the same socioeconomic status. In other words, when social scientists perform macro analyses, those with one or more ADLs often get lumped in with the nondisabled and counted in the same way, even though their everyday lives may be completely different. Disabled people, who depend on caretakers in their everyday lives, are often abused by their caretakers.

The US Department of Health and Human Services' Office on Women's Health (2011) reported that women with disabilities are especially likely to suffer domestic abuse:

> Research suggests that women with disabilities are more likely to suffer domestic violence and sexual assault than women without

disabilities. And women with disabilities report abuse that lasts longer and is more intense than women without disabilities. Like other women, women with disabilities usually are abused by someone they know, such as a partner or family member. In addition, women with disabilities face the risk of abuse by health care providers or caregivers. Caregivers can withhold medicine and assistive devices, such as wheelchairs or braces. They can also refuse to help with daily needs like bathing, dressing, or eating. (Office of Women's Health, US Department of Health and Human Services 2011)

Disabled women are most likely to be abused by romantic partners and family members, and they are more likely than nondisabled women to suffer abuse from health care workers and strangers. "Compared to women without disabilities, women with disabilities were more likely to report more intense experiences of abuse, including the combination of multiple incidents, multiple perpetrators, and longer duration (Office of Women's Health, US Department of Health and Human Services 2011).

Staff malfeasance in nursing homes and other similar settings have experienced a few periods of intense media scrutiny since the 1990s, with TV investigative news shows immersing themselves into the topic, often with the aid of hidden cameras. In 2011, the *New York Daily News* ran a story on how a man caught staff members abusing his elderly mother at the nursing home where she lived. The man had formally complained to the facility about abuse prior to hiding a camera and catching staff in the act. In the video, which can be seen at (http://www.nydailynews.com/news/national/man-plants-camera-elderly-mother-nursing-home-captures-brutal-abuse-caregivers-video-article-1.125509), the aid is seen treating the elderly lady, who suffers from Alzheimer's and needs care for a variety of ADLs, "like a rag doll"; she is pushed, punched in the face, and has her face slammed against the wall, among other abuses (Caulfield 2011).

Residents do not have to be immobile to be abused; those with mostly mental deficits are also apt to be mistreated (e.g., see Brown, Stein, and Turk 1995). Often though, those who are abused have both mental and physical deficits. For example, a news release[4] filed on May 7, 2012, by the *Virginia Attorney General's Office* noted that the owner of a group home for adults had been convicted of acts that contributed to the death of a man with Parkinson's disease and an intellectual deficit. The report details the disturbing events:

[The victim] was placed under a faucet running scalding water and suffered second- and third-degree burns on his legs, face, buttocks, and arm. Ten days later, Mr. Tuggle was found dead in his bed with scabbed burns. The medical examiner determined that Tuggle died from sepsis and pneumonia secondary to thermal injury. His death was ruled as a direct result of the injuries he sustained on February 8, 2011. Caregivers failed to call 911 and, at Wagoner's orders, did not transport Tuggle to the hospital. "Not only did Wagoner fail to properly prevent conditions in which an incapacitated and helpless patient could suffer from such abject neglect and abuse, he also explicitly and deliberately deprived Mr. Tuggle of the care he needed to survive these injuries," said Virginia's Attorney General Ken Cuccinelli. (WDBJ7 2012)

Victims in circumstances like these are unable to reach out for help, and, even if they are able, their diminished physical and mental abilities make it hard for them to document the abuse they have received, file a police report, testify on their own behalf at a trial, etc. Even researchers are often limited by only being able to investigate cases that are reported to professionals (Pedrick-Cornell and Gelles 1982). Scholars who conducted a random-digit-dialing survey of adults over the age of sixty (the individuals *did not* need to be in an assisted living facility) found that one in ten of these adults had been abused or neglected in the last year (Acierno et al. 2010).

The social context of nursing homes and the characteristics of the caretakers also play a role in the manifestation, sustainment, and hidden nature of abuse. Just as weak or vulnerable patients inhabit a sociospatial position and often possess compromised cognitive abilities, both of which foster abuse, the employee hierarchy, preparedness, and esteem also contribute to the likely occurrence of abuse. Charles Stannard (1973) observed the patterns and interactions that took place in a sixty-five-bed nursing home, concluding that the everyday work environment sealed nurses off from the abuse of patients by others, as nurses were not often directly involved in caring for the patients. He argued that those providing daily care for the patients were of a low social class and had little education. Their culture, according to Stannard (1973), saw fighting or the threat of violence as a useful and legitimate way to get others to conform to their demands: "Because of their social class and low levels of education, these people do not entertain sophisticated and complex notions about human motivation and mental illness. Their interpretations of patients' actions are likely to be based on lay rather than medical ideologies" (Strauss et al. 1964, 95–6).

This increases their likelihood of using already established and familiar means of handling difficulties with patients, namely force.

To fulfill their duties, the orderlies and aides relied on the resource they had a disproportionately large amount of compared to the patients: physical strength. Thus, various resource imbalances, most importantly those regarding physical strength and ability, which exist in interpersonal relationships between caretakers and those dependent on them for ADLs, create a fertile environment for abuses of power to grow unimpeded by other forces (calls for help, government oversight, physician diagnosis, etc.).

As many studies concur, there is no concrete way to measure the full extent of the abuse suffered by the elderly and or disabled people because many of the victims do not have the ability to recognize and/or report the abuse, so even victimization studies—the usual way for social scientists to measure crime incidences—are reasoned to miss an unknown, but likely substantial, amount of the abuse that is actually occurring.

Again, because it is hard for many victims in this realm to take action against their abusers, some organizations, law enforcement, journalists, concerned family members etc. have placed stealth monitoring devices in the room of the person thought to be suffering from abuse. In early 2011, the *San Gabriel Valley Tribune* (2011) reported on the sexual assaults of disabled individuals living in group homes:

> More than 100 hours of video footage, which was dropped off at Sheriff's Headquarters Bureau in Monterey Park in March, show what appear to be 10 female patients at residential care facilities being raped. At least one of the suspects was believed to be an employee of a residential care facility and another of the suspects appeared to be a patient. All of the victims appear to be severely disabled. One of the suspects also appears to have been disabled because he used a wheelchair. The attacks involved force with no consent from the disabled victims. (San Gabriel Valley Tribune 2011)

While seemingly even less reported, perhaps due to a lack of oversight, these types of abuse also occur in traditional private family homes. In January 2010, Wisconsin's *Kenosha News* reported insidious abuse within a family home:

> Authorities found an emaciated 38-year-old woman, half-naked and shivering on a urine-soaked blanket, chained to a weight bench, covered in feces and unable to communicate or use her legs,

according to charges filed Monday against her mother and brother. The mentally disabled woman, who reportedly has the mind of a 5-year-old but had once lived normally, weighed 60 to 70 pounds when she was found. When rescuers cut the chain around her left ankle, authorities said the woman could not straighten her legs or walk. (Stephen 2010)

Another case, from Mississippi, involved a developmentally delayed woman and her housemates:

Banished to the basement, the 29-year-old mother with a childlike mind and another baby on the way had little more than a thin rug and a mattress to call her own on the chilly concrete floor. Dorothy Dixon ate what she could forage from the refrigerator upstairs, where housemates used her for target practice with BBs, burned her with a glue gun and doused her with scalding liquid that peeled away her skin. Her attackers/housemates included Michelle Riley, 35, who they said befriended Dixon but pocketed monthly Social Security checks she got because of her developmental delays, Judy Woods, three teenagers (including Riley's 16-year old daughter), and Riley's 12 year old son. They torched what few clothes she had, so she walked around naked. They often pummeled her with an aluminum bat or metal handle. Dixon—six months pregnant—died after weeks of abuse. Police have charged two adults, three teenagers and a 12-year-old boy with murder in the case that has repulsed many in this Mississippi River town. Riley and Dixon, police said, had lived in Quincy, a Mississippi River town about 100 miles north of St. Louis, Mo. Quincy is where Riley worked as a coordinator for a regional center that helps the developmentally disabled with housing and other services. Dixon was a client. (Suhr 2008)

These are not isolated incidents. The US Department of Justice reported that younger disabled individuals experience twice as much violence as their able-bodied counterparts (Bureau of Justice Statistics 2008). ABC News has reported that one in three nursing home residents are abused, citing a large two-year study conducted by the Special Investigations Divisions of the House Government Reform Committee (Ruppe 2001). The activist group Barrier Free Living (2012), which began as a federally funded project, argued that the biggest concern of women with disabilities is domestic abuse. Additionally, it argued that four out of five people within this demographic have been sexually abused, and that, each year, around five million disabled people in the United States are victims of crime. Of course, weak or vulnerable men also fall victim to abuses of power.

Using data from Adult Protective Services case files on seventeen men who were sexually abused in Virginia, Roberto, Teaster, and Nikzad (2007) found that the victims had trouble caring for themselves and managing their finances. More notably, the characteristics of the men who were abused were very similar to those of abused women who were documented in an earlier study. For both men and women, a relative lack of resources served as a precursor to abuse. It is clear that a relative lack of physical strength of the victims influences their chances of being victimized, whether the victim is an elderly person, a woman, a child, or even a man.

However, in order for this to fit the thesis of our book, these offenses must occur under the cover of an HMV, within one social unit, and, in this way, be somewhat hidden from rank-and-file social science. Barrier Free Living (2012) reports that around 98 percent of the perpetrators sexually abusing a disabled person are "well known to, trusted by, and in a care providing position to the victim." A third of the abusers are family or friends; almost half of the abusers are caretakers (Barrier Free Living 2012). Family and caretakers are regularly in very intimate and isolated relationships with handicapped individuals, giving them a chance to abuse (Hoog 2003). Both the abusers and those being abused are likely to share the same race and live in the same area or even home; they are likely to be conceptualized the same way by macro studies, even macro studies on dependency. A study by Valenti-Hein and Schwartz (1995) documents that abusers usually abuse ten, twenty, thirty, or even seventy people before they get caught, if they get caught at all. Most abuse towards disabled people is not reported to police, and even if it is, it is much less likely to be prosecuted than are crimes against able-bodied people. So even using arrest and/or conviction records as a variable in a study will only catch a sliver of these dynamics.

Although all domestic violence has consequences, abuse is compounded for individuals who lack resources: they need to realize the abuse is wrong, physically remove themselves from the situation, reach out for help, explain the abuse, testify against the abuser, etc. Furthermore, because most abuse is doled out by those with intimate, personal, and, in many ways, private relationships with the victim—people the victim relies on to assist him or her with ADLs—the victim can ill afford to offer resistance, as, with their especially vulnerable position, the consequences can be quick and deadly (e.g., the purposeful withholding of needed medications). The Center for Research on Women with Disabilities at the Baylor College of Medicine illustrates how hard it is for women, especially disabled women, to alert someone to their abuse (which may account for part of the reason why the abuse of disabled people is so much less likely to be reported than the abuse of able-bodied people):

> [Domestic abuse is] a highly stigmatizing phenomenon that most women are reluctant to discuss. Fear of mandatory reporting and consequent retaliation by the perpetrator further serve to discourage answering such questions candidly. For women with disabilities there may be the added dimension of dependence on the perpetrator for personal care. A woman with severe functional impairments can little afford to disclose abuse and face having the perpetrator prosecuted when she is dependent on that person for her daily survival, with no back up available. (Baylor College of Medicine, n.d.)

Not only are disabled people a prime target for abuse, but their limitations in performing ADLs and IADLs also limit their ability to seek out and secure help. Even when abused disabled individuals are able to be seen by medical and/or social work professionals, it is easy to have the damage sustained from the abuse seen as just another manifestation of their disability or illness. So, while domestic abuse leads to depression, anxiety attacks, back pain, sleep and appetite disturbance, emotional imbalance, low self-esteem, sexual dysfunction, etc., medical professionals often attribute these issues to the original handicap. This makes it unlikely that they will seek out alternative causes for these symptoms (Baylor College of Medicine n.d.).

In some cases, the disabled individuals are even abused by their primary care providers, who may injure service animals, withhold medication, break medical equipment, etc. If disabled and abused persons do seek out help, they are putting themselves in a precarious position, as medical professionals and the state may decide to institutionalize them, taking away some of their basic autonomy (Barrier Free Living 2012). Even if the disabled and abused person is able to seek out help, receives quality help with no abuse, and does not get institutionalized, they still have to fear retaliation by their abuser(s) and carry around the stigma associated with having been involved in an abusive relationship.

Domestic Abuse of Vulnerable, Able-Bodied Family Members

Of course, a person does not have to fit the label of "disabled" to be taken advantage of in their dwelling: they may just be physically weaker, or at least perceived to be less physically strong, than another.

Any strength imbalance within a family has the ability to facilitate the infliction of harm on those who do not possess the ability to equal the power of abusers. Spousal and child abuse are often the result of a variety of variables (e.g., psychological control, disparate ownership of family wealth, and societal norms), but physical strength certainly plays a role in facilitating these tragic and usually recurring incidents. Sometimes, backed by a potential physical threat or with an antecedent of actual physical violence, a strong family member can dictate what other members of the family must do.

Indeed, the abuser often benefits from the backing of others, even if he created this backing through threatened or actual power abuses ("If you snitch, I'll whoop you too!"). The extant cultural milieu also provides both latent and, at times, manifest backing of the abuser. So, the adults in a neighborhood will support the rules other adults impose on their children and will believe the version of events presented by parents over contradictory accounts offered by children. With increasing awareness and disdain of child abuse at the macro level, this layer of backing may be thinning over time.

Similarly, the presence of laws and their jurisdiction regarding domestic abuse have changed over the years. In the early United States, women and children had little legal recourse when attacked by someone within their family. It was not until the mid-nineteenth century that any US state made wife battering illegal (Kleinberg 1999), and only much later did marital rape enter the penal code. (In 1980, fewer than 10 percent of states had made marital rape illegal; Allison and Wrightsman 1993.) In addition to a soft legal stance on marital rape throughout history, there has been a strong social stigma attached to victims who went public (Browne 1993). As with abuses of power against disabled family members, most scholars agree that the true amount and degree of spousal abuse and rape remains unknown. The physical, psychological, and sexual abuse suffered within the family when one member exerts physical dominance over another is largely hidden from the scope of macro social science and the implementation of HMVs.

While most of the research in this area has been elucidating the abuse perpetrated by males on their female intimate partners, domestic spousal abuse can also be perpetrated by women on men (although this is estimated to be much less common) and in the realm of homosexual relationships. Waterman, Dawson, and Bologna (1989) found that in their sample of people in homosexual relationships "12% of the gay men and 31% of the lesbians reported being victims of forced sex by their current or most recent partners."

The family is one of the most private institutions in modern day society, and members of a family possess a disparate amount of many resources, one of which is physical strength and capability. These differences in resource allocation create situations where family members need to be dependent on other family members. In the case of physical strength, those with disabilities need help with activities of daily living, and those less strong in general are dependent on the whims and demands of stronger individuals in order to avoid abuse. Because these power abuses occur within a social unit, this type of inequality is not as studied in the social sciences as that which exists between different groups at the macro level.

Physical Strength in Schools

In schools, we see small initial physical advantages yielding compound social interest. Kids from the same neighborhoods, of the same age, and going to the same school will eventually individually evolve into the social hierarchy so commonly seen coexisting with the youth of America. Elementary students with a high level of physical strength will generally excel at sports, be free from fear of attack from peers, have the option to use physical ability to intimidate and extract favors from others, and will develop self-confidence and esteem. These attributes will enhance his attractiveness to others, make teachers form favorable impressions of him, and lead administrators to track him down the more lucrative curriculum. These people will associate positive feelings with physical activity, which will lead to even more physical activity and the commensurate boosts to mental health—a reinforcing loop. Linking physical activity with mental health and cognitive ability has been well documented. Tomporowski, Davis, and Naglieri (2008) reviewed the literature in this area in regards to children, which included both cross-sectional correlational studies and experimental studies parsing out causation. Although the results varied in magnitude, the studies pointed to a positive overall correlation between exercise and cognitive functioning, with a large portion of the correlation attributed to exercise causing increased mental ability. Dwyer et al.'s (2001) study on Australian schoolchildren aged seven to fifteen had similar results. Measures of children's physical fitness (sit-ups, pushups, long jump, hand grip, etc.), cardio-respiratory efficiency (50 meter sprint, 1.6 kilometer run, and submaximal measure of VO$_2$), and general activity (self-report questionnaire) were correlated with ratings of scholastic achievement provided by school personnel. Small but significant positive associations were found between scholastic achievement and physical fitness and general activity measures. The California Department of Education (2005) found a stronger positive correlation in their study on the relationship between the physical fitness and academic performance of fifth, seventh, and ninth graders.

Those who are more physically fit/strong will exercise more, becoming even more fit and strong, and do better in school/have higher cognitive functioning abilities. Thus, an initial edge in physical strength can strongly influence the forming social hierarchy within schools, not to mention the direct effects on popularity and power gained from being able to be relationally aggressive, and good-looking, and a sports star as a result of superior fitness garnered from the genetic lottery or an organizational nuance such as a decision on when students may start formal schooling and/or sport league play.

In *Outliers*, Malcolm Gladwell (2008) highlighted the power of the confluence of birthdays and league or division cutoff dates for school-aged kids. At most schools, one needs to be within a certain age range to be placed in a specific grade (e.g., a student would have to be thirteen years old on September first to be in the eighth grade). Hence, one student could be a day shy of being a full year older than another student in the same grade. While this difference would seem to get less important as time moved on (i.e., the difference between being thirteen years old and thirteen years and 364 days old is more significant than the difference between being twenty-three years old and twenty-three years and 364 days old), we cannot ignore the influence the initial effects have on later life. A boy, almost fourteen, with 364 days more days of puberty than his competition for the starting center position on the basketball team, will be more likely to make inroads toward sports, social, and academic success compared to his younger counterparts: he will be granted the more prestigious role on the team, excel at the role, and experience all of the tangential effects of being a star athlete (e.g., attention, romantic interests, self-esteem, more athletic opportunities, and favorable impressions on teachers).

Later on down the line, we would expect that the older kid would be more likely to earn a college scholarship, have a fulfilling social life, be employed at a well-paying job, etc. This will not always be the case, of course, but the kids with the initial advantage, even if it is small, will have recurrent advantages that compound upon one another; the differences in the end are much more dramatic than they were in the beginning.

Gladwell (2008) used the case of hockey players, setting the mood by describing a National Hockey League game in which the players' names were replaced with the month and day of their birthdays. Reading, you start to notice that the majority of the players were born at the beginning of the year (specifically in January). Gladwell (2008) argued that this trend can be traced back to youth hockey leagues that have a December thirty-first cut-off line, and so those born in January will be the oldest on their respective teams. When eight- or nine-year-olds play hockey, the slightly older kids—those born in January, February, and March—will, in general, be better players. They will be singled out for more instruction and get invited to compete on select teams, which involve playing more hockey games with and against better competition. Because they excel, they will be more likely to practice and will practice harder; others will help push them. The December-born kids may quit or play just for fun.

Most of the kids born in January will not make it into the NHL ranks, but, when looking at NHL rosters, we see a disproportionately high number of players who were born in the early months of the year. That initial competitive advantage, most likely those extra bits of size, strength, and speed, will pay dividends. None of the usual HMVs can predict a young child's sports success as accurately as will his birthday vis-à-vis the age group cut-off date.

This initial edge in physicality not only yields compound competitive gains (including the manufacture of an even greater strength imbalance) but also creates dependent relationships. In the contemporary United States, strength (or its appearance), level of sexual desirability, sexual success, sports success, and fighting (even if play-fighting or fighting as sport, as in wrestling or boxing) are all tied to popularity, especially for males. Being strong, sexy, and sexual (these become important around puberty), a sports star, and someone who commands physical respect on the playground, in the locker room, and/or at parties helps a person become popular, which comes with its own set of advantages (e.g., a large social circle to call on for assistance).

Dijkstra et al. (2010) used a subsample from the cohort study "Tracking Adolescents' Individual Lives Survey" to document that physical attractiveness, athletic ability, and physical aggression all predicted popularity. Other studies have shown that popularity is associated with influence, leadership, admiration, dominance, and resource control (Dijkstra et al. 2010). Being popular affords an individual power over the unpopular.

If others wish to align themselves with those who possess the above attributes as a result of their physical strength/fitness, they must be accepted by the popular kids. In many ways, without the sanctioning of those who hold premium social status, those lacking physical strength cannot successfully participate in certain sports, date in certain circles, expect protection from bullies and to not be their target, etc.

Those on the weaker end of the spectrum are, thus, dependent on their stronger counterparts. This dynamic allows the strong to exploit the dependence of others. So, the strong and popular may sanction the inclusion of a weaker person under the condition that the weaker person provides services for him. The dependent, weaker members will confess to actions they did not do in order to save the stronger members from punishment or a tarnished reputation. They will carry out acts under the direction of the stronger members—acts which the stronger member does not have time for (e.g., completing homework, doing household chores), does not feel like doing (again, homework and chores), cannot do for fear of spoiled identity (e.g., renting an embarrassing movie) or possible negative sanction (e.g., buying beer with a fake ID, theft), or which the stronger member finds amusing (e.g., telling off a teacher, doing something embarrassing in front of a large audience of school members). The stronger member can threaten violence if the tasks are not done to his liking, although just the threat of losing membership in the social group is often enough to ensure compliance.

Physical strength and aggression help individuals not only to attain the powerful position popularity brings within a school setting but also to maintain their status. Adler and Adler (1998) illustrated how those atop the social hierarchy used physical aggression or the threat of physical aggression to prevent others from dethroning them.

Physical Strength in the Military

In the military, a minimum level of physical capability needs to be met in order for one to be accepted and retained. To achieve inclusion in an elite group (e.g., Navy Seals, Green Berets, or Army Rangers), one has to be even more physically impressive relative to others. For example, in order to qualify for Ranger School, a candidate must be able to complete forty-nine pushups in two minutes, fifty-nine sit-ups in two minutes, six pull-ups, a two-mile run in less than fifteen minutes and twelve seconds, a five mile run in less than forty minutes, and a sixteen-mile hike carrying sixty-five pounds in five hours and twenty minutes. And these are the *minimum* requirements (Smith n.d.). Becoming a Ranger comes with an increased likelihood of future promotions; a lucrative signing bonus; access to state-of-the-art training, housing, and dining facilities; and a considerable bump in everyday status (Army.com 2013). While the standards are lower for the basic enlisted man (some of the standards vary by age and gender), they still pose a considerable threat to curtailing a prospective soldier's military career. Individuals who repeatedly cannot meet the basic level of fitness will be dismissed from the service because the US military feels that:

> All military personnel, regardless of occupational specialty, unit assignment, age, or gender should acquire a base level of general physical fitness. This physical fitness promotes a standard of physical readiness commensurate with the active life style and deployability of the military profession. Such a DoD-wide generalized fitness standard will enhance overall health, physical well-being, military readiness, and appearance. This base level of fitness can then be used as a springboard to train the personnel for further physically demanding occupational unit assignments and deployable combat readiness. (Military Operational Medicine Research Program 1999)

While a certain baseline of strength and fitness is required to enter the military, possessing a relatively high degree of strength and fitness also gives a soldier an advantage over the competition in ascending through the various levels of military leadership. The military is tightly hierarchical—a low-level soldier reports to her commanding officer, who reports to his commanding officer, who reports to her commanding officer, and so on. Additionally, soldiers have a legal obligation to follow the orders of their superiors as long as these orders are "lawful." A soldier is dependent on his commanding officer, who may be around the same age, from the same socioeconomic circumstances, from the same country, of the same race, etc. In this way, strength influences status attainment, which bestows rational-legal power. This may even flow all the way to the top; US presidents, who take on the role of commander-in-chief during their presidency, have been taller on average than other US men born around the same time (Stulp et al. 2013).

However, there are even power differences among military members of the same rank, some of which are, at least partially, the result of disparate strength. Obviously, all other things being equal (including rank), the physically dominant member of a collective in the battlefield can exert his will on the others, forcing them to place themselves in precarious positions (e.g., being the first to walk through a minefield), donate their food rations to the stronger member(s), or perform the daily "grunt" work needed by the team (e.g., cleaning).

Soldiers have been raped not only by those with superior ranking, who can use their authority over the person to coerce her to conform to his request ("If you do not do this, I will have you written up for poor job performance"), but also by their peers of the same rank. When the victims of these acts recount the events, we often notice the victim's lack of ability to physically overcome her attacker. Granted, rapists attacking their peers also utilize other modes of control in performing their acts, such as threats of future action against the victim or someone the victim cares about ("If you don't let me have sex with you, I will kill you/have you fired/tell everyone what you did/spread a lie about you/hurt your children/tell your husband you are cheating on him."), psychological manipulation ("You are a slut, and this is what sluts do."), and drugging.[5] However, a key component in many rapes is the ability for the rapist to use his superior strength to subdue his victim. Of course, a group of rapists acting together can use their collective strength against an outmatched victim as well.

While the prevalence of rape and the rape culture in the military has received quite a bit of recent media and scholarly attention, for a long time (and still, to a large degree), these incidents were hidden because victims did not feel comfortable coming forward and/or, when they did come forward, their allegations were swept under the rug, deemed hearsay, resulted in an extremely mild punishment, were met with internal disciplining of the *victim*, etc. The victims feared that they would be harassed and abused even more if they spoke up. Many victims of rape/sexual harassment in the military were given stigmatizing and discrediting psychiatric diagnoses after making it known they had been raped (Nelson 2008). All of these issues may be even more threatening when the individual is a victim of homosexual rape in an antigay military culture. One Army veteran victim of sexual abuse explained what happened to her after lodging a complaint:

> They made me feel like I was crazy. All I needed was a little support. Instead, they locked me up in psych with some really, really sick people, drugged me to where I could barely walk, and never, not once,

got me in to see a counselor. They said I had a personality disorder and then they discharged me. The counselor I see now is really good, but she doesn't think I have a personality disorder. I think they screwed me till the end. (Nelson 2008, 129)

The fact that the military creates cohesive groups of people who swear to a code of honor and allegiance to one another is an additional factor in why the abuses within the military are often kept hidden. In addition, it still seems that the cases that are currently coming to light may only be the tip of the iceberg, with some studies pointing to the rate of sexual assaults in the military being twenty times the rate of those occurring in other government jobs (Murdoch and Nichol 1995).

An abused Marine is quoted in Nelson's (2008) text, describing a situation that highlights how pervasive these acts can be in the military:

Apparently, there were far too many incidents of men forcefully entering the women [marines'] bedrooms at night. It seems that many of these men enter these rooms uninvited and often through the windows while the women sleep. Upon breaking and entering into the private sleeping quarters of the service women, the male marines get on top of the women and then force sex upon them. These marines are raping their fellow female marines and threatening them not to tell anyone. (Nelson 2008, 31)

Conclusion

An individual's relative possession of physical strength still influences his or her life in the twenty-first century. Within families, military barracks, and junior high hallways, those who possess superior physicality are privy to benefits, while those with a lack of physical ability are not only denied such benefits but also susceptible to abuse. The dynamic is especially ripe for abuse when an individual is dependent on another due to a strength imbalance, whether it is a wife depending on her husband to not physically beat her, a smallish adolescent dependent on his more physically mature classmates to accept him into their prestigious social circle, or a frail, elderly family member depending on his grandchildren to cook his meals and administer his medications. In each situation, the stronger individuals have the ability to use their superior strength to extract personal benefits. In the macro studies of modern social science, this type of inequality—that which occurs within social units—is often passed over.

Notes

1. For a fairly recent review and critique of the various manifestations of this theory, see Ghosh 2001.
2. In a Vanity Fair article titled "Hollywood's Vial Bodies," Ned Zeman (2012) characterizes the phenomenon:

   "Two inside sources, a movie producer and a studio executive, can rattle off a list of Hollywood H.G.H. users, starting with several top-shelf movie stars of both genders. H.G.H.—or 'H,' as jocks call it—is an equal-opportunity employer, except as pertains to age. Although one particularly ripped twenty-something heartthrob is said to be on the needle, H.G.H. is largely the domain of stars who wish they were still under 35. The surest giveaway? 'Any actor over 50 you're still seeing with a ripped stomach and veins in his forearms is probably taking H.G.H.,' says a talent manager who represents one famously veiny TV star."
3. Similarly, some have expressed great worry that the sequencing of the human genome would reintroduce eugenics to mainstream society (e.g., see Garver and Garver 1994).
4. The four following block quotes were compiled in VOR 2013. We have cited the original press reports in the text.
5. One of the first female US Naval Air Crew members tells of her 1989 rape on the activist site www.mydutytospeak.com: "Eventually, I was sent on another deployment to Greece. I felt I could manage my interactions with people to ensure what happened on my first deployment, didn't happen again. So one evening, when I was asked by a quiet, married crew member to join him for a drink, I felt it was a safe, low-risk opportunity to socialize. The last thing I remember is having one drink with this man. I am confident I was drugged. The following morning I woke up black, blue and purple from head to toe. I had severe bruising and swelling between my legs. My vagina was raw. I was covered with vomit and bodily fluids. The man I had had one drink with was still there. But the bruising and the mess that was made in the night told me, there had been more than one visitor to my room. I soaked in a bath to rid myself of the disgustingness that was done to my body. I put on a turtle neck under my flight-suit to hide my bruised neck, and went to work broken."

References

Acierno, Ron et al. 2010. "Prevalence and Correlates of Emotional, Physical, Sexual, and Financial Abuse and Potential Neglect in the United States: The National Elder Mistreatment Study." *American Journal of Public Health,* 100(2):292–7.

Adler, Patricia and Peter Adler. 1998. *Peer Power: Preadolescent Culture and Identity.* New Brunswick, NJ: Rutgers University Press.

Allison, Julie A. and Lawrence S. Wrightsman. 1993. *Rape: The Misunderstood Crime.* Thousand Oaks, CA: Sage Publications.

Anderson, Kristin L. 1997. "Gender, Status, and Domestic Violence: An Integration of Feminist and Family Violence Approaches." *Journal of Marriage and the Family,* 59(3):655.

Arling, Greg and Arthur R. Williams. 2003. "Cognitive Impairment and Resource Use of Nursing Home Residents: A Structural Equation Model." *Medical Care,* 41(7):802–12.

Army.com. 2013. "Ranger Benefits and Lifestyle." http://army.com/info/spec-ops/rangers/life (accessed September 4, 2013).

Baumeister, R. F., Kathleen D. Vohs and Dianne M. Tice. 2007. "The Strength Model of Self-Control." *Current Directions in Psychological Science,* 16:396–403.

Baylor College of Medicine. n.d. "Violence Against Women with Disabilities." http://www.bcm.edu/crowd/?pmid=2143 (accessed September 4, 2013).

Barrier Free Living. 2012. "An Innovative New Method for Measuring Safety." http://www.bflnyc.org/about-us/domestic-violence-disability (accessed September 4, 2013).

Bourdieu, Pierre. 1977. *Equisse D'une Théorie de La Pratique.* Cambridge, MA: Cambridge University Press.

Bourdieu, Pierre. 2013. *Distinction: A Social Critique of the Judgement of Taste.* Abingdon, UK: Routledge.

Bourdieu, Pierre, and Loïc J. D. Wacquant. 1992. *An Invitation to Reflexive Sociology.* Chicago, IL: University of Chicago Press.

Brown, Hilary, June Stein, and Vicky Turk. 1995. "The Sexual Abuse of Adults with Learning Disabilities: Report of a Second Two-Year Incidence Survey." *Mental Handicap Research,* 8(1):3–24.

Browne, Angela. 1993. "Violence Against Women by Male Partners: Prevalence, Outcomes, and Policy Implications." *American Psychologist,* 48(10):1077–87.

Bureau of Justice Statistics. 2008. "Crimes Against People with Disabilities, 2008." (http://www.bjs.gov/content/pub/pdf/capd08.pdf).

California Department of Education. 2005. "A Study of the Relationship Between Physical Fitness and Academic Achievement in California Using 2004 Test." http://www.cde.ca.gov/ta/tg/pf/documents/pft2004resultsv2.doc (accessed September 4, 2013).

Cartledge, Paul. 2003. *Spartan Reflections.* Berkeley, CA: University of California Press.

Caulfield, Philip. 2011. "Man Plants Camera in Elderly Mother's Nursing Home, Captures Brutal Abuse by Caregivers." *NY Daily News,* June 29. (http://www.nydailynews.com/news/national/man-plants-camera-elderly-mother-nursing-home-captures-brutal-abuse-caregivers-video-article-1.125509#ixzz2d-wYTfgzP).

Center for Disease Control. 2008. "Summary Health Statistics for the U.S. Population: National Health Interview Survey, 2006." http://www.cdc.gov/nchs/data/series/sr_10/sr10_236.pdf (accessed September 4, 2013).

Colvin, Geoff, Tary Tobin, Kelli Beard, Shanna Hagan, and Jeffrey Sprague. 1998. "The School Bully: Assessing the Problem, Developing Interventions, and Future Research Directions." *Journal of Behavioral Education* 8(3):293–319.

Dijkstra, Jan Kornelis, Antonius H. N. Cillessen, Siegwart Lindenberg, and René Veenstra. 2010. "Basking in Reflected Glory and Its Limits: Why Adolescents Hang Out with Popular Peers." *Journal of Research on Adolescence,* 20(4):942–58.

Dion, Karen, Ellen Berscheid, and Elaine Walster. 1972. "What Is Beautiful Is Good." *Journal of Personality and Social Psychology,* 24(3):285–90.

Dosomething.org. 2013. "Disability Rights." http://www.dosomething.org/issues/disability-rights (accessed September 4, 2013).

Dwyer Terrence, James F. Fallis, Leigh Blizzard, Ross Lazarus, and Kimberly Dean. 2001. "Relation of academic performance to physical activity and fitness in children." *Pediatric Exercise Science,* 13:225–37.

Felson, Richard B. 1996. "Big People Hit Little People: Sex Differences in Physical Power and Interpersonal Violence." *Criminology,* 34(3):433–52.

Gallup, Andrew C., Daniel D. White and Gordon G. Gallup, Jr. 2007. "Handgrip Strength Predicts Sexual Behavior, Body Morphology, and Aggression in Male College Students." *Evolution and Human Behavior,* 28:423–9.

Garver, K. L., and B. Garver. 1994. "The Human Genome Project and Eugenic Concerns." *American Journal of Human Genetics,* 54(1):148–58.

Ghosh, B. N. 2001. *Dependency Theory Revisited.* Farnham, UK: Ashgate.

Gladwell, Malcolm. 2005. *Blink: The Power of Thinking Without Thinking.* New York: Back Bay Books.

Gladwell, Malcolm. 2008. *Outliers: The Story of Success.* New York: Back Bay Books.

Hoog, C. 2003. "Model Protocol on Screening Practices for Domestic Violence Victims with Disabilities." Washington State Coalition Against Domestic Violence. http://www.wscadv.org/docs/protocol_disability_screening.pdf (accessed September 4, 2013).

Judge, Timothy A., and Daniel M. Cable. 2004. "The Effect of Physical Height on Workplace Success and Income: Preliminary Test of a Theoretical Model." *The Journal of Applied Psychology,* 89(3):428–41.

Kaur, Ravneet, and Suneela Garg. 2008. "Addressing Domestic Violence Against Women: An Unfinished Agenda." *Indian Journal of Community Medicine: Official Publication of Indian Association of Preventive & Social Medicine,* 33(2):73–6.

Kennis, Mitzy, Arthur R. Rademaker, and Elbert Geuze. 2013. "Neural Correlates of Personality: An Integrative Review." *Neuroscience & Biobehavioral Reviews,* 37(1):73–95.

Kleinberg, S. J. 1999. *Women in the United States, 1830–1945.* Basingstoke, UK: Macmillan.

Koenig, Michael Alan et al. 2003. "Women's Status and Domestic Violence in Rural Bangladesh: Individual- and Community-Level Effects." *Demography,* 40(2):269–88.

Krahn, Gloria L., and Charles E. Drum. 2007. "Translating Policy Principles into Practice to Improve Health Care Access for Adults with Intellectual Disabilities: A Research Review of the Past Decade." *Mental Retardation and Developmental Disabilities Research Reviews,* 13(2):160–8.

Levendosky, Alytia A. et al. 2004. "The Social Networks of Women Experiencing Domestic Violence." *American Journal of Community Psychology,* 34(1–2): 95–109.

Lindemann, Danielle. 2012. *Dominatrix: Gender, Eroticism, and Control in the Dungeon.* Chicago, IL: University of Chicago Press.

McDougall, Christopher. 2009. *Born to Run: A Hidden Tribe, Superathletes, and the Greatest Race the World Has Never Seen.* New York: Vintage.

Military Operational Medicine Research Program. 1999. "Summary Report: Research Workshop on Physical Fitness Standards and Measurements within the

Military Services." http://www.dtic.mil/cgi-bin/GetTRDoc?AD=ADA466590 (accessed September 4, 2013).

Murdoch, M., and K. L. Nichol. 1995. "Women Veterans' Experiences with Domestic Violence and with Sexual Harassment While in the Military." *Archives of family medicine* 4(5):411–8.

Nelson, Terri Spahr. 2008. *For Love of Country: Confronting Rape and Sexual Harassment in the U.S. Military*. Abingdon, UK: Routledge.

Office of Women's Health, US Department of Health and Human Services. 2011. "Violence against women with disabilities." http://www.womenshealth.gov/violence-against-women/types-of-violence/violence-against-women-with-disabilities.cfm#pubs (accessed September 4, 2013).

Ogburn, William Fielding. 1957. *Cultural Lag as Theory*. Indianapolis, IN: Bobbs-Merrill.

PBS. 2013. "Survivors Share Experiences of Sexual Assault in the Military." *PBS NewsHour*, March 13. http://www.pbs.org/newshour/bb/military/jan-june13/sexualassualt_03-13.html (accessed August 12, 2013).

Pedrick-Cornell, Claire, and Richard J. Gelles. 1982. "Elder Abuse: The Status of Current Knowledge." *Family Relations*, 31(3):457.

Perilla, Julia L., Roger Bakeman, and Fran H. Norris. 1994. "Culture and Domestic Violence: The Ecology of Abused Latinas." *Violence and Victims*, 9(4):325–39.

Petersen, Michael Bang, Daniel Sznycer, Aaron Sell, Leda Cosmides, and John Tooby. 2013. "The Ancestral Logic of Politics Upper-Body Strength Regulates Men's Assertion of Self-Interest Over Economic Redistribution." *Psychological Science*, 24(7):1098-1103. http://pss.sagepub.com/content/early/2013/05/13/0956797612466415 (accessed July 15, 2013).

Reischer, Erica, and Kathryn S. Koo. 2004. "The Body Beautiful: Symbolism and Agency in the Social World." *Annual Review of Anthropology*, 33(1):297–317.

Roberto, Karen A, Pamela B. Teaster, and Katherina A. Nikzad. 2007. "Sexual Abuse of Vulnerable Young and Old Men." *Journal of Interpersonal Violence*, 22(8).

Ruppe, David. 2001. "Elderly Abused at 1 in 3 Nursing Homes: Report." *ABC News*, July 30. http://abcnews.go.com/US/story?id=92689&page=1 (accessed September 4, 2013).

San Gabriel Valley Tribune. 2011. "At Least Two Suspected of Sex Assaults on Disabled Identified." http://www.sgvtribune.com/20110107/at-least-two-suspected-of-sex-assaults-on-disabled-identified (accessed September 4, 2013).

Shuttleworth, Russell, and Helen Meekosha. 2013. "The Sociological Imaginary and Disability Enquiry in Late Modernity." *Critical Sociology*, 39(3):349–67.

Smith, Stew. n.d. "Preparing Americans to Serve in the Military, Special Ops, Law Enforcement, & Fire Fighting." http://www.stewsmith.com/linkpages/ranger.htm (accessed September 4, 2013).

Stannard, Charles I. 1973. "Old Folks and Dirty Work: The Social Conditions for Patient Abuse in a Nursing Home."*Social Problems*, 20(3):329–42.

Stephen, Jessica. 2010. "Two Sent to Prison for Chaining Up Relative." *Kenosha News*, May 19. http://www.kenoshanews.com/home/two_sent_to_prison_for_chaining_up_relative_150122923.html (accessed September 4, 2013).

Stobbe, Mike. 2011. "Horrific US Medical Experiments Come to Light." *AOL News*, Feb 27. http://www.aolnews.com/2011/02/27/horrific-us-medical-experiments-come-to-light (accessed September 4, 2013).

Strauss, Anselm L., Leonard Schatzman, Rue Bucher, Danuta Ehrlich, and Melvin Sabshin. 1964. *Psychiatric Ideologies and Institutions*. New York: The Free Press.

Stulp, Gert, Abraham P. Buunk, Simon Verhulst, and Thomas V. Pollet. 2013. "Tall Claims? Sense and Nonsense about the Importance of Height of US Presidents." *The Leadership Quarterly*. http://dx.doi.org/10.1016/j.leaqua.2012.09.002.

Suhr, Jim. 2008. "Pregnant Woman's Death by Torture Described." *Boston.com*, March 22. http://www.boston.com/news/nation/articles/2008/03/22/pregnant_womans_death_by_torture_described (accessed August 13, 2013).

The Telegraph. 2009. "Taller Men Earn More Money." *Telegraph.co.uk*, May 18. http://www.telegraph.co.uk/science/science-news/5344766/Taller-men-earn-more-money.html (accessed July 29, 2013).

Thomas, Raji, and Michael Barnes. 2010. "Life Expectancy for People with Disabilities." *NeuroRehabilitation* 27(2):201–9.

Tomporowski, Phillip D, Catherine L. Davis, and Jack A. Naglieri. 2008. "Exercise and Children's Intelligence, Cognition, and Academic Achievement." *Educational Psychology Review*, 20(2):111–31.

United States Census Bureau. 2006. "Population Estimates." https://www.census.gov/popest/data/historical/2000s/vintage_2006/index.html (accessed September 4, 2013).

Valenti-Hein, D., and L. Schwartz. 1995. *The Sexual Abuse Interview for Those with Developmental Disabilities*. Santa Barbara, CA: James Stanfield Company.

Waterman, Caroline K., Lori J. Dawson, and Michael J. Bologna. 1989. "Sexual Coercion in Gay Male and Lesbian Relationships: Predictors and Implications for Support Services." *Journal of Sex Research*, 26(1):118–24.

WDBJ7. 2012. "Martinsville Group Home Owner Convicted in 2011 Death." http://articles.wdbj7.com/2012-05-07/group-home_31614913 (accessed September 4, 2013).

Zeman, Ned. 2012. "Hollywood's Vial Bodies." *Vanity Fair*, March 15. http://www.vanityfair.com/hollywood/2012/03/human-grown-hormone-hollywood-201203 (accessed August 7, 2013).

4

Wealth

Inequality has been a popular topic in sociology since the field's nascent stages. Karl Marx and Max Weber focused on inequality, although with different emphases. Marx highlighted the nefarious outcomes of resource disparities in capitalism, where the ownership of the means of production concretely relegated the bourgeoisie and proletariat to different social, economic, and cultural spheres. Weber added disproportionalities in social and political status to the mix, arguing that these variables—which were often more ascribed than achieved—greatly influenced the life chances of an individual. Later scholars would highlight the fact that these two well-educated European men, and others who were similarly positioned, had a great deal of influence on the sociological canon, whereas women, ethnic minorities, and those without formal education failed to have their views legitimized (e.g., see Lengermann and Niebrugge-Brantley's 1998 textbook *The Women Founders: Sociology and Social Theory, 1830–1930*, which argued that the important contributions of women have been ignored and tried to work toward correcting this misappropriation).

While studying a variety of kinds of inequality—social (e.g., Beck 2010), incarceration (e.g., Wakefield and Uggen 2010), educational (e.g., Tyler 2011), health (e.g., Scambler 2012), etc.—sociologists have remained interested in economic inequality, both as a stand-alone classification (e.g., when comparing the poor with the rich; e.g., Blau and Blau 1982) and as a marker exhibiting the results of other types of inequality (e.g., to illustrate pay gaps between men and women; e.g., Marini and Fan 1997). Economists and political scientists have also tended to focus on wealth inequality/economic class in their analysis of spending, voting behaviors, and the like (e.g., Gelman 2009 points out that while Democrats tend to win rich states, rich people tend to vote Republican).[1]

We can examine economic inequality across the globe, looking at both sides of a global poverty line, the percentage of people living on

71

one dollar a day or less, the number of billionaires, etc. and how these positions affect life chances (e.g., correlations have been established between the average health of individuals in a country and that nation's GNP, and between individual income and health; Marmot 2002). There are also studies operating at the intercountry level. Some compare rich and poor countries, others compare countries based on the level of wealth inequality within their borders (e.g., Solt, Habel, and Grant 2011 found a positive correlation between a country's wealth inequality and the religiosity of its citizenry), and still others compare different countries' relationships with the global economy. We can examine the debt that is passed from country to country, the currency market, the economic ramifications of colonialism, or world political power as related to wealth (e.g., who gets to be on the U.N. Security Council, have a seat at the G8 conference, or host the Olympics).

Within the United States, economic class has been found to be related to a variety of behaviors and outcomes. One example is political participation. Bartels (2009, 167) posited:

> Wealthier and better-educated citizens are more likely than the poor and less-educated to have well-formulated and well-informed preferences, significantly more likely to turn out to vote, much more likely to have direct contact with public officials, and much more likely to contribute money and energy to political campaigns.

Perhaps the fact that wealth is related to so many other behaviors and outcomes in the United States should be given even more attention. According to a 2011 Harvard Business School survey (see Gudrais 2011; for an illuminating video entitled "Wealth Inequality in America" based on this and other data, see https://www.youtube.com/watch?v=QPKKQnijnsM), the wealth/income gap within the country is wider than people think (Americans think the top 20 percent of wealth holders hold a little less than 60 percent of the total wealth, while they actually hold a little over 80 percent), wider than they think it should be (the top 1 percent actually have more than 90 percent of what people think the top *20 percent* should have), and growing increasingly polarized. (The Pew Research Center reports that "[f]rom 2009 to 2011, the mean wealth of the 8 million households in the more affluent group rose to an estimated $3,173,895 from an estimated $2,476,244, while the mean wealth of the 111 million households in the less affluent group fell to an estimated $133,817 from an estimated $139,896" [Fry and Taylor 2013]).

While economic inequality can be found around the world, it is especially pronounced in the United States when compared with other Westernized countries. According to World Bank Indicators, in the late 2000s, the United States had the most inequitably dispersed income among the OECD countries (World Bank Development Indicators 2013). Wealth inequality is part of the socioeconomic climate of the modern United States.

However, wealth/income is usually measured at the household, business, or other social unit level. This yields inter–social unit comparisons: like in the Pew data above, households are compared to other households (e.g., the 99 percent to the 1 percent; those below the poverty line to those above it), businesses to other businesses (e.g., Fortune 500 to local family run entities; Walmart to mom and pop groceries), whites to blacks (e.g., white households are reported to have *twenty times* as much wealth, on average, as black households [Kochar, Fry, and Taylor 2011]; on average, blacks make less than 60 percent of the income of whites in the United States [Christie 2010]).

Of course, there are good reasons for measuring income/wealth this way. For example, parents' income is a strong predictor of their children's eventual adult income (even more so in the United States than in other Westernized countries (The Economist 2010)), but the degree to which this is cultural or based purely on wealth is debated (Dubner 2013[2]). While this relationship is at least partially because of the formal, traditional continuation of wealth mechanisms involving inheritance, lineage, etc., it is also related to the transference of social and cultural capital: parents paying for college, teaching their progeny how to invest in the stock market, providing kids with a nice interview suit. Further cementing the argument for the utility of using the household as the unit of measurement for measuring wealth (especially for the younger members of the family) is the empirical data stating that the differences in wealth dispersal to children between families is bigger than the differences in wealth dispersal to different children within one family (Henretta, Voorhis, and Soldo 2013).

Not only is wealth distributed unequally (even if this inequality is considered by many to be a fair outcome—the result of better, smarter, and/or harder work)—but wealth is extremely influential in shaping people's everyday life and the character of the social structure that guides them. Wealth influences elections, or at least most of us think it does (the causality is hard to sort out[3]). Income has been shown to correlate with happiness (e.g., Diener et al. 1993 showed positive correlations between people's income and subjective well-being, both within the United States and in country-to-country comparisons), but only at moderate levels, with the relationship waning past culturally relative subsistence levels (Duncan 2013).

Some of our major politico-ideological differences are fully entangled with our disparate views on the proper distribution of wealth and/or the desired conditions of people's opportunity to acquire wealth. Major differences in capitalism, socialism, communism, anarchism, etc.—in all of their manifestations—are largely based on how each system views wealth, together with its determinations of the proper role of government (including government's role in the economy).

Disproportionate Distribution of Wealth Within the Family

Although wealth is often conceptualized at the family or household level, it is not always distributed evenly to the individuals within these entities. Furthermore, the family structure has shifted from a relatively stable, single-earner situation toward something more fluid and varied in regard to which/how many people earn income outside of the home, and which/how many people are supported by these funds. These reasons, among others, make "household income/wealth" a less than ideal measure of individual wealth. Operating with the concept of household income, social science has displayed a tendency to overlook not only the inequalities in wealth possession within the home but also the potential for abuse that is derived from this unequal distribution of wealth.

Jan Pahl has been one of the few to point out the inadequacy of referring to the household as an individual unit. She refers to this as the "black box model of the household" because it treats the household as one static entity while ignoring the inner complexities and conflicts that take place within it: "income is earned by individuals, not households, and goods and services are purchased not by households, but by individuals" (Pahl 1990, 120). If we "open up" the black box, Pahl claims that we will gain a more dynamic understanding of the transfer of resources between the earner(s) and spender(s)/receiver(s) in relationships within the family. Furthermore, a closer inspection will allow us to articulate the distinction between personal spending and household spending norms and sanctions. Among many other inequalities of wealth within the home, different pieces of the pie are given to each parent (those who work outside of the home and those who do not); to the adults and the children; to biological, step, and adopted children; and to the first-born and the second-born.

Couples

Opening the black box in search of wealth-inequality-driven dependency and abuse, we see spouses having separate bank accounts, often with the poorer spouse at the mercy of his/her richer counterpart for paying major bills, securing new clothes, participating in paid leisure activities, etc. This dependency can easily lead to extortion (e.g., one member demanding sexual favors from the other member in exchange for money for a haircut), even going so far as preventing the poorer member from being able to leave the relationship for fear of extreme financial difficulty (which makes the ground fertile for the most severe forms of abuse). The prospect of dire financial straits upon separation is exacerbated by the fact that the couple's valuable possessions may only be in the name of one of the spouses, especially when the couple is not married (which is a path that more couples are taking of their own volition or because of a lack of options [e.g., same-sex couples or polygamous/polyamorous groups]). Moreover, if it is expected that the separation and subsequent allocation of wealth will funnel through legal channels, and if one member of the couple has superior financial means to exert influence during the legal process (e.g., securing a more effective lawyer), the less wealthy member will have even more reason to stay in the relationship. Of course, a shared bank account is no panacea. Research shows that one spouse often has much more control over a shared bank account than the other does (Volger 1994); wealth may be shared "in name only."

Exploring some of these dynamics, Pahl (1990) interviewed 102 heterosexual British couples (all but one couple were married) to gain better knowledge of the allocation and control of money within their households. Each of these couples had at least one dependent child. Furthermore, each of the individuals who participated, each husband and each wife, had a source of income—through wages, salary, social security benefits, etc. The 102 couples were sorted into four categories based on the wives' responses to the question of "who controls the money that comes into the house?" In most cases, the study reported that couples had joint bank accounts. Answers were coded into four categories: (1) "wife-controlled pooling"—twenty-seven instances—where the couple had a joint account and the wife was more responsible for control over finances and took charge of paying the bills, rent, etc. (in most of these cases, neither member had a separate bank account); (2) "husband-controlled pooling"—thirty-nine instances—where the couple had a joint account and the husband controlled the finances, or there was joint control and the husband took on the majority of responsibility for paying bills; (3) "husband controlled"—twenty-two cases—included cases where the husband had his own personal account or just cash and took responsibility for the main bills; (4) "wife controlled"—fourteen instances—where the wife controlled the finances and was responsible for major bills but usually only had cash.

"Husband control" was associated with relatively high income levels compared to "wife control," which represented very low levels of income in most cases. "Wife controlled pooling" was associated with medium income levels, while "husband controlled pooling," once again, usually occurred in couples with high levels of income. In the realm of controlling finances, the study concluded that where women took control over finances, they were responsible for making ends meet in the household; they had to pay bills, buy food, etc. In cases where husbands took more control, they delegated housekeeping duties and expenses to their wives.

The study also examined the relationship between financial control, management, and patterns of spending. It examined three different areas of spending: food, leisure expenditures, and poll tax bills. In a joint interview, each couple was given a long list of items and asked who was responsible for spending on each item. Wives were more likely to pay for food as well as child- and school-related expenses, whereas husbands handled expenses related to cars, repairs, etc.

Overall, the study concluded that although men, in absolute income terms, contributed more to the household economy, women were more likely to contribute a higher percentage of their income. Elsewhere, scholars have found that, on average, the more money women bring into the household, the higher their decision-making power. Similarly, wives with paid employment seem more instrumental in decision making than wives without paid employment. Members of a couple have different disposable incomes as well as different amounts of freedom in spending that income and making general household decisions (Pahl 1995).

Couples fight over money more than any other issue (Dew, Britt, and Huston 2012). They argue about how money should be spent vis-à-vis how it is earned, what bill to pay off with this month's allotment (this issue is not limited to those considered poor, as there are relative quibbles over what to buy and how much to spend in most families), who is better/works harder at finding deals, etc. Using the 1987 *National Survey of Families and Households* as a baseline and then tracking marriage longevity from there, researcher Jeffrey Dew found that couples who fought once a week about finances divorced 30 percent more often than those who fought only a few times a month (there was a generally positive correlation between frequency of financial fights and likelihood of divorce). Additionally, of all the variables collected through individual self-reporting—how often fights occurred about chores, quality time together, relatives, sex, and money—financial disputes were the best predictor of divorce (Rampell 2009).

Part of this fighting may be due to the taboo nature of talking about money in our culture. In a 2013 *New York Times* article, Professor Terri Orbuch noted that most couples do not discuss finances prior to marriage[4] and only do so within marriage once a problem emerges. Orbuch's research with the University of Michigan's Institute for Social Research, which involves a sample of over three hundred couples who have been followed for decades, has illustrated that money "is even more taboo [than sex], because these days friends talk about sex, but we don't usually know how much our friends make" (Vanek Smith 2013).

Further complicating the matter, there are no set rules for how wealth should be distributed within a couple and what role, if any, the relative incomes the parties bring into the household should play. This taboo, together with the inequality in collection and dispersal of family funds and the propensity of money issues to lead to fights, is the reason that about one-third of Americans in combined-finance relationships say they have committed financial infidelity (Linn 2012). In her insightful article in the prestigious journal *Gender and Society*, "The Power of the Purse: Allocative Systems and Inequality in Couple Households," Catherine Kenney showed how couples' allocation of material resources varied based on socioeconomic status (SES), race, ethnicity, and family structure, among other factors. She argued that the interpersonal dynamics occurring within families, which are gendered and situated within the overarching culture, influence the distribution of wages earned by members of the home—trumping prevailing market or cultural norms (Kenney 2006). In discussing the way couples navigate these matters, Kenney, drawing on the work of her peers, contended:

> Such personal relations of distribution, or "household allocative systems" (Pahl 1983) may "match, reinforce, or even reverse the principles that govern money's distribution outside the household" (Burgoyne 1995, 422). Evidence drawn from largely qualitative research conducted in Europe and Oceania suggests that the use of particular allocative systems varies systematically by factors that

include not only women's and men's relative and combined earnings but also the couples' legal relationship, the presence of children, regional or ethnic subculture, and gender attitudes (Burgoyne and Morison 1997; Elizabeth 2001; Morris 1993; Pahl 1983, 1990; Singh and Lindsay 1996; Vogler 2005; Vogler and Pahl 1993). (Kenny 2006)

Pahl (1983) had reached a similar conclusion, underlining the importance of understanding the overarching historical and cultural context to the way money (and, thus, power) is allocated between the members of a couple. Pahl (1983) also relayed an important caveat regarding money allocation and power; she argued that sometimes the ability to pawn off money—and the attached responsibility to fulfill certain duties using the money, such as paying bills and buying groceries—is indicative and more producing of power and control than actually holding the money. How this works within the home may largely be influenced by how the culture views the importance of money possession. Pahl (1983) summarized the importance of understanding both the macro- and micro-sociological variables involved in the inequality that produces and is the result of household income allocation:

> Finally, it is important to see the relationship between patterns of allocation and patterns of inequality within marriage in terms of social processes which may change over time; these social processes may or may not be in phase. Thus, for example, much social and economic policy at the present time is based on the assumption that the 'normal' family is composed of a breadwinner husband and a dependent wife—what Poster called the 'bourgeois family' (Poster, 1978). Similarly, much popular thinking about the allocation of money within the household appears to regard the 'housekeeping allowance' as the normal form for money transfers to take. It may be that one particular historical configuration, at its most powerful among the middle classes in the first half of the twentieth century, has moulded thinking on this topic. This configuration was characterised by the dominance of the bourgeois family form, by a high degree of segregation between husband and wife, limited opportunities for women to earn in their own right, a rising standard of living which gave rise to the existence of financial 'surpluses' in family budgets, and the predominance of the allowance system. In its turn the allowance system reinforced inequality between the sexes by increasing the financial dependence of the wife and the autonomy of the husband; and the assumption that the allowance system would be the norm both reflected, and reinforced, the significance of the bourgeois family form. The fact that financial arrangements within marriage were regarded as essentially a private matter reflected the importance of privacy as a way of maintaining,

by concealing them, particular power relations within the household. This same phenomenon can also be seen at work in the concealment of violence within the family, by laying stress on the sanctity of the home and the privacy of the married couple. (258)

Children

Inequalities in wealth access also trickle down to children within family homes. Their spending power has steadily increased since the middle of the twentieth century (McNeal 1999). Of course, the assumption, and its utility, that all children within a given home have equal monetary access is largely on point (e.g., research shows that there is more variation in wealth dispersion to children between families than within families; see Henretta, Voorhis, Soldo 2012). This is especially true when we consider the substantial evidence that household/parental wealth greatly influences the course of the lives of children. Susan Mayer starts off her 1997 book *What Money Can't Buy: Family Income and Children's Life Chances* with a summary of the literature on the topic:

> Poor children have more than their share of problems. They usually weigh less than rich children at birth and are more likely to die in their first year of life. When they enter school, poor children score lower on standardized tests, and this remains true through high school. Poor children are also absent from school more often and have more behavior problems than affluent children. Poor teenagers are more likely than teenagers from affluent families to have a baby, drop out of school, and get in trouble with the law. Young adults who were poor as children complete fewer years of schooling, work fewer hours, and earn lower wages than young adults raised in affluent families. As a result, children raised in poverty are more likely to end up poor and in need of public assistance when they become adults (1).

Mayer's (1997) ultimate point in her empirically sensitive and ideologically neutral book is that the direct causal link between parental income and child success is not as clear as many had characterized because some of the attributes correlated with high incomes (e.g., good health and steadfastness) are also causally related, in and of themselves, to increased life chances for children. In other words, when a poor family has characteristics that the rich tend to have more of (besides wealth, obviously), the children of the poor family are more likely than the children of other poor families to be upwardly socially and economically mobile. Nonetheless, even in Mayer's critique, she concludes that parental money *does* affect children's life chances.

However, Mayer was looking at parental money and its effect on children at the household level. While we know that these funds exert an effect, not as much attention is paid to how financial resources are used on individual children. Indeed, there are cases where children under the same roof have disproportionate access to wealth. Additionally, the household income marker fails to recognize the varying proportions of spending power held by children or by children in different homes with parents with the same household income.

Birth-order matters. Over a century ago, Francis Galton published *English Men of Science* (1874). The text depicted a study in which he selectively chose famous and/or influential scientists based on certain external markers of success and then asked these scientists about their birth order among other things. Galton found that first borns and only sons were more likely to have been selected into his sample than would have been expected perchance. Altus (1972) summarized Galton's thoughts on the causal mechanisms involved in this disparity:

> Through the law of primogeniture, the eldest son was likely to become possessed of independent means and to be able to follow his own tastes and inclinations. Further, Galton argued, parents treated an only child and a first-born child (who is an only child for a period of time) as a companion and accorded him more responsibility than other children were given. Thus first arrivals on the family scene were favored from the start. (44)

Decades later, other researchers added more nuance to this finding by arguing that, while oldest sons seemed to be the most advantaged, youngest sons had an advantage over middle sons (Yoder 1894; McKeen Cattel 1917). Altus (1972) also pointed to studies showing positive correlations between being first born and becoming a university professor, a Rhodes Scholar, and scoring three standard deviations above the mean on high school aptitude tests, among other things. Clarke (1916) found that it was, again, the first and last born who became "men of letters" in America. He reasoned:

> First-born and last-born children frequently enjoy greater educational opportunity than do their intermediate brothers and sisters. First borns often succeed in getting a start before adversity befalls the family or before the expense of caring for an increasing family of young children becomes so great that it is necessary to curtail the education of some of the older children.

While first-born children have been found to have different per-sonalities than their latter born counterparts—for example, being more conscientious, more driven by the need to affiliate, and more curious—these differences seem to act in concert with those related to wealth distribution, and not against them (i.e., they are both related to the same social context, and the parenting styles and decisions bred from it) (Altus 1972). Thus, birth order affects how parents treat their kids (e.g., how they spend their money on their children; how strictly they discipline their children) and the social context into which the kids are born (e.g., is he or she the only child needing to be financially supported?).

A first born might have more access to family wealth for school projects, sports participation, dates, college applications, etc. than a second born does. Or, last borns might reap the benefits of their parents being at the peak of their money-earning lives and/or having older siblings becoming financially independent just as they comes into an age where financial support is extremely advantageous.

This initial difference in access to wealth can lead to a disparity in resource possession among children within one family; this is one application of the well-known *Matthew Effect* (Merton 1968). For example, the eldest, due to having funds to play in pay-for-play sports, may have more social networks and thus more job opportunities than his younger brothers and sisters. He may be able to secure a job based on these connections, while his younger brother, devoid of these types of connections, will depend on his older brother's recommendation to be able to get the same job. This scenario supplies the oldest brother with an opportunity to exploit his younger brother (e.g., the older brother makes the younger brother perform embarrassing tasks at school for his own entertainment in exchange for recommending his brother to his employer).[5]

Of course, birth order is far from the only reason why parents might treat their children differently in regards to guiding their access to family wealth. For example, parents might, consciously or otherwise, provide more financial support to their biological children than their step or adopted children, or to their sons than their daughters. While the data supports the assertion that step-children are treated worse than biological children within the same home (e.g., Barber [2009] contended that "[c]hildren growing up in step families are about 40 times as likely to be abused and 140 times as likely to be murdered as children growing up with both natural parents (murder still being a low probability)."), there are also a litany of studies that argue that adopted children are actually treated better (or at least no worse) than biological children. This includes adopted children receiving more money and material items from their adopted parents.

Hamilton, Cheng, and Powell's 2007 study, published in the *American Sociological Review,* provided evidence against established sociological and evolutionary thinking regarding parental investment. The researchers found that adopted parents invested more in their children than did biological parents by comparing data from the Early Childhood Longitudinal Study, Kindergarten–First Grade Waves (ECLS-K). Barber (2009) summarized:

> Adoptive parents were more likely to provide computers for their children, more likely to eat meals with them, and more involved in sports, science projects, and so forth. This falsifies the fairy-tale claim that parents cannot treat genetically unrelated children as well as their own kin.

Controlling for socioeconomic status closed this gap, but adopted children with two parents still had their parents investing in them on a par with biological children with two biological parents, and much more so than those in other family arrangements (Hamilton, Cheng, and Powell 2007).

Of course, for the purposes of this book, we are more interested in disparity of resources within a single home—and in this case, in the differential parental investment in children within the same household. Armed with adoption agency records covering over two decades, Kyle Gibson looked at households with both an adopted (unrelated) and a biological child. Leaving the more often studied negative markers—such as physical abuse—aside, Gibson focused on comparing the amount of investments parents made in their children. He concluded that adopted children received more personal and educational investments, but that this was most likely because adopted children needed more support than biological children did; the adopted children were also more likely than the biological children to experience a slew of negative outcomes, such as drug addiction and future divorce (Gibson 2007); additionally, birth children end up attending around one more year of school than do nonbirth children (Case, Lin, and McLanahan 2001; see the article for more on the possibility of these differences being based on initial biological variations). Barber (2009) summed up

Gibson's findings, writing that "parents invested more in the adopted child than in [their] own offspring. Adopted children were more likely to attend preschool and to receive private tutoring. Adoptees had a better chance of receiving cars and personal loans. Parents also spent more time at their sports events."

Still, we may be overemphasizing the role that parental wealth investment, and even parental time investment, plays with children. Judith Harris, in her book *The Nurture Assumption: Why Children Turn Out the Way They Do* (2011), argues that parents have little influence on the socialization of their children, despite the incessant and lucrative messages arguing otherwise. She contends that other children are more influential in socializing children. However, parental wealth and the willingness to focus that wealth on children by moving to neighborhoods and school districts conducive to successful child development still play a role, as the social settings in which socialization occurs are variable.

Parents and Children

Despite variations in wealth possession by the adults in a family or in the amount of parental investment in individual children, young children are dependent on their parents for financial support, except in the rare cases where they earn enough income independently to financially support themselves. Children rely on their parents to provide for them in rich or poor households; as a step, adopted, or biological child; with two parents bringing in income, or only one parent working outside of the home, or even with only one parent in the home at all. Parents may withhold money and goods from their kids in order to elicit certain actions from them. These actions occur often and are not necessarily nefarious: "you can't have your allowance until you do *all* of your chores," or "I will get you the new PlayStation *if* you make the honor roll."

However, because of the great power bestowed upon parents by their relative access to wealth compared to their children, and the children's dependency on their parents for a piece of that wealth, abuses of power can occur. (What is considered abuse is certainly quite subjective; for example, some children would see tying access to a PlayStation on school performance as a cruel and unusual punishment, whereas the law would see something like demanding sexual favors for lunch money as infinitely more menacing.)

Disproportionate Wealth Possession Within Schools

As we know, schools, even public schools, have radically different comparative wealth. Some are housed in multimillion dollar, state-of-the-art facilities, equipped with smart boards, acoustically impressive auditoriums, ornate shrubbery, a low faculty-to-student ratio, and fresh paint. These schools have the latest computers, a wide variety of extracurricular options, a well-stocked library and cafeteria, and students who tend to perform better on standardized tests (not to mention college admissions) than their counterparts at the poorer, crustier, less technologically advanced, old-paint-decorated schools. This inequality and its presumed effect on the students' later life chances is well documented in the scholarly literature. Here are some of the bullet points that have been found by researchers in comparing private to public schools:

- Among students with similar backgrounds, those at private schools outperform those at public schools in vocabulary and mathematics (Coleman, Hoffer, and Kilgore 1982).
- Among students with similar backgrounds, those at private schools outperform those at public schools in reading and social studies (Gamoran 1996).
- Public school graduates acquire more cultural capital, whereas private school graduates acquire more social capital (Zweigenhaft 1993).

While recent scrutiny (see Cloud 2007) has compellingly questioned the presence of a disparity in outcomes due to attendance at public compared to private schools (Center on Educational Policy President Jack Jennings asserted: "it appears that private schools simply have higher percentages of students who would perform well in any environment based on their previous performance and background" [Cloud 2007]), the evidence remains strong that students at richer schools tend to outperform those at poorer schools.

For example, when looking at over three hundred secondary schools in Australia, Perry and McConney (2010) found a relationship between increases in a school's SES and the academic achievement of the students at that school, whether the students were from rich or poor families. Ellen Brantlinger's 2003 book *Dividing Classes: How the Middle Class Negotiates and Rationalizes School Advantage* (written in the vein of Macleod's famous work *Ain't No Makin' It* [2008]) not only reviewed the literature on the power of class advantage in schools but also performed an ethnographic analysis of an Indiana town, illuminating the process by which some of these advantages were reinforced and justified by those gaining from them.

Schools in the United States spend different amounts of money per student (Orfield 2000), and children from wealthier families do better in school than students from less wealthy families; they end up getting more prestigious and higher-paying jobs as well (e.g., Coleman 1988). At the macro level, the inequality in educational and subsequent life success between the rich and the poor is often attributed to the type of schools poor and rich kids attend and to tracking within these schools (i.e., the process by which lower-class kids are placed into curriculum that is thought to lead to lower-paying jobs, while the opposite is true of upper-class kids [Ansalone 2001]). However, some of the differences in outcomes between students at rich and poor schools is no doubt due to the individual socioeconomic class of the individual students (White 1982), and some may also be due to biological/genetic differences (Johnson, McGue, and Iaconu 2006).

Leaving aside the powder-keg conversation of assessing the possible role of biological differences in social stratification, we can focus on the influence of the relative wealth of individuals in a school environment. As someone once said, "I've been poor and not so poor, and not so poor is better." Although it is hard to untangle the role of wealth from, say, the role of social networks or social status, it seems that whether in a rich or poor school, the relatively wealthy possess advantages, from having the basic necessities, such as food, clothes, school supplies, a place to study at home, etc., to social hierarchy enhancers, such as access to sport leagues, access to parties, coat tailing on parents' social circles, likelihood of having siblings in college, knowing people in high places for jobs, reputation, access to a car, and leniency in punishment.

For a person with less relative wealth, access to the above is somewhat—and, at times, exclusively—dependent on individuals with more wealth. Thus, a poor student might ask to do his homework at his friend's house because his friend has a computer, a well-lit quiet room, a video camera, extra pizza, etc., or he might try to get a ride from a friend who has a car to a job interview, or a school dance, or a party, or even a college. The student with relatively more resources may offer these services benevolently but may also do so as part of an exchange where he expects some service to be rendered for his assistance. So, in exchange for letting a friend use her car, a girl might require her friend to finish her math homework. Of course, following the laws of supply and demand, when the less resourceful member of the exchange has no alternatives, *and is dependent on the supplier for the good or service*, the supplier can manipulate the terms of the exchange into his deep favor. So, when the person in need of a car or car ride to get to sports practice or to his job lives in a town with no affordable public transportation, does not have parents or relatives who can assist, and lives too far to walk or bike, then he is almost completely at the mercy of his benefactor even if these students go to the same school in the same town—rich or poor, public or private, urban or rural.

While these differences between students certainly correlate with differences in the households the students come from, there is variation: students with relatively high wealth may come from a poor family, and those with relatively little wealth may come from a rich family. One reason for this is simply because we are discussing *relative* wealth. Kids from wealthy homes relative to the whole of US households may be from relatively poor households in their school district; the needed car ride may become the needed private jet ride or Super Bowl ticket. Another reason is that students may gain access to or engineer wealth apart from their families. Take, for example, the small-town drug dealer. He may only be fifteen years old and from a poor family, but he can potentially dominate the market and become independently wealthy.

Wealth differences manifest themselves in college too. While, for the most part, kids from richer homes have more options for where to go to school, more spending money while there, and less loan debt upon leaving, this is not always the case. As we know, the amount of money parents give to children varies, even among those parents making the same incomes. Because general federal financial aid for college is based on the parents' income and their expected contribution (which is not their actual contribution), some students find themselves with little financial aid *and* little parental financial help. Macro analysis will group these students with those who do get significant parental financial help, even though their experiences and opportunities at university might be vastly different. Here too, this inequality can lead to abuse. One roommate might depend on the other to buy food or to share books, which can turn into, "I'll let you use my book, but you have to do my homework." Of course, kids from poor families and rich families at the same school may run into the same dynamic; however, this is an example in which there is the potential for abuse based on dependence stemming from wealth inequality not only within one school but also within one household income level.

Just as household income does not articulate the inequalities regarding wealth within the family, merely concentrating on which school a student attends fails to pay heed to the vastly different experiences students have within a single school, some of which are the result of the individual wealth of the different interacting students.

Conclusion

Economic inequality is one of the most talked about areas of sociology, economics, and even politics. It is divisive not only in practical, tangible terms but also in how we perceive and feel about economic inequality. These dynamics are well studied. However, the role of the inequitable distribution of wealth within social units is less studied, even though this social setting is fertile for abuses of power, and these power abuses are unlikely to be detected by scholars of social stratification and/or policymakers and enforcers heading humanistic intervention programs.

Wealth, like physical strength or status, is a powerful resource held by individuals within a family or a school, as when it is measured as a characteristic of the family or the school. Couples fight, lie, and divorce over money in part because they do not agree on expectations about who gets to or has to spend the money (these expectations themselves are based upon gendered cultural norms and the jobs/earnings brought into the home by the different individuals). A spouse in a rich family may have to beg his wife (though more often the wife is begging her husband) for an allowance to get groceries or see a movie with friends. When one spouse controls all household income, the other spouse is dependent on the first for all monetary needs, especially if he or she has no other option to secure money. This dependence breeds the possibility for abuse. A similar scenario happens with children, who also do not share wealth evenly, and with parents versus children, or with kids in schools. These dynamics can occur in households with incomes in the millions, and those with incomes in the hundreds, and at the most prestigious and expensive Ivy-track prep school or the poor and outdated small rural high school, as the term *inequality* is tied to relativity.

Notes

1. In this chapter, both "wealth" and "income" will be considered as constituting information about a person's, household's, business's, etc. spending power. Some cited studies only measure income as it shows up on a paycheck, while others take a more holistic view of wealth. While conceptually separating these terms will provide a more nuanced analysis, we did not feel it was

worth the added complexity, as the application of both markers meshes with our overall framework and arguments.

2. In their *Freakonomics* podcast from September 26, 2013, Stephen Dubner and Steven Levitt considered whether or not a "big bucket of cash" would really change someone's life. To answer this seemingly hypothetical question, they peered into some research concerning an early nineteenth century Georgia state land lottery where large pieces of land were awarded via a lottery that rich and poor alike (although presumably not women or slaves) could enter. Around 20 percent of entrants were awarded land. While the money gave the initial recipients a big boost in wealth, their descendants, after a few generations, mostly floated back to the economic class their ancestors had inhabited *before* the lottery. In other words, the big pot of money did not do much in terms of lessening long-term economic inequality.

3. Economist Jeff Milyo: "It is true that winning candidates typically spend more on their campaigns than do their opponents, but it is also true that successful candidates possess attributes that are useful for both raising money and winning votes (e.g., charisma, popular policy positions, etc.). This 'reverse causality' means that campaign spending is potentially as much a symptom of electoral success as its cause" (Dubner 2012).

4. Nevertheless, Schneider (2011) illustrated that the wealth of the individuals in a couple predicts the likelihood of that couple marrying.

5. It is important to note that the oldest son suffers some relative disadvantages as well, like, in the instance of pursuing a job, not having an older brother's recommendation as an asset.

References

Altus, William D. 1972. "Birth Order and Its Sequelae." *Science*, 7:44–49.

Ansalone, George. 2001. "Schooling, Tracking, and Inequality." *Journal of Children and Poverty*, 7(1):33–47.

Barber, Nigel. 2009. "Do Parents Favor Natural Children Over Adopted Ones?" http://www.psychologytoday.com/blog/the-human-beast/200906/do-parents-favor-natural-children-over-adopted-ones (accessed November 13, 2013).

Bartels, Larry M. 2009. "Economic Inequality and Political Representation." *The Unsustainable American State*. New York: Oxford University Press.

Beck, Ulrich. 2010. "Remapping Social Inequalities in an Age of Climate Change: For a Cosmopolitan Renewal of Sociology." *Global Networks*, 10(2):165–81.

Blau, Judith R., and Peter M. Blau. 1982. "The Cost of Inequality: Metropolitan Structure and Violent Crime." *American Sociological Review*, 47(1):114.

Brantlinger, Ellen. 2003. *Dividing Classes: How the Middle Class Negotiates and Rationalizes School Advantage*. Abingdon, UK: Routledge.

Case, Anne, I. Fen Lin, and Sara McLanahan. 2001. "Educational Attainment of Siblings in Stepfamilies." *Evolution and Human Behavior*, 22(4):269–89.

Christie, Les. 2010. "Pay Gap Persists for African-Americans." *CNN Money*. http://money.cnn.com/2010/07/30/news/economy/black_pay_gap_persists (accessed May 6, 2014).

Clarke, Edwin L. 1916. *American Men of Letters: Their Nature and Nurture*. New York: Columbia University, 72(1):1–180.

Cloud, John. 2007. "Are We Failing Our Geniuses?" *TIME Magazine*, August, 16.

Coleman, James S. 1988. "Social Capital in the Creation of Human Capital." *American Journal of Sociology,* 94:95–120.

Coleman, James, Thomas Hoffer, and Sally Kilgore. 1982. "Achievement and Segregation in Secondary Schools: A Further Look at Public and Private School Differences." *Sociology of Education,* 55(2/3):162.

Dew, Jeffrey, Sonya Britt, and Sandra Huston. 2012. "Examining the Relationship Between Financial Issues and Divorce." *Family Relations,* 61(4):615–28.

Diener, Ed, Ed Sandvik, Larry Seidlitz, and Marissa Diener. 1993. "The Relationship Between Income and Subjective Well-Being: Relative or Absolute?" *Social Indicators Research,* 28(3):195–223.

Dubner, Stephen J. 2012. "How Much Does Campaign Spending Influence the Election? A Freakonomics Quorum." Freakonomics. http://freakonomics.com/2012/01/17/how-much-does-campaign-spending-influence-the-election-a-freakonomics-quorum (accessed May 6, 2014).

Dubner, Stephen J. 2013. "Would a Big Bucket of Cash Really Change Your Life? A New Freakonomics Radio Podcast." Freakonomics. http://freakonomics.com/2013/09/26/would-a-big-bucket-of-cash-really-change-your-life-a-new-freakonomics-radio-podcast (accessed May 6, 2014).

Duncan, Grant. 2013. "Should Happiness-Maximization Be the Goal of Government?" In *The Exploration of Happiness, Happiness Studies Book Series,* ed. Antonella Delle Fave. Dordrecht, Netherlands: Springer, 303–20. http://link.springer.com/chapter/10.1007/978-94-007-5702-8_16 (accessed November 8, 2013).

Economist. 2010. "Upper Bound." *The Economist,* April 15. http://www.economist.com/node/15908469 (accessed February 8, 2014).

Fry, Richard, and Paul Taylor. 2013. *A Rise in Wealth for the Wealthy; Declines for the Lower 93%.* Washington, DC: Pew Research Center.

Gamoran, Adam. 1996. "Student Achievement in Public Magnet, Public Comprehensive, and Private City High Schools." *Educational Evaluation and Policy Analysis,* 18(1):1–18.

Gelman, Andrew. 2009. *Red State, Blue State, Rich State, Poor State: Why Americans Vote the Way They Do (Expanded Edition).* Princeton, NJ: Princeton University Press.

Gibson, Kyle. 2007. "Different Parental Investment in Families with Both Adopted and Genetic Children." *Evolution and Human Behavior,* 30(3):184–9.

Gudrais, Elizabeth. 2011. "Loaded Perceptions: What We Know About Wealth." *Harvard Magazine,* Nov/Dec. http://www.bflnyc.org/about-us/domestic-violence-disability (accessed May 6, 2014).

Hamilton, Laura, Simon Cheng, and Brian Powell. 2007. "Adoptive Parents, Adaptive Parents: Evaluating the Importance of Biological for Parental Investment." *American Sociological Review,* 72(1):95–116.

Harris, Judith. 2011. *The Nurture Assumption: Why Children Turn Out the Way They Do.* New York: Free Press.

Henretta, John C., Matthew F. Van Voorhis, and Beth J. Soldo. 2013. "Parental Money Help to Children and Stepchildren." *Journal of Family Issues,* doi: 10.1177/0192513X13485077.

Johnson, Wendy, Matt McGue, and William G. Iacono. 2006. "Genetic and Environmental Influences on Academic Achievement Trajectories during Adolescence." *Developmental Psychology,* 42(3):514–32.

Kenney, Catherine T. 2006. "The Power of the Purse Allocative Systems and Inequality in Couple Households." *Gender and Society,* 20(3):354–81.

Kochhar, Rakesh, Richard Fry, and Paul Taylor. 2011. "Wealth Gaps Rise to Record Highs Between Whites, Blacks, Hispanics." July 26. *Pew Research: Social and Demographic Trends.* http://www.pewsocialtrends.org/2011/07/26/wealth-gaps-rise-to-record-highs-between-whites-blacks-hispanics (accessed May 6, 2014).

Lengermann, Patricia M., and Jill Niebrugge-Brantley. 1998. *The Women Founders: Sociology and Social Theory, 1830–1930: A Text/Reader.* Boston: McGraw-Hill.

Linn, Allison. 2012. "Sometimes We Cheat on Our Partners About Money" *TODAY.* http://www.today.com/money/sometimes-we-cheat-our-partners-about-money-survey-shows-731779 (accessed November 8, 2013).

MacLeod, Jay. 2008. *Ain't No Makin' It: Aspirations & Attainment in a Low-Income Neighborhood.* Boulder, CO: Westview Press.

Marini, Margaret Mooney, and Pi-Ling Fan. 1997. "The Gender Gap in Earnings at Career Entry." *American Sociological Review,* 62(4):588.

Marmot, Michael. 2002. "The Influence of Income on Health: Views of an Epidemiologist." *Health Affairs,* 21(2):31–46.

Mayer, Susan E. 1997. *What Money Can't Buy: Family Income and Children's Life Chances.* Cambridge, MA: Harvard University Press.

McKeen Cattell, J. 1917. "Families of American Men of Science." *The Scientific Monthly,* 4:248–62.

McNeal, James U. 1999. *The Kids Market: Myths and Realities.* Ithaca, NY: Paramount Market Publishing.

Merton, Robert K. 1968. "The Matthew Effect in Science The Reward and Communication Systems of Science Are Considered." *Science,* 159(3810):56–63.

Orfield, Gary. 2000. "Policy and Equity: Lessons of a Third of a Century of Educational Reforms in the United States." In *Unequal Schools, Unequal Chances: The Challenges to Equal Opportunity in the Americas,* ed. Fernando Reimers. Cambridge, MA: Harvard University Press and David Rockefeller Center for Latin American Studies, 401–426.

Pahl, Jan. 1983. "The Allocation of Money and the Structuring of Inequality Within Marriage." *The Sociological Review,* 31(2):237–62.

Pahl, Jan. 1990. "Household Spending, Personal Spending and the Control of Money in Marriage." *Sociology,* 24(1):119–38.

Pahl, Jan. 1995. "His Money, Her Money: Recent Research on Financial Organisation in Marriage." *Journal of Economic Psychology,* 16(3):361–76.

Perry, Laura B., and Andrew McConney. 2010. "Does the SES of the School Matter? An Examination of Socioeconomic Status and Student Achievement Using PISA 2003." *Teachers College Record,* 112(4):1137–62.

Rampell, Catherine. 2009. "As Layoffs Surge, Women May Pass Men in Job Force." *New York Times,* February 5.

Scambler, Graham. 2012. "Health Inequalities." *Sociology of Health & Illness* 34(1):130–46.

Schneider, Daniel. 2011. "Wealth and the Marital Divide." *American Journal of Sociology,* 117(2):627–67.

Solt, Frederick, Philip Habel, and J. Tobin Grant. 2011. "Economic Inequality, Relative Power, and Religiosity." *Social Science Quarterly,* 92(2):447–65.

Tyler, William. 2011. *The Sociology of Educational Inequality*. Abingdon, UK: Routledge.

Vanek Smith, Stacey. 2013. "Money Talk Before Marriage a Tip You Can't Disparage." *New York Times*, March 25. http://www.nytimes.com/2013/03/26/your-money/money-talk-before-marriage-a-tip-you-cant-disparage.html?pagewanted=all&_r=0.

Wakefield, Sara, and Christopher Uggen. 2010. "Incarceration and Stratification." *Annual Review of Sociology*, 36(1):387–406.

White, Karl R. 1982. "The Relation Between Socioeconomic Status and Academic Achievement." *Psychological Bulletin*, 91(3):461–81.

World Bank Development Indicators. 2013. "Wealth Distribution and Income by Country." *New York: Global Finance*. http://www.gfmag.com/tools/global-database/economic-data/11944-wealth-distribution-income-inequality.html (accessed October 29, 2013).

Yoder, A. H. 1894. "The Study of the Boyhood of Great Men." *The Pedagogical Seminary*, 3(1):134–56.

Zweigenhaft, Richard L. 1993. "Prep School and Public School Graduates of Harvard: A Longitudinal Study of the Accumulation of Social and Cultural Capital." *Journal of Higher Education*, 64(2):211–25.

5

Social Status

Social status—the umbrella term for the achieved and ascribed components of an individual that are used to make judgments about that person relative to others—is entangled with dependency and power. The concept fits the purview of this book nicely not only for this reason but also because of its relation to other resources (including those we have concentrated on so far—strength and wealth) and its possible conceptualization as a resource in its own right.

Ball et al. (2001) kept this notion in mind while defining social status: "[Social status is] a ranking in a hierarchy that is socially recognized and typically carries with it the expectation of entitlement to certain resources" (161). Elsewhere, social status is seen as a typology of the charismatic, rational-legal, and traditional bestowals of status; or by the sorts of status that one is born with and that one comes by through one's actions; or that which is steeped in a hierarchy of awards or a hierarchy of displays (Riahi-Belkaoui 2009).

We can also define social status in relation to other similar classifications: socioeconomic status (SES), popularity, leadership, and power. SES is a function of wealth, job classification, and level of education attained. Popularity is about being liked by others. Power concerns the relative control of resources. While all of these concepts are related to social status, they are not complete overlaps. Thus, someone may have a high SES but low social status, or low social status but a tremendous amount of power (e.g., a high-ranking official at the Federal Reserve). Still, it is usually the case that these concepts coincide with one another.

Like other resources studied in social science, social status is often thought of and operationalized at the group or social unit level (the term *social class* is regularly, but not always, used synonymously in this manifestation). Weber argued that social status represented a coherent marker, albeit an implicit one, that people used to group themselves communally (Weber 1946). These groups and their shared, or at least perceived to be common, social positions were seen by Weber as more influential (while still retaining parsimony) and ripe for study than basic economic classifications. Thus, social class was a more meaningful marker of one's life chances than unadorned economic class. Yet, Weber saw economic class/status as a strong input in determining social status; he also saw relevance in including attributes such as religious affiliation, neighborhood lived in, and lifestyle in determining social status, and he even placed different values on different types of wealth (e.g., old wealth versus new wealth, real estate holdings versus cash on hand).

In large-scale studies, social class has been found to be significantly related with being respected and valued (Berger, Rosenholtz, and Zelditch 1980); the likelihood/length of jail time (D'Alessio and Stozenburg 1993); body mass index (BMI; relationship is curvilinear with low social status coinciding with very low and very high BMIs; Jeffrey et al. 1989); and jury decisions in criminal trials (Devine et al. 2001), although whether social status is correlated with criminality remains hotly contested (see Thornberry and Farnworth 1982 for a summary and response to the classic debate; see Clinard, Quinney, and Wildeman 2010 for a thorough recent assessment of sociological variables related to criminal activity). Social class and going to/graduating from college have also been documented as having a strong relationship (see Walpole 2003). Somewhat surprisingly, social status has only been weakly linked to happiness (Anderson et al. 2012). Because of the breadth of the term and its treatment as an index, it is easy to find many variables that correlate with social status. However, these findings may only be showing tautological relationships (e.g., social status predicts wealth, but wealth is only one part of social status).

There are a couple of other important and robust correlations we feel should be mentioned. Social status/standing/class influences our health; people with a higher social status live longer and are healthier during their lives (Adler et al. 2000). Michael Marmot examined this dynamic in his 2004 book *The Status Syndrome: How Social Standing Affects Our Health and Longevity*, arguing that the relationship goes well beyond the health disparities found when comparing the global poor to the global not-so-poor:

> You are not poor. You are employed. Your children are well fed. You live in a decent house or apartment. You turn on the faucet and drink the water in the secure knowledge that it is clean. The food you buy is similarly not contaminated. Most people you come across in your daily routine also fit this description. But, among these people, none

of whom is destitute or even poor, you acknowledge that some are higher than you in the social hierarchy: they may have more money, bigger houses, a more prestigious job, more status in the eyes of others, or simply a higher class way of speaking. You also note that there are other people lower than you on these criteria, not just the very poor or the homeless, but people whose standing is merely lower than yours, to a varying extent. The remarking finding is that among *all* of these people, the higher the status in the pecking order, the healthier they are likely to be. In other words, health follows a social gradient. I call this the status syndrome (Marmot 2004, 1)

The famous multidecade Whitehall study that looked at the health of thousands of British civil servants over a period of time provided good evidence to support this point. Marmot and colleagues found that the higher a government employee's employment status was, the less chance he would contract and/or die from a variety of illnesses, including angina, ischaemia as shown by electrocardiogram (EKG), and chronic bronchitis (Marmot et al. 1991).

Social Status by Context

Social status is socially constructed. Although the presence of the concept of social status is nearly culturally universal, this social construction means that the character of social status varies by time and space. The attributes, styles, achievements, tastes, etc. that contribute to social status in one era and/or in one place are different than those in other places and times. Moreover, the ways in which these characteristics are evaluated also vary by context. Being a skinny woman comes with more social status in the United States in 2013 than it did in 1913, whereas having a compelling web presence relates to social status now but certainly did not in 1913—and still does not in some remote parts of the world.

Alain de Botton's insightful book *Status Anxiety* (2004), which wove together social history, literature, art, and philosophy in examining contemporary society's obsession with status and its elusiveness, denoted the characteristics that have brought the most status during different time periods. In Sparta, around 400 BCE, those with the most status were the physically fit, sexually bi-curious fighters who cared little for family life or money. About one thousand to two thousand years later, after the Roman Empire had fallen and Christianity had taken hold of Western Europe, those who were deemed to be the most Christ-like derived the highest reverence from their contemporaries; nonviolence and sexual suppression were in vogue. The monk-like stars of that time were then surpassed by the wealthy knights who waged war in the Crusades and pursued sexual relationships with many women, especially virgins. A couple hundred years later, across an ocean, the most high-status individuals were jaguar hunters. Indeed, the Amazonian Cubeo tribe rewarded hunting prowess with power; those who had killed the most jaguars (and, thus, those with the most jaguar teeth in their necklaces) had the best chance of becoming the head of the tribe.[1]

So, while social scientists study how social status relates to life outcomes and opportunities, they also compare and contrast the way status is determined in different cultures (Young 1965), time periods (De Botton 2008), and countries (Huberman, Loch, and Onculer 2004), among other comparisons. For example, Howard Becker's popular ethnography of professional jazz musicians (1973) characterized the different value systems in the jazz culture and the mainstream music culture, which were so diametrically opposed that it was impossible to hold high status in both. One could not resist "squares" and treat the music as art (which gave you a high rung among the jazz ladder) while simultaneously commercializing his sound in accordance with mainstream culture, thereby gaining employment at the highest paying gigs and pleasing "squares" (which moved one rung up the mainstream music status ladder): "To sum up, the emphasis of musicians on freedom from the interference inevitable in their careers creates a new dimension of professional prestige which conflicts with the previously discussed job prestige in such a way that one cannot rank high in both" (Becker 1973, 113).

What brings status is variable, not only across countries, cultures, and time-periods, but also within interpersonal associations, even those that are fleeting. A person's relative status is context specific. Within different social units, the same person can be dependent upon others for status-related considerations while also being the one some other person depends on.

Bourdieu's "Distinction"

We would be remiss to not mention Pierre Bourdieu's work in this area. In *Distinction: A Social Critique of the Judgment of Taste* (1984), the eminent French sociologist investigated the relationship between taste and social class, arguing that the interests, hobbies, favorite form of entertainment, etc. of people are inextricably linked to their social class (he was looking at French culture in the 1960s, but much of the analysis seems to apply widely). People learn these things as part of early socialization, and these differences in taste among different social groupings serve to clearly demarcate the boundaries of one social class from another. Furthermore, because this programming is instilled at such an early age, it appears to be naturally occurring to the conscious self, if the individual becomes conscious of it at all. In this sense, those who possess the "right" of cultural capital possess an advantage, in most settings, over those who like and prefer to do other things.

Within our framework, a person adopted by a wealthy, wine-drinking, golf-playing, theatre-going, Mahler-listening family at the age of sixteen from a poor, malt liquor–drinking, dice-playing, Judge Judy–watching family will gain cultural, social, and economic capital through the adoption but will still be likely to have less of it than his siblings and parents. Furthermore, he will be dependent on those around him to steer him toward refining his tastes, if he chooses to use his new social class as a means to a "better" life.

Thus, when prepping for the Ivy League interview and trying to live a more aristocratic life, he may rely on his siblings to teach him which topics are appropriate to chat with the interviewer about, how to tie a Windsor, how to talk about sailing, etc. He may be a Rockefeller or a Kennedy, but he is dependent on those around him for the acquisition of cultural capital.

Social Status as a Resource Disproportionately Possessed Within Social Units

Inside families, schools, military barracks, sports teams, and even nursing homes, a social status hierarchy emerges. There are "cool" kids, sports "stars" (who do not necessarily need to be more proficient than others at their sport; e.g., tennis's Anna Kournikova or soccer's David Beckham), and elderly men, who have been shown to hold more social status in nursing homes than elderly women as the result of being more in demand for romance, sex, and companionship because of their relative scarcity (Hardcastle 2012; Span 2012).

Social status has been measured at this individual level in the past—as an individual's perception of her own social standing using the MacArthur Scale of Subjective Social Status (see http://www.macses.ucsf.edu/research/psychosocial/subjective.php) or as someone's place in the social hierarchy as determined by a researcher using some sort of formula. It is often connected to a larger unit of analysis. So, we know that the New York Yankees hold more social status than the

Cleveland Indians, and that kids from the wealthier/better-at-sports high school have more social status in the larger general society than their counterparts from the other side of the tracks. Doctors hold more social status than highway construction workers, and scrubs indicate a higher-ranking than Carhartts (this is, of course, an average; in some places, such as working-class bars, Carhartts come with more status than scrubs).

When social status is measured at the macro/aggregate level, resource distribution can only be asserted as an important variable by drawing correlations with other variables at the macro level. We can list the average incomes of different professions and the prestige rankings of those occupations; these types of crosstabs are commonly found in introductory sociology textbooks. So, we can list the average income of MDs and compare it with the average income of construction workers, and then ask a sample of everyday people which type of person they would trust more, respect more, listen to more, etc. Positive correlations can be found between the income of a person and how others think of them.

However, these analyses of the dynamics surrounding social status do not delve deep enough to uncover the role of social status stratification within a group of doctors, construction workers, students at the same school in the same town, or residents of a nursing home. Additionally, although we can have *master statuses*, they, too, are subject to some context effects. For example, a man with AIDS might be known as the man with AIDS at the law firm where he works, at his children's school, and at his favorite restaurant, but not at his AIDS patient support group.

Social Status in Schools: A Resource Perspective

"Everyone who has ever gone to school is aware that there is a social status hierarchy in school. It is very painful to think that our own children are being ranked in some way by the group, but it happens," says Michael Thompson, an expert on the subject and co-organizer (with Lawrence Cohen) of a typology of school social groupings reported by PBS (see http://www.pbs.org/parents/education/going-to-school/social/cliques/). They focus on six different positions in the hierarchy: very popular kids, accepted kids, average or ambiguous kids, neglected kids, controversial kids, and rejected kids (PBS Parents n.d.)

We could delve into the specifics of the different types of students and their commensurate social rankings, but, like Dr. Thompson asserted, if you've been to school, then you know these classifications exist.

Compared to the other resources this book has considered in depth (e.g., strength and wealth), there is more evidence and awareness that social status exerts great influence within social units. Scholarship is especially rich in its delineation of social status within schools; perhaps this is to match the extremely powerful role social status plays in this domain.

While social status has been called a resource by others (e.g., Huberman, Loch, and Onculer 2004), an analysis of its relative distribution in creating dependency and abuse has not been made explicit. In other words, we know that some kids rank higher than others, and that these rankings are correlatively and causally entangled with certain life chances (e.g., the likelihood of going to college, the likelihood of the criminal justice system being lenient in the kid's favor) and life outcomes (e.g., longitudinal studies have shown that peer status in school predicts long-term health, even controlling for things like initial health, family SES, and future employment [e.g., Almquist 2009]), but we do not often analyze the micro context of the interpersonal dynamics that facilitate these differences, especially through the lens of resource distribution.

In schools, there are groups whose members are afforded a special status relative to other groups. Analyzing the relationship between the members of these different groups fits the thesis of the book, as schools are so often used as major explanatory variables in analyses of social inequality (e.g., those from rich schools get good jobs, while those from poor schools do not). So, the first part of this section will look into that. Still, we can go deeper with the theory and reach into the different groups within schools to search for the dynamics regarding resource distribution, dependency, and abuse that we have found elsewhere. As Rosalind Wiseman illustrated in her extremely popular sociological self-help book *Queen Bees and Wannabees* (2009), which was the basis for the popular Hollywood movie *Mean Girls*, a hierarchy exists even among the most popular kids in school. In the "girls' world," there is the "Queen Bee" who rules over her "Wannabees," all of whom reside at the top of the social status mountain (this group was depicted as "the Plastics" in the film). Wiseman characterized a similar dynamic in her newer book about the "boys' world," calling the leader the "Mastermind" and his popular followers "Wingmen."

To look at the role of social status within the social unit of a school, we can revisit a classic study. In the 1970s, William Chambliss set forth to study the relationship between self-image and delinquency by hanging around and talking to high school students. While at the school trying to get a feel for the social climate, Chambliss (1973) noticed a few students ducking out and leaving campus. Curious, he followed these students, met them, gained their trust, received consent to hang out *by* them, and did so for a couple of years. These students, and their compatriots, would come to be called the "Saints" and were compared with another group, who Chambliss named the "Roughnecks." Chambliss's highlighting of the disparity in the treatment of these two groups, both of whom performed similarly delinquent acts, would become a seminal work in the sociology of deviance and is still included in most introduction to sociology textbooks today. The scene is set:

> The Saints were a group of eight promising young men from "good" white upper-middle class families. They attended Hannibal High [the names are pseudonyms]: a moderate size high school in a suburb near a large metropolitan area. The Saints were active in school affairs, were enrolled in the pre—college program and received good grades. At the same time, they were some of the most delinquent boys at Hannibal High.
>
> The teachers, their parents, and people in the community knew that these boys occasionally sowed a few wild oats. They were totally unaware, however, of the extent to which the Saints engaged in delinquency. No one realized that "sowing their wild oats" completely occupied the daily routine of these young men. The Saints were constantly occupied with truancy, drinking, wild driving, petty theft and vandalism. Yet not one was officially arrested for any misdeed during the two years I observed them.
>
> This record was particularly surprising in light of my observations during the same two years of another gang of Hannibal High School students, six lower—class white boys I call the Roughnecks. The Roughnecks were constantly in trouble with police and community even though their rate of delinquency was about equal with that of the Saints. (Chambliss 1973)

Due to the high social status of the Saints—which was derived from their clothing, curriculum, official involvement in extracurricular activities (six played sports), grades (as a group, they averaged a "B"), and families—they were trusted and given the benefit of the doubt by authority figures. The teachers even felt that these kids would go on to do good things with their lives, and accepted their excuses and favorably graded their assignments. At least some of the eight Saints would skip school each day, telling teachers a fabricated "legitimate" reason for needing to leave class (e.g., for drama club rehearsal). The boys would then head somewhere concealed from their families and school personnel, although still in public, and would behave mischievously, but the proprietors usually put up with them because they were paying customers.

On weekends, they would go to the big city and party: get drunk at clubs, drive drunk, vandalize, steal public property, and put other people in danger (e.g., by adding a roadblock around the sharp bend of a road). Over the two years, there was only one arrest incident, and, after paying a five dollar fine, this did not stay on the boy's permanent record. Otherwise, both in school and with the police, if they were ever caught doing something wrong, they would be contrite and ask for forgiveness, which they were almost always granted.

The community generally had a negative view of the Roughnecks. They were poorer, wore shabbier clothing, behaved more coarsely than their counterparts, and were seen in run-ins with the police more than the Saints were (there was a tense, trustless relationship between the Roughnecks and the police). The Roughnecks engaged in lots of fighting, usually weaponless, and these melees were well known to the public. They also frequently engaged in (usually petty) theft, but these actions were largely not detected by the general public. Differently from the Saints, the Roughnecks' "thefts were for profit, not just thrill." The boys also did some drinking, but because their drinking was so often done out in the open—on the sidewalk in front of a convenience store, for example—the community perceived these individuals to be perpetually drunk. In school, the Roughnecks were not purposively destructive, nor did they ditch nearly as often as the Saints (most likely due to lack of access to an automobile).

While the two groups were clearly treated differently by law enforcement, teachers, and the community, the underlying reasons for this disparate treatment were harder to discern:

> Evaluating the relative seriousness of the two gangs' activities is difficult. The community reacted as though the behavior of the Roughnecks was a problem, and they reacted as though the behavior of the Saints was not. But the members of the community were ignorant to the array of delinquent acts that characterized the Saints' behavior. Although concerned citizens were unaware of much of the Roughnecks' behavior as well, they were much better informed about the Roughnecks' involvement in delinquency than they were about the Saints'. (Chambliss 1973)

In addition to the severity of their relative transgressions, Chambliss put forth a few other reasons for the disproportionate treatment of the two differentially placed groups: visibility of group delinquency, demeanor of the group, and a bias in framing the groups' acts by outsiders. The Roughnecks could not escape the local community like the Saints could; they could not drive to a different town or pay their way into a private establishment. The Roughnecks malfeasance was on display more often and more directly than that of the Saints. Additionally, while the Saints were very polite and contrite in their interactions with authority figures when confronted for their wrongdoing, and often made a point of making it seem like they were following the rules (perhaps due to the cultural capital instilled in them by their family and friends), the Roughnecks were not as successful, able, or willing to produce a similar veneer. The police, public, and school officials saw the transgressions of the Roughnecks as representing serious delinquency and saw the transgressions (when they were detected) of the Saints as the "sowing of wild oats." The Saints' social status in school afforded them more opportunities and leniency than was afforded to the Roughnecks. They were popular, well-liked by their peers, and respected by teachers; the Roughnecks were not.

A key point of this analysis is that the status of students within the social unit of the school was based, in part, on their associations with others. The Saints maintained their elevated status not only through their strategic actions but also through their associations with others. Students gain social cache through their associations. Furthermore, by being part of the Saints, a student could rely on others for manufacturing and executing "legitimate" excuses for ditching class, providing transportation to other towns, and having the ability to use money to cover up some of their sins.

In this way, each member of the Saints was dependent on his other members for upholding the standards of the group, reinforcing their collective "clean" image, and not polluting this image. Additionally, there were signs of a hierarchy within the Saints, which placed certain members at the mercy of higher-ranking members, similar to how the Wannabees were dependent on the Queen Bee. Chambliss illustrated what happened when one Saint was left behind by the others:

> The only Saint who did not complete college was Jerry. Jerry failed to graduate from high school with the other Saints. During his second senior year, after the other Saints had gone on to college, Jerry began to hang around with what several teachers described as a "rough crowd."

> At the end of his second senior year, when he did graduate from high school, Jerry took a job as a used—car salesman, got married and quickly had a child. Although he made several abortive attempts to go to college by attending night school, ten years after he graduated from high school, Jerry was unemployed and had been living on unemployment for almost a year. His wife worked as a waitress. (Chambliss 1973)

Comparatively, the other Saints experienced more professional success. All of the others went to college right out of high school, all graduated, and three went on for professional degrees. All secured well-paying and highly respected jobs. Of course, perhaps Jerry was just a bad apple. While this notion cannot be completely refuted, Chambliss noted that Jerry's lack of cover from other Saints during his second senior year—and his new group of rougher friends—put him in a disadvantageous position to achieve what is deemed by wider society as "success" during that year of high school and beyond:

> For one of the Saints (Jerry), his parents' divorce and his failing to graduate from high school brought about significant changes in his interpersonal relationships. Being held back in school for a year and losing his place among the Saints had sufficient impact on Jerry. It altered his self—image and virtually [assured] that he would not go on to college as his peers did. Although the experiments of life rarely can be reversed, it is likely that if Jerry had not experienced the "special consideration" of his teachers that kept him from graduating with his peers that he too would have "become something" had he graduated as anticipated. (Chambliss 1973)

We can sort out dependency in a couple of different ways in this example, depending on how we measure the social unit. Starting with a school as a social unit, which is what many studies on inequality do, we can see a disproportionate possession of status between the two groups: the Saints had more status, and the Roughnecks less. Although it is only a periphery issue in the Chambliss analysis, one can see how a member of the Roughnecks would be dependent on the Saints, a Saint, or some other high-status individual(s) in order to improve his own status level; these people would have to accept him into their circle. Thus, lower-status individuals are dependent on higher-status individuals, all other things being equal, for upward mobility in status. In seeking out higher-status, individuals on the low end of the social spectrum may face having daunting physical and emotional trauma exacted upon them by those in higher-status positions. Some of this may serve as rite-of-passage hazing, where it is expected that the individual will gain acceptance into the new group following the abuse. However, there does not have to be any guarantee of this; the high-status individuals might just wish to exploit the lower-status individual.

While lower-status individuals are, perhaps, particularly susceptible to abuse when they are motivated to transcend their social class status, they are also at the mercy of the higher-class kids even when they have no wish to move up in the social rankings. This is because of the advantages bestowed on the higher-class students by the power brokers within the community and the school. A lower-status individual may have to face the shame of backing down from a fight because he knows that if he engages in it, he will go to jail or get suspended, whereas the higher-class kid can engage in the fight knowing that he is risking much less. This difference in the cost–benefit calculus creates an environment ripe for abuse (although some might argue that the higher-ranking individuals would have more to lose because they have farther to drop, the likelihood of dropping must be figured into the scenario—a detention for fighting will not remove a Saint's halo). As the research shows, the Saints could get away with almost everything.

Research also shows that status attainment and maintenance are tangled with aggression (mostly reputational) for almost all of the participating students—not just those on the margins as was/is commonly thought. In a recent article in the *American Sociological Review*, Faris and Felmlee (2011) argued that "aggression is intrinsic to status and escalates with increases in peer status until the pinnacle of the social hierarchy is attained." The authors also argued that having a disproportionately high amount of social status facilitates the ability, and perhaps the motivation, to abuse one's peers of lesser status: "Our results underscore the argument that attaining and maintaining group status likely involves some degree of antagonistic behavior." In talking about the high-social-status kids, Faris and Felmlee contended that "[t]he characteristics that make them central—affluence, attractiveness, athleticism, or charisma—should enable them to influence, manipulate, or otherwise dominate their peers. In addition, occupying a central position within a school's social network, as compared to a more isolated position, directly increases the opportunities to engage in aggressive interactions with one's peers" (2011).

Of course, thinking about the interactions and relationships between high- and low-social-status students at the school level is only one way to show how status is a powerful resource within social units.

We can also look at the Saints as their own social unit. They depended on one another to carry on the façade and gave each other credibility through their associations. Furthermore, research like that of Rosalind Wiseman has illustrated how there are even hierarchies adorned with power differentials within popular groups in America's schools.

The Roughnecks and Saints had different social statuses within their high school and community; the overall perceptions of the groups by the town and teachers were vastly dissimilar. They were treated differently by teachers and law enforcement. Some of this was certainly related to the different initial economic conditions of the two groups and perhaps their current abilities and/or innate biology, but there were also other contributing features. In sum, their social status mattered, not only in their immediate treatment by others but also in their ultimate life outcomes. (Note that the Roughnecks secured less-prestigious and lower-paying jobs and held fewer degrees later in life than did the Saints.)

The wealth/income of one's parents has regularly been cited as having a predictive utility in determining one's own wealth/income in adult life (e.g., Behrman and Taubman [1990] suggest around a 0.5 correlation between the two indicators). The Saints may have just been rich kids who stayed rich. However, there is compelling evidence that popularity not only is associated with SES but also predicts someone's likelihood of continuing on to new levels of education reasonably well (Almquist, Modin, Ostberg 2010), which of course predicts future earnings (Card 1999).

Conclusion

Status, like wealth and physical strength, is a powerful variable that exerts influence over interpersonal relationships within social units. Not only is status related to life chances and outcomes, but it also steers the interactions of individuals at the micro level. Students with different levels of status encounter dissimilar social contexts within the same school. The penalties and awards that authority figures—including other students—dole out are done through the prism of social status; high-status kids have it easier, generally speaking. Lower-status kids may also be dependent on higher-status kids for entrée into certain important circles or opportunities (e.g., the opportunity to make a varsity sports team, attend a high-status party, or gain the teacher's permission to miss class). Moreover, because status is largely contingent upon associations, lower-status individuals are at the mercy of the whims of those of higher status. These high-ranking kids can exploit this dependency and abuse the lower-ranking kids. All of this may happen at schools that are rich or poor, among kids of the same race, religion, gender, etc.

Note

1. These examples show almost exclusively male examples of people with high status. While there are and were places throughout human history where certain females held high social status, this has not been the norm. Of course, this relative dearth of examples of high status is just as important to our analysis as the alternatives, especially if the likelihood of finding examples illuminates the objective historical record.

References

Adler, Nancy E., Elissa S. Epel, Grace Castellazzo, and Jeannette R. Ickovics. 2000. "Relationship of Subjective and Objective Social Status with Psychological and Physiological Functioning: Preliminary Data in Healthy, White Women." *Health Psychology,* 19(6):586.

Almquist, Ylva. 2009. "Peer Status in School and Adult Disease Risk: A 30-Year Follow-Up Study of Disease-Specific Morbidity in a Stockholm Cohort." *Journal of Epidemiology and Community Health,* 63(12):1028–34.

Almquist, Ylva, Bitte Modin, and Viveca Östberg. 2010. "Childhood Social Status in Society and School: Implications for the Transition to Higher Levels of Education." *British Journal of Sociology of Education,* 31(1):31–45.

Anderson, Cameron, Michael W. Kraus, Adam D. Galinsky, and Dacher Keltner. 2012. "The Local-Ladder Effect: Social Status and Subjective Well-Being." *Psychological Science,* 23(7):764–71.

Ball, Sheryl, Catherine Eckel, Philip J. Grossman, and William Zame. 2001. "Status in Markets." *The Quarterly Journal of Economics,* 116(1):161–88.

Becker, Howard. 1973. *Outsiders: Studies in the Sociology of Deviance.* New York: Free Press.

Behrman, Jere R., and Paul Taubman. 1990. "The Intergenerational Correlation Between Children's Adult Earnings and Their Parents' Income: Results from the Michigan Panel Survey of Income Dynamics." *Review of Income and Wealth,* 36(2):115–27.

Berger, Joseph, Susan J. Rosenholtz, and Morris Zelditch. 1980. "Status Organizing Processes." *Annual Review of Sociology,* 6:479–508.

De Botton, Alain. 2008. *Status Anxiety.* Random House Digital, Inc. http://books.google.com/books?hl=en&lr=&id=83ZCBa9hXLQC&oi=fnd&pg=PR5&dq=Botton+status+anxiety&ots=SVD6y1QQjU&sig=KuijvN6FO1V_UZdEuw-5S9uknyCM (accessed January 31, 2014).

Bourdieu, Pierre. 1984. *Distinction: A Social Critique of the Judgement of Taste.* Cambridge, MA: Harvard University Press.

Card, David. 1999. "The Causal Effect of Education on Earnings." In *Handbook of Labor Economics, Volume 3, Part A,* ed. Orley C. Ashenfelter and David Card. Philadelphia: Elsevier, 1801–63. http://www.sciencedirect.com/science/article/pii/S1573446399030114 (accessed January 25, 2014).

Chambliss, William J. 1973. "The Saints and the Roughnecks." *Society,* 11(1):24–31.

Clinard, Marshall B., Richard Quinney, and John Wildeman. 2010. *Criminal Behavior Systems: A Typology.* Boston, MA: Newnes.

D'Alessio, Stewart J., and Lisa Stolzenberg. 1993. "Socioeconomic Status and the Sentencing of the Traditional Offender." *Journal of Criminal Justice,* 21(1):61–77.

Devine, Dennis J., Laura D. Clayton, Benjamin B. Dunford, Rasmy Seying, and Jennifer Pryce. 2001. "Jury Decision Making: 45 Years of Empirical Research on Deliberating Groups." *Psychology, Public Policy, and Law,* 7(3):622–727.

Faris, Robert, and Diane Felmlee. 2011. "Status Struggles Network Centrality and Gender Segregation in Same-and Cross-Gender Aggression." *American Sociological Review,* 76(1):48–73.

Hardcastle, Jessica. 2012. "Sexuality in Senior Homes." *Monterey County Weekly,* May 10. http://www.montereycountyweekly.com/news/cover/article_efda960f-812d-5add-8817-0e3980c2d0bc.html (accessed January 30, 2014).

Huberman, Bernardo A., Christoph H. Loch, and Ayse ÖNçüler. 2004. "Status as a Valued Resource." *Social Psychology Quarterly,* 67(1):103–14.

Jeffery, R. W. et al. 1989. "The Relationship Between Social Status and Body Mass Index in the Minnesota Heart Health Program." *International Journal of Obesity,* 13(1):59–67.

Marmot, M. G. et al. 1991. "Health Inequalities Among British Civil Servants: The Whitehall II Study." *Lancet* 337(8754):1387–93.

Marmot, Michael. 2004. *The Status Syndrome: How Your Social Standing Affects Your Health and Life Expectancy.* London: Bloomsbury.

PBS Parents. n.d. "Cliques." http://www.pbs.org/parents/education/going-to-school/social/cliques (accessed January 30, 2014).

Riahi-Belkaoui, Ahmed. 2009. *Social Status Matters.* Charleston, SC: BookSurge.

Span, Paula. 2012 "Fewer Beds for Men Entering Nursing Homes." *The New Old Age Blog.* http://newoldage.blogs.nytimes.com/2012/01/30/fewer-beds-for-men-entering-nursing-homes (accessed January 30, 2014).

Thornberry, Terence P., and Margaret Farnworth. 1982. "Social Correlates of Criminal Involvement: Further Evidence on the Relationship Between Social Status and Criminal Behavior." *American Sociological Review,* 47(4):505.

Walpole, MaryBeth. 2003. "Socioeconomic Status and College: How SES Affects College Experiences and Outcomes." *The Review of Higher Education,* 27(1):45–73.

Weber, Max. 1946. "Class, Status, Party." In *From Max Weber: Essays in Sociology.* Oxford, UK: Oxford University Press, 180–95.

Wiseman, Rosalind. 2009. *Queen Bees & Wannabes: Helping Your Daughter Survive Cliques, Gossip, Boyfriends, and the New Realities of Girl World.* New York: Three Rivers Press.

Young, Frank Wilbur. 1965. *Initiation Ceremonies: A Cross-Cultural Study of Status Dramatization.* Indianapolis, IN: Bobbs-Merrill.

II

Help

6

General Help

Jeff Oliver

How Are "Weak" People Helped?

Weak or vulnerable individuals in possession of a relative scarcity of key resources compared to others within their social units—due to their position in the societal structure and the norms of social science, politics, and political thinking—face daunting challenges in ridding themselves of their resource-poor position and overcoming the abuse that may have followed from it. Of course, those in disadvantageous positions in macro society must overcome similarly difficult obstacles. However, the two groups—not to mention those who are downtrodden in both macro and micro space—must fight to improve their lot in different contexts.

The spouse of a wealthy but abusive and money-controlling husband will not be able to get much government aid for college or rent-subsidized housing. If she tries to divorce, she might incite more abuse, have any communal funds or goods completely taken away from her, and face an army of powerful lawyers intent on securing all household wealth for their client. To her local community, the wife might be seen in a negative light, as a diva, as greedy, as a "gold-digger;" she is subject to being ostracized by her friends and community. Some will see her lack of family values as a pollutant to their wholesome communities, while others might fear she will start a trend and wish to silence or delegitimize her as quickly as possible. They will not help her.

A member of a poor family, from a poor community, may be able to get financial aid for college and other government resources allocated for the poor if he can overcome any cultural resistance and paranoia regarding the government and college, can procure government-issued ID, access the Internet, find transportation, etc. Once at college, he will be competing with kids who hail from highly ranked high schools in wealthy communities (where one could take classes such as *Disease and Society*[1] and *Electricity and Magnetism* as well as field trips to world-class museums), who have personal iPads, and who study under highly rated teachers with PhDs. He may need to learn to talk differently, to leave all etchings of his underclass roots behind. The bit of financial assistance cannot be directly exchanged for cultural capital, social capital, or knowing how to use what Steve Jobs called a "magical and revolutionary device" (Huffington Post 2011). He will need help.

While they may still be obscure to, or denied by, the general public, the problems of direct and institutional discrimination, cultural stereotypes, the "it's not what you know, but who you know" corporate ladder, and other social mobility–stymieing mechanisms are well documented in the social sciences (e.g., McCrudden 1982; Shih, Pittinsky, and Ambady 1999; Bagilhole 1993; Nardi, Whittaker, and Schwarz 2000) (even if there is disagreement, which often falls along political lines, as to the degree of influence these various phenomena represent). Putting aside the process, one can also look at the end result: parental income while one is growing up is a fairly reliable predictor of one's individual adult income (Wells and Lynch 2012; Sewell, Hauser, and Wolf 1980) and is even more robust in the "American Dream," rags-to-riches United States than in many other first-world countries. In 2010, the *Economist* ran a story documenting the reality of the American Dream: "Compared with people in other rich countries, Americans tend to accept relatively high levels of income inequality because they believe they may move up over time. The evidence is that America does offer opportunity; but not nearly as much as its citizens believe."

Parental income is a better predictor of a child's future in America than it is in much of Europe, implying that social mobility is less powerful (Economic Mobility Project 2013). Different groups of Americans have different levels of opportunity. Those born to the middle class have about an equal chance of moving up or down the income ladder, according to the Economic Mobility Project. But those born to black middle-class families are much more likely than their white counterparts to fall in rank. The children of the rich and poor, meanwhile, are less mobile than the middle class's. More than 40 percent of those Americans born in the bottom quintile remain stuck there as adults (Economic Mobility Project 2013).

Family background is not insurmountable, according to Isabel Sawhill and Ron Haskins of the Brookings Institution. In particular, earning a degree and marrying before having children can help someone climb to a higher rung. However, family background influences the likelihood of education and marriage (Economist 2010).

So, the poor person at the rich college becomes dependent on others for status and transfer of social and cultural capital. The major macro-economic disparity inhibiting the poor student from reaching the expensive and esteemed school is addressed by local and national scholarships, need-based and performance-based fellowships, federal financial aid, etc. The money helps, but only so much. And what about the poor student at the rich high school? Who helps him with transportation and clothes? Is he able to see a doctor? Who does he depend on? What hidden barriers does he face in trying to get to a college or secure a high-paying job?

Of course, much of the same phenomena are present for physically weak kids who are bullied in school or at home by strangers, or for prison inmates who lack status, affiliation, and/or physical strength to be protected from beatings and rapes by fellow inmates. The people deemed weak in macro society receive help to overcome their condition from a variety of channels, including those that expose and illuminate the injustices they face. Similarly, weak people in micro space get help from the government, civil society, and individuals. However, the challenges the two groups face, the type of help they receive, and the specific sources of that help differ.

Just as the conditions of the relatively resource deprived within social units are understudied, so are the types of help they receive. Moreover, the types of help they receive may be limited by the lack of attention given to the situation by the general society and by scholarly and political bodies interested in inequality.

In the last third of this book, we felt it prudent to delineate the type of help that is available for the weak people we have discussed in the text so far for two primary reasons. First, help can improve these people's lives. Maybe not all efforts towards helping these people have the desired effect, or are worth the economic and opportunity cost in developing and implementing when that time and money could go toward other actions (e.g., macro-level programs) that might be higher yield. Still, we should at least sort through the extant help process for these people, assess it, and see if it can be made better.

Second, because of their place within the social structure and the general public as well as scholarly and political opinion toward examination of the world at certain levels of analysis (e.g., the household), the process of helping the relatively resource deprived within social units faces unique roadblocks (legal, political, individual, public perception based, etc.) not usually encountered or highlighted when talking about helping marginalized groups at the macro level (e.g., how do you address the retaliation by the person the victim is dependent on in their social unit?).

Interpersonal abuse requires assistance from outside the abusive relationship (although we will also highlight the options for resistance that those being abused can use themselves). In forthcoming chapters, we will look at two special types of outside help: aid from civil society and government assistance (while also remaining cognizant of the role individuals play in helping). Perhaps that most commonly thought of is government assistance. However, civil society and individuals also protect the vulnerable from their abusers of the past, present, and potentially the future, and some types of help are more effective in certain situations than others.

The lines drawn between these three types of help we will look at (i.e., government, civil society, and individual) are somewhat ambiguous and overlapping. For example, in the nationally publicized case of Karen Klein (Associated Press 2012), a bus monitor from upstate New York, her abuse came at the hands of bully students. These young students ridiculed her, called her names, and posted their abuse on the Internet. However, when her case became known, support poured in. The support began as an influx of apparently semi-organized individual financial donations. These individual donations soon were organized into a fundraising campaign on indiegogo.com and facebook.com, with a goal to earn $5,000 to send Karen on a much-needed vacation. Soon the campaign had easily cleared half a million dollars from over 30,000 donors. Part of these donations went on to fund the eponymous Karen Klein Anti-Bullying Foundation. In the case of Karen Klein, what began as individual-level help soon became an official organization in civil society. In this way, individual help can often turn into a formal organization (Stevenson 2013).

Another point of overlap among these three types of help is the way the government sometimes subsidizes nonprofit charitable endeavors. In 2005, writing for charity watchdog group Charity Navigator, Emily Navarro stated the different funders of charity:

> We all know that charities receive their funding from multiple sources. The majority of contributions come from individuals; foundations and corporations also give significant amounts to nonprofits each year. What most of us don't realize is that another considerable source are taxpayer dollars, or government funding. While overall it represents

a small percentage of a charity's contributed income, government funding is a generally reliable source that is typically renewed each year, or even increased. However, in recent years this funding has become less and less predictable. (Navarro 2005)

The notion that the government, through direct funding, tax breaks, charitable giving subsidies, and other ways, steers money into what are traditionally thought of as nongovernment entities muddles the lines between individual, civil, and government even more. Many helping organizations progress from individual-level help; if formalized, they can become a nonprofit or other organization (part of civil society) and ultimately may go on to receive government funding or subsidies. In this way, many large and highly influential nonprofits in the United States today are government-funded organizations that began from individual-level helping behavior. Women's shelters are an excellent example of this process, often being organized in civil society but later thriving on government funding in order to remain in operation.

The government may also directly fund individuals who wish to help those in need. Foster parents, for example, represent individual-level help that is subsidized as part of a government program. Nevertheless, foster parents certainly do not make money off of their children, save for some rare parents spotlighted by need-a-villain, sensationalized media shows (which certainly may not reflect reality).

> Licensed foster parents are usually reimbursed expenses accrued throughout the month by way of monthly stipend, sent from the state or agency you're working with. It is not uncommon for parents to spend well beyond the monthly allotment in order to care for the children in their care, so ensuring your ability to care for children is a very important step when deciding to become licensed. However, that stipend will help considerably. ("Foster Parenting" n.d.)

So the government has a hand in much of the types of help available to weak people. For some types of vulnerable people, all three types of help seem to play a meaningful role. For example, the homeless, who may be the closest thing to truly resource-less, receive financial assistance from the kindness of strangers on street corners and may be the beneficiaries of shelters and soup kitchens—agencies that are often both government sponsored and run by civil society.

The interconnections of the three spheres of helpers we are focused on can be illustrated through a discussion of the *Not in Our School* movement (Not in Our School n.d.[a]), which involves schools (government), civil collectives, and a reliance on the effort of individuals. An offshoot of Not in Our Town, a campaign to stop hate using media, resources, and engagement programs, Not in Our School (NIOS) is a national effort to create schools free of stereotypes, intolerance, and hate.[2] The campaign varies from school to school, with students being encouraged to define the local problems and identify solutions. To start a NIOS campaign, a coalition is first created by whoever initiates the campaign, be it students or others. The coalition could consist of students, teachers, administrators, and outside community members and organizations. The broader the scope of support, the more effective the campaign may be. In addition to the coalition, or instead of if the case may be, a NIOS club is formed. A NIOS club is entirely student led.

Working with the coalition, the students identify the issues that are occurring in their school, including bullying, harassment, hate, or exclusion based on anything from gender, race, religion, sexual orientation, appearance, or disability. The coalition identifies the most pertinent issue and works toward its resolution. The idea behind NIOS is not simply to have adults and those in charge tell students what should not be happening, but to have students identify what is really going on and propose their own solutions, followed by the entire school community uniting against this issue. Each school that participates is encouraged to upload a video of their efforts to the NIOS website. These videos serve as inspiration and testimonials to the work that students can do to end hate in their schools. Not in Our Town also includes videos, subject- and grade-appropriate lesson plans,[3] and other activities to get a NIOS campaign going.

In these videos, the creativity and endless possibilities of the students dedicated to a NIOS campaign is evident. The videos address not only bullying but also diversity, hate crimes, immigrants, faith, racism, stereotypes, and sexual identity. Students from one school in Ohio sent a survey out to students of the school asking where they had witnessed bullying. With these results, a map was created showing that bullying occurred in the vast majority of the school, while also identifying "bullying hotspots." In one of these hotspots, the cafeteria, the NIOS club coordinated a flash mob–type demonstration to raise awareness of the different forms of bullying. Posters were also placed around the school saying how many students reported witnessing bullying in said location (Not in Our School n.d.[d]).

A California school took on the perception of immigrants. With the slogans "Don't Drop the I-Bomb" and "No Human Was Born Illegal," students organized a lunch-time demonstration to teach that the term *illegal* is hurtful. In response to two teen suicides, students set up activities across twenty schools in a California county for a week of action, including signing pledges to not bully, reading personal stories about victims of bullying, enacting bullying role-playing in the elementary schools, and setting up presentations telling the teachers where in the school bullying occurs and the actions they wish teachers would take. These students spoke about how simply hearing the term *Not in Our School* has stopped bullies in the act. (Not in Our School n.d.[b]). At the University of Mississippi, traditions stemming from segregation and the confederacy were challenged. The chant "The South will rise again" is popular on campus, creating a sense of pride in the campus and its southern origins, but has historically been used by the Ku Klux Klan (KKK) and separates students on campus, particularly white and black students. The student legislation passed a vote banning the chant, though with only a 51 percent majority. When protestors from the KKK came to the university, students planned a counter-protest by bringing in community members, wearing shirts saying "Turn your back on hate," and reciting the University of Mississippi creed that encourages academic freedom and respect for all. In response, the protestors from the KKK ended their protest and left (Not in Our School n.d.[c]).

While we acknowledge the complexities inherent in separating one type of help from the others, each chapter in this section attempts to focus on the different types of help (help from individuals, civil society, and the government) in order to better understand its role in interpersonal abuse. Additionally, we seek to understand the extent of help available and the efficacy of each type of help based on circumstance.

The Government

The government has programs for the regulation of everything from food assistance for women and children to regulating the interference an electronic device can or cannot receive. When it comes to its role in interpersonal or micro-level abuse, the efforts of the government, when present, are not able to fully address the problems inherent in inter-social-unit abuse.

For example, the Special Supplemental Nutrition Program for Women, Infants, and Children, more commonly known as WIC (a food assistance program for low-income women and their children;

see http://www.fns.usda.gov/wic/women-infants-and-children-wic for official information about the program), does not detect or hinge upon the occurrence of abuse in the family relationship for those women and children. However, it does provide resources (specifically food) that may be used by the women and children to hopefully prevent or terminate abuse, even if the program's intended purpose is much broader. The program "provides Federal grants to States for supplemental foods, health care referrals, and nutrition education for low-income pregnant, breastfeeding, and nonbreastfeeding postpartum women, and to infants and children up to age five who are found to be at nutritional risk" (United States Department of Agriculture n.d.).

So, while WIC does not directly help a woman who may not feel able to leave an abusive partner due to a lack of money, it does provide a path to food or shelter in the case that the woman breaks away, which may make her more likely to do so.

Still, the government often needs individuals to be its "eyes and ears" in cases of micro-level abuse. The government has a rather good pulse on disadvantaged *groups*; even disadvantaged *neighborhoods* are almost fully mapped out nationwide. However, the specific individuals who are being abused (among all classes, wealth levels, and races) may be hard to detect. As we have noted in the theoretical chapter of this book, interpersonal abuse is often covert; it is not brought into the open, as, for example, the debate between the rich and the poor is.[4]

The highly bureaucratic nature of government structures and processes is rather slow to react to situations of abuse. Just as the government was criticized for its slow response during the Hurricane Katrina crisis of 2005 (see ABC News 2005 for a discussion of who was to blame for the slow response time), the same issues haunt government response to aid those who are the victims of interpersonal (micro-level) abuse. In the forthcoming government chapter, we offer an example of this regarding school bullying. While there are laws and protocols in place specifically targeting bullying, they have just recently been created and do not seem to have filtered down into any measurable difference at the micro level.

The United States may well benefit from the new agenda implemented in the United Kingdom to find all kinds of vulnerable adults and assess the type of assistance that they need. While the United States has recently endeavored to make all individuals the eyes and ears of child abuse and elder abuse, the United Kingdom has taken that notion to a higher level. The Safeguarding Vulnerable Adults initiative is based on bringing covert abuses into the open: "There can be no secrets and no hiding places when it comes to exposing the abuse of vulnerable adults" (Department of Health n.d.). This initiative in the United Kingdom led to nearly 300,000 identified vulnerable adults being placed under various government care organizations. In the United Kingdom, the public mentality that there can be "no secrets" when it comes to vulnerable adults is in contrast with the American way of thinking. Indeed, even some constitutional rights, such as the Fourth and Fifth Amendments, grant a certain degree of secrecy of speech and property (see https://www.gov.uk/government/uploads/system/uploads/attachment_data/file/194272/No_secrets__guidance_on_developing_and_implementing_multi-agency_policies_and_procedures_to_protect_vulnerable_adults_from_abuse.pdf for the full document). Although the authors of this book do not advocate that the constitutional rights be repealed, we argue that taking greater interest in those individuals who may be victims of covert interpersonal abuse is a key to greater protection for all vulnerable Americans. Making certain types of individuals the eyes and ears of child abuse and elder abuse in the country is a step in this direction and may well be better incorporated in the detection of other types of abuse. Similarly, both the federal and state governments have enacted directives aimed at thwarting school bullying by advocating/requiring intervention at the school or individual level. One piece of this is teaching individuals how not to bully, report it/or stop it when it happens, and how to prevent others from doing it (Swearer, Espelage, Vaillancourt, and Hymel 2010). One way the government compels schools to act in accordance with their guidelines is by making general funding contingent upon the implementation of particular programs (more will be said on this topic in the Bullying section of the Government Help chapter).

Still, there are some abusive situations in which individual-level reporting is nearly impossible. For example, in situations of spousal abuse, the victim is often a woman who has been cut off from virtually all resources. The role of the government in providing women with resources that are both preventative as well as alleviatory is essential. Similarly, in situations such as abuse in the military, government intervention for the protection of the weak is vital, as outside individuals can easily be kept out of the inner circles of military operations. Furthermore, the very overt and highly organized power dynamic in the military is sanctioned by the government (specifically, some are designated as having more power than others). This power dynamic makes the abuse of power easy because the perpetrator has enough power to control the victim and to hide the acts. It is estimated that 26,000 cases of sexual abuse happened in the US military in 2012, though only 10 percent were reported through official channels (Associated Press 2013a). Weak individuals in the military have trouble avoiding/ reporting abuse exacted upon them for a number of reasons: (1) There is a "boys will be boys" culture in the military. (2) Power structures are so ingrained in military life that they can almost not be fought against or resisted. (3) The military does not leave much access to outsider groups or services. (4) Those in the military are seen as strong and able to defend themselves, so programs have not looked to defend them.

In such circumstances as rape within the military, individual and even civil help are unlikely to be of assistance because their access to the victims is very limited and the power structures are predetermined. In fact, the government is aware of the massive incidence of inter-personal abuse in the military; however, they are struggling to make improvements. The number of victims of sexual abuse is estimated to be increasing, and even those individuals who have been put in charge of the project have themselves been accused of being sexual predators (Kube and Black, 2013). President Obama has called for stricter penal-ties for those found guilty of sexual abuse in the military (O'Brien 2013); however, the way abusers are able to exercise their power to commit the abuse and to cover it up may limit the effectiveness of increased penalties for those found guilty of such abuses.

Another area in which government assistance is vital (along with organizations of civil society as mentioned earlier) is in prisons. Prisons are what Erving Goffman called "total institutions" (Goffman 1961). Basically, they are self-contained. Fellow inmates and even prison officials can easily abuse prisoners who have basically no resources besides their comparative physical strength. In total institutions, such as prisons, individuals often act by their own rules in a way that is largely unseen by the outside world. In many ways, prisons epitomize the covert nature of interpersonal abuse. Total institutions must have greater transparency and greater levels of accountability for misdeeds related to interpersonal abuse. Perhaps due to the way prisoners are seen as a sort of underclass in society, there has not been a priority to end these abuses; however, nothing short of the resources, authority, and legitimacy of the government can provide that (although individual and civil protests may raise enough awareness to get the government to act if there was enough interest in the welfare of prisoners).

Civil Society

Referred to as the "third sector," civil society can be defined as simply as any nongovernmental organization, or as intricately as the space occupied by the public in between the home, market, or business and the state. Generally, any organization or institution that is constituted outside of the state or government is recognized as a component of civil society. Examples include nongovernmental organizations (NGOs), nonprofit organizations (NPOs), professional and community organizations, faith-based organizations, academia, labor unions, activist groups, clubs, charities, and voluntary associations. Social movements are also considered a part of civil society, as they typically bring together multiple organizations and many individuals all with the same common cause.

Civil society is often able to help where the government cannot or will not, and in cases where individuals lack the resources or level of organization necessary to help the victims in question. For example, in Dallas, New York, Detroit, and other big cities with a large homeless "problem," the local government has paid to put homeless people on a bus and ship them out of the city. In a recent case, the city of Ft. Lauderdale "offered" to give the homeless a one-way ticket out of the city as well (Winter 2011). In preparation for the Olympic Games, the city of Atlanta endeavored to ship out the homeless as part of a clean-up effort (Associated Press 1996).

Some startup businesses and nonprofits see it the opposite way. For example, in San Francisco a startup venture is looking to repurpose old buses as free showers for the homeless (Associated Press 2013b). Another company, called the Homeless Bus, provides free transportation, blankets, and meals to the homeless, especially during stormy weather (Landgrebe 2010). Of course, this is not to say that the government is always an enemy to the homeless, and civil society their champion; it simply means that in many cases where the government cannot assist either due to logistics, "manpower," or finances, civil society is often able to step in and provide aid to individuals who are without resources to defend themselves.

Similarly, religious organizations do much work seeking to help vulnerable individuals in society. For example, the Church of Jesus Christ of Latter-day Saints has implemented an extensive welfare system intended to teach self-reliance. The Church owns canneries, farms, and factories throughout the United States through which mostly volunteers provide needed items and teach individuals how to grow and store foodstuffs ("Church Welfare Program" 2008).

Abuse of prison inmates is another area that is well served by civil society. While the United States government has recently expressed a commitment to crack down on prison rape and inmate abuse (both by prison officials and other inmates; see the *Prison Rape Elimination Act* of 2003), prisons are a difficult case due to the perception that inmates are less deserving (or a lower class of human beings). Some even argue that helping prisoners removes the deterrent effect of incarceration (see Andenaes 1966 for a popular classic look at the preventative effects of incarceration). The American Civil Liberties Union (ACLU) Prison Project is one group that does seek to advocate for the protection of prisoners against interpersonal abuse (see https://www.aclu.org/prisoners-rights for more information). The Center for Constitutional Rights (CCR) and Ethecon are other civil rights organizations that have made efforts to protect prison inmates against exploitation (see http://ccrjustice.org and http://www.ethecon.org/en/1635, respectively). These organizations believe they are in a position to advocate for prisoners to ensure that their civil rights are honored and that they are not becoming the victims of abuse within the prison system by other inmates or prison officials.

Still, civil society has not perfected its craft of aiding the weak in situations of *interpersonal* or micro-level abuse. Much of what has actually been accomplished by these groups is the prevention of exploitation of inmates by large corporations (for example, those that charge monumental fees for providing phone services that inmates must pay for). Nevertheless, these organizations are interested in and well positioned to assist inmates against interpersonal abuse and supportive of a key notion of this book—that the abuses that occur within an organization are often ignored in favor of inveterate notions of abuse between large, powerful, elite groups and marginalized groups in society.

Interestingly, civil society not only fills undesirable niches among the more despised of society but also has a large presence in situations where a lot of people feel compassion for the victims. Orphans are a great example of this. There are several large charities that support orphaned children. God's Kids, World Vision, Orphan Voice, Christian Foundation for Children and Aging (recently renamed Unbound), and SOS Children's Village are only a few of the organizations created for the support of orphans (see https://www.godskids.org, http://www.world vision.org, http://www.orphanvoice.org, http://www.unbound.org, and http://www.sos-usa.org for more information.) Many of these organizations effectually solicit, encourage, and facilitate individual-level giving (e.g., donations or sponsorships) and, in turn, manage the distribution of the money. These organizations, though technically classified as civil society, hinge upon the efforts of direct individual donations.

Finally, because organizations in civil society have access to more resources than the average individual does, they can provide help that individuals in some ways cannot. Many women's shelters are a good example of this. They are usually able to provide food, shelter, and childcare as well as help finding a permanent job or home (Smith and Segal 2012). Of course, these and other services are no panacea for domestic violence victims. One (2012) survey recently revealed that in a twenty-four-hour period, victims of domestic violence in the United States made ten thousand requests for services that could not be granted due to a lack of resources (NNEDV 2012). Additionally, a number of charitable organizations are at risk of being shut down as government funding is being slowly and systematically reduced in various locations across the country, threatening the continued operations of many organizations in civil society (and illustrating the complex and common relationship between the government and civil institutions). In a strange way, civil society has come to depend deeply on the government in the United States, even to the degree that some argued the visible relationship between the two has reduced private giving because of the perception that the government will provide the needed funds for an organization to continue to operate (Horne, Johnson, and Van Slyke 2005).

The role of civil society fills an important place between government and individual assistance. It is in touch and passionate enough to somewhat personalize its assistance to those in need yet has greater access to resources than the average individual does. This is an important combination, especially for helping those who are abused at the micro level and who are somewhat more likely to go unnoticed by large bureaucratic organizations such as the federal government.

Additionally, while budget cuts threaten the continued operations of many charities in civil society, the Internet appears to be playing a growing role in the growth of civil society's organizations. For example, the "modest" fundraiser put together for bullied bus monitor Karen Klein (described earlier) raised roughly three-quarters of a million dollars at the time of this writing, and the earthquake in Haiti in 2010 was answered with billions in donations largely garnered through social media websites, even though this aid does not seem to be resulting in marked progress in the ravaged country (Huffington Post 2012). The role of the Internet in these organizations is very promising and may be the future of such organizations in many ways.

Individual Help

Individual help is often regarded as less effective than that which comes from organized civil society or the government due to the comparative lack of resources of the average individual relative to an organization. Nevertheless, individual help has an irreplaceable position in helping the vulnerable (including the idea of the victim helping him or herself). The government and civil society may be more highly organized, be more highly legitimized, and possess more resources; however, individual help can reach abused persons in a way that a large organization cannot. Individual help is often the "eyes and ears" of interpersonal abuse that would otherwise go undetected. The role of individual help in bullying is one of the best examples.

The government is showing increasing interest in prevention of bullying in schools. This interest has been substantiated as antibullying legislation and awareness programs throughout the country. However, it appears that the antibullying efforts are not enough, as a large bureaucracy is inefficient and largely ineffective at detecting some types of bullying. Individual help may be a better remedy for bullying.

An interesting case study is that of Chy Johnson of Arizona (Reilly 2012). Chy was repeatedly bullied due to her lower cognitive abilities caused by a medical condition (microencephaly), and her reduced cognitive resources caused her to be exploited by her peers. Chy's mother became concerned at the extensive reports of bullying. However, the Johnson family's appeals to teachers and administrators were completely ineffective, and the bullying continued unabated. Chy's mother decided to turn to the individual-level sphere of support—a local football player who she knew, starting quarterback Carson Jones. Chy's mother asked Carson to "keep his ear to the ground" to try and figure out who the bullies were. Carson decided to do more than that. He began to invite Chy to eat with him and his friends at lunch and to walk with her in the halls. Carson reasoned that if the bullies saw Chy with him and his high-status football player friends that they might start treating Chy better, adding that, "Telling on kids would've just caused more problems." Soon, Chy was surrounded by a host of popular football players, and the bullying largely stopped (Reilly 2012).

The nationally publicized case of Chy Johnson illustrates the way that bullying can most effectively be remedied by individual-level help. As Carson notes, even if administrators enforce nationally installed anti-bullying practices against bullies, it may only result in "more problems" such as retaliation from the bullies (perhaps in more subtle or crafty ways, even possibly threatening the bullied child that if he reports the bully again, terrible things will happen).

Researchers of bullying similarly find that the best way to beat bullies is not by reporting them to teachers or administrators, but by finding and befriending nonbullied students (or students who are themselves bullies of others) (Swearer, Espelage, Vaillancourt, and Hymel 2010). There is a powerful TV commercial produced by Values.com, a foundation set on seeking a better life, that advocated this approach. In the commercial, a high school student has his books slapped to the ground and a seemingly popular kid comes over to help him (Values.com n.d.; the video can be seen at http://www.values.com/inspirational-stories-tv-spots/72-Locker). While it is not the intention of these researchers, or of the current authors, to advocate that bullied children remain quiet and not report the abuse, it is very relevant to the case of individual-level help that the most effective strategies for bullying prevention relate to the help that can come from individuals (often other students).

Chy's lack of cognitive strength became the means of exploitation by her peers. Chy was defenseless against the abuse (even her appeals to teachers and administrators failing) until she received outside resources—in this case, the increase in status by virtue of her new association with the popular football players.

In many ways, the most effective type of outside help (individual, civil, or government) is determined by the resources needed in order to overcome the abuse. The case of Chy Johnson (and the research that supports it) provides evidence of this phenomenon. Specifically, in the case of bullying in schools, status can be seen as one of the most effective resources in overcoming bullying. It is unlikely that the government or even a civil society organization would be able to provide a boost in status like befriending another nonbullied child would.

A common theme among the current body of literature on interpersonal (or micro-level) abuse is awareness as a means for prevention of abuse. This is reflected in the case of Chy Johnson and is also commonly seen in cases of child and elder abuse, in which individual awareness is a key to preventing or stopping abuse.

The incidence of elder abuse has been increasing in American society for decades (National Center on Elder Abuse n.d.), accompanying the increasing geographic mobility of families (as jobs take people all across the nation rather than families remaining geographically close together), the general decrease in respect for elders, and the continued "graying of America" (the term among social scientists to indicate an increase in the number of people who are living longer and, thus, becoming a larger percentage of the population). In cases of elder abuse, the abuser is usually a family member, professional caregiver, or co-resident in a care facility (National Center on Elder Abuse 2005).

The government and civil society have no doubt tried to reduce the prevalence of elder abuse. However, much of the effort has gone to encouraging individual-level assistance in the form of awareness. Through the lens of scarce resource, the individual is providing a resource that the victims, government agencies, and civil organizations cannot—a voice. That voice is also rendered effective by the possession of another resource: information (concerning the abuse that is occurring). In this way, the helping person's clear mind, freedom of expression, and possession of knowledge about the abuse are vital in the prevention thereof. Without those individual-level resources, the abuse would most likely continue unabated.

Many civil organizations have campaigned and promoted awareness about elder abuse, as has the government, but individual-level assistance has become an invaluable part of the campaign against elder abuse. Shortly after the government redoubled its focus on ending elder abuse, the federal government began requiring that certain individuals (e.g., doctors) report any suspicion of elder abuse to a special hotline or website. Some may see this as a government-level action primarily; however, if viewed through the lens of resources that the helping individual possesses, one can see the necessity of individual help in the prevention of elder abuse. In most cases of elder abuse, the voice of the victim is stifled by threats from the abuser or through confusing the victim, who may have some cognitive impairment. The victim, who is either threatened or confused, is not able to raise her voice in favor of her own well-being. Indeed, in most cases, the elder has full access to the lines of communication (such as the telephone) but is usually threatened or convinced that the abuser must do what he is doing for some reason ("You do not understand, but it is for your good").

The effort to have individuals provide a voice for a victim, who has been effectually dispossessed of his own, has also recently been seen in the case of child abuse, in which certain individuals in certain positions of trust are required to report any possible indication of child abuse to the authorities. (See https://www.childwelfare.gov/systemwide/laws_policies/statutes/manda.pdf for a state-by-state list of mandated reporters.) A child is definitely a case of a victim who lacks an important resource that could be used to stop abuse, a voice. In this case, small children also lack knowledge about bureaucratic systems, such as the 911 emergency reporting system. Like many elderly victims, abused children often have full access to a phone but lack the knowledge that it can be used (and about how to use it) to set themselves free. In this case, individuals who possess knowledge about the system can be a voice for those children and use the resource of knowledge to aid an abused child.

In summary of these last two cases (i.e., the cases of elder abuse and child abuse), a current trend is the pairing of government initiatives with individual assistance to help the victims. Individual-level help has been so effective in these two cases that it will likely continually be employed in detecting interpersonal abuse. The resource the individual helper possesses is often simple and nonmaterial, such as status or knowledge of legal or governmental reporting systems (such as 911 or Internet reporting sites). It is clear that individual assistance is invaluable in reaching victims at the "grassroots" level in ways that the government and civil society often cannot. In a way, the government is asking individuals (as did Chy Johnson's mom) to "keep an ear to the ground" to help detect some kinds of micro-level abuse.

In the case of spousal abuse, the opposite is true—individual help is extremely limited. This is due to the way that the abuse usually occurs. In situations of spousal abuse, the abuser is usually male and begins the pattern of abuse by removing all resources from a female partner. Abusers usually cut off contact with family and friends, bank accounts, and even reduce the mental and emotional capacities of their female partner through a degrading cycle of verbal abuse. In these conditions, it becomes almost impossible for an "outside" individual to even detect the abuse or, consequently, to provide resources that could put an end to the abuse. Women's shelters are currently the most common refuge for nearly resource-less women to overcome their abuse. Individual help is currently largely ineffective at preventing abuse that cuts the victim off from the rest of society.

Still, the role of individual help (especially in being the eyes and ears of interpersonal abuse) appears to be so effective in other circumstances that it is likely to continue to be billed as an important opponent of abuse for years to come.

Conclusion

Help from individuals, civil society, and the government all play different, yet essential, roles in assisting the weak in interpersonal groups. Individual help is essential in identifying victims of interpersonal abuse, as this abuse would be rather hard for large bureaucratic organizations to detect. The government has tried to combat interpersonal abuse by deploying individuals to be its eyes and ears, as is the case with teachers and religious leaders reporting child abuse to government authorities or bank tellers reporting suspected elder abuse.

The government is often the necessary level of assistance when a vast amount of organized resources are needed, although many government programs are currently directed toward groups rather than vulnerable *individuals,* as is the case in the United Kingdom. Additionally, organizations as large as the government are quite ineffective at detecting individual-level vulnerability. Government assistance will be essential in the military and in prisons where activities are rather closed off from the rest of the world, making abuse nearly impossible to detect by individuals or civil society. Furthermore, in cases such as abuse in the military, the legitimacy of the government is essential.

Civil society can provide a balance between the other two types of help, as it is more in touch with the "ground level" of abuse than is the government, but has more resources than does the average individual. Civil society also often fills in the gaps where the government or individuals do not want to or cannot assist.

As a whole, detection and elimination of interpersonal (micro-level) abuse is largely neglected. Many programs and organizations are geared toward the assistance of underprivileged groups, such as racial, class, or wealth-based groups, rather than on individuals in need. The Protecting Vulnerable Adults program in the United Kingdom (discussed earlier) provides an interesting comparison in which, rather than looking to provide assistance based only on some group membership, vulnerable adults are identified based on a spectrum of vulnerabilities (such as mental, emotional, physical, or age based factors; of course, the designation of these attributes may just lead to new group classifications, e.g., "young and emotionally vulnerable"). Much work is needed to better identify and strategically help those who are in need due to resources they lack relative to close others.

Notes

1. A 2011 *New York Times* article about Calhoun, a private NYC high school depicts a study session: "At noon, the students were still at it. They had moved on from deconstructing the novel, by Geraldine Brooks, to hashing out topics for research papers in the science and social studies class, called Disease and Society: one wanted to tackle 17th-century grave digging in London; another would explore the obligation midwives had to report illegitimate children" (Anderson 2011).
2. Not on Our Campus are campaigns to address similar issues on college campuses.
3. Lessons are particularly relevant for English, Language Arts, Social Studies, Health, and Visual and Performing Arts courses and curriculums.
4. Indeed, this has been the basis of the highly publicized Occupy Wall Street movement and various other political battles entrenched in ideas about the proper dispersal and means of acquiring wealth in society.

References

Anderson, Jenny. 2011. "At Elite School, Longer Classes to Go Deeper." *New York Times*, June 1. http://www.nytimes.com/2011/06/02/education/02calhoun.html?pagewanted=all&_r=0) (accessed February 8, 2014).

Andenaes, Johannes. 1966. "The General Preventive Effects of Punishment." *University of Pennsylvania Law Review*, 114(7):949.

ABC News. 2005. "Katrina Response: Who's to Blame?" *ABC News*. http://abcnews.go.com/WNT/HurricaneKatrina/blame-delayed-response-katrina/story?id=1102467 (accessed December 19, 2013).

Associated Press. 1996. "Olympics – Atlanta 'Cleanup' Includes One-Way Tickets for Homeless." *Seattle Times*, March 22. http://community.seattletimes.nwsource.com/archive/?date=19960322&slug=2320280 (accessed February 8, 2014).

Associated Press. 2012. "Bullied Bus Monitor Receives $700k Check." *CBS News*, September 11. http://www.cbsnews.com/news/bullied-bus-monitor-receives-700k-check (accessed December 19, 2013).

Associated Press. 2013a. "More than 85,000 Veterans Treated Last Year Over Alleged Military Sex Abuse, Report Says." *Fox News*, May 20. http://www.foxnews.com/us/2013/05/20/more-than-85000-veterans-treated-last-year-over-alleged-military-sex-abuse (accessed February 8, 2014).

Associated Press. 2013b. "Old San Francisco Muni Buses to Be Converted into Homeless Showers." *NBC Bay Area*, October 15. http://www.nbcbayarea.com/news/local/Old-SF-Muni-Buses-to-be-Converted-Into-Homeless-Showers-227694011.html (accessed February 8, 2014).

Bagilhole, Barbara. 1993. "How to Keep a Good Woman Down: An Investigation of the Role of Institutional Factors in the Process of Discrimination Against Women Academics." *British Journal of Sociology of Education*, 14(3):261–74.

"Church Welfare Program Helps People Help Themselves During Tough Economic Times." 2008. *The Church of Jesus Christ of Latter-day Saints,* September 17. http://www.mormonnewsroom.org/article/church-welfare-program-helps-people-help-themselves-during-tough-economic-times (accessed December 6, 2013).

Department of Health. n.d. *No Secrets: Guidance on Developing and Implementing Multi-agency Policies and Procedures to Protect Vulnerable Adults from Abuse.* https://www.gov.uk/government/uploads/system/uploads/attachment_data/file/194272/No_secrets__guidance_on_developing_and_implementing_multi-agency_policies_and_procedures_to_protect_vulnerable_adults_from_abuse.pdf.

Economic Mobility Project. 2013. "Moving On Up: Who Do Some Americans Leave the Bottom of the Economic Ladder, But Not Others?" *The Pew Charitable Trusts,* November 7. (http://www.pewstates.org/research/reports/moving-on-up-85899518104).

Economist. 2010. "Upper Bound." *The Economist,* April 15. http://www.economist.com/node/15908469 (accessed February 8, 2014).

"Foster Parenting." n.d. *Adoption.com.* http://www.fosterparenting.com (accessed February 8, 2014).

Goffman, Erving. 1961. *Asylums.* New York: Doubleday.

Horne, Christopher S., Janet L. Johnson, and David Van Slyke M. 2005. "Do Charitable Donors Know Enough—and Care Enough—About Government Subsidies to Affect Private Giving to Nonprofit Organizations?" *Nonprofit and Voluntary Sector Quarterly,* 34(1):136–49.

Huffington Post. 2011. "Apple iPad Features: 13 Tings You NEED to Know." *Huffington Post,* April 4, 2010, ed. May 25, 2011. http://www.huffingtonpost.com/2010/01/28/ipad-features-what-you-ca_n_439232.html#s64162title=No_Multitasking (accessed February 8, 2014).

Huffington Post. 2012. "Haiti Earthquake Recovery: Where Did All the Money Go? (INFOGRAPHIC)." *Huffington Post,* January 11. http://www.huffingtonpost.com/2012/01/11/haiti-earthquake-recovery_n_1197730.html (accessed February 11, 2014).

Kube, Courtney, and Jeff Black. 2013. "Army Sergeant Assigned to Sex-Abuse Prevention Being Investigated for Pimping, Sexual Assault." *NBC News,* May 14. http://usnews.nbcnews.com/_news/2013/05/14/18258681-army-sergeant-assigned-to-sex-abuse-prevention-being-investigated-for-pimping-sexual-assault?lite (accessed February 8, 2014).

Landgrebe, Mark. 2010. "Meet *the* Director." *Homeless Bus, Inc,* November 20, 2010, ed. November 27, 2010. http://www.homelessbus.org/meet-the-director.html (accessed February 8, 2014).

McCrudden, Christopher. 1982. "Institutional Discrimination." *Oxford Journal of Legal Studies,* 2(3):303.

Nardi, Bonnie A., Steve Whittaker, and Heinrich Schwarz. 2000. "It's Not What You Know, It's Who You Know: Work in the Information Age." *First Monday,* 5(5). http://ojphi.org/ojs/index.php/fm/article/view/741/650.

National Center on Elder Abuse. n.d. "Statistics/Data." *National Center on Elder Abuse Administration on Aging.* http://www.ncea.aoa.gov/Library/Data/index.aspx (accessed February 8, 2014).

National Center on Elder Abuse. 2005. "15 Questions & Answers About Elder Abuse." *National Center on Elder Abuse Administration on Aging.* http://www. ncea.aoa.gov/Resources/Publication/docs/FINAL%206-06-05%203-18-0512-10-04qa.pdf.

Navarro, Emily. 2005. "Government Funding for Charities: When It Declines, the Charities Lose Twice." *Charity Navigator.* http://www.charitynavigator. org/index.cfm?bay=content.view&cpid=281 (accessed December 19, 2013).

NNEDV. 2012. "Domestic Violence Counts 2012: A 14-Hour Census of Domestic Violence Shelters and Services." *National Census of Domestic Violence Services.* http://nnedv.org/resources/census/2012-report.html.

Not in Our School. n.d(a). "About Not in Our School." Not in Our Town. http:// www.niot.org/nios/about (accessed February 8, 2014).

Not in Our School. n.d.(b). "No Human Was Born Illegal." Not in Our Town. http://www.niot.org/nios-video/no-human-being-was-born-illegal (accessed February 8, 2014).

Not in Our School. n.d.(c). "Ole Miss: Facing the Change." Not in Our Town. http:// www.niot.org/nios-video/ole-miss-facing-change (accessed February 8, 2014).

Not in Our School. n.d.(d). "Students Map Bully Zones to Create a Safer School." Not in Our Town. http://www.niot.org/nios-video/students-map-bully-zones-create-safer-school (accessed February 8, 2014).

O'Brien, Michael. 2013. "Obama: 'No Tolerance' for Military Sexual Assault." *NBC News,* May 7. http://nbcpolitics.nbcnews.com/_news/2013/05/07/18107743-obama-no-tolerance-for-military-sexual-assault?lite (accessed February 8, 2014).

Reilly, Rick. 2012. "Special Team." *ESPN,* November 1. http://espn.go.com/espn/ story/_/id/8579599/chy-johnson-boys (accessed December 19, 2013).

Sewell, William H., Robert M. Hauser, and Wendy C. Wolf. 1980. "Sex, Schooling, and Occupational Status." *American Journal of Sociology,* 86(3):551–83.

Shih, Margaret, Todd L. Pittinsky, and Nalini Ambady. 1999. "Stereotype Susceptibility: Identity Salience and Shifts in Quantitative Performance." *Psychological Science,* 10(1):80–3.

Smith, Melinda, and Jeanne Segal. 2012. "Domestic Violence and Abuse: Signs of Abuse and Abusive Relationships." http://www.helpguide.org/mental/domestic_violence_abuse_types_signs_causes_effects.htm (accessed February 11, 2014).

Stevenson, Seth. 2013. "Mob Justice." *Slate,* March 11. http://www.slate.com/ articles/technology/the_browser/2013/03/karen_klein_bullied_bus_monitor_why_did_a_bunch_of_people_on_the_internet.html (accessed December 19, 2013).

Swearer, Susan M., Dorothy L. Espelage, Tracy Vaillancourt, and Shelley Hymel. 2010. "What Can Be Done About School Bullying? Linking Research to Educational Practice." *Educational Researcher,* 39(1):38–47.

United States Department of Agriculture. n.d. "Women, Infants, and Children (WIC)." *United States Department of Agriculture Food and Nutrition Service.* http://www.fns.usda.gov/wic/women-infants-and-children-wic (accessed December 19, 2013).

Values.com. n.d. "Enjoy the Pass It On No Bullying Commercial and Share Your Own Story." http://www.values.com/inspirational-stories-tv-spots/72-Locker (accessed February 11, 2014).

Winter, Michael. 2011. "Fort Lauderdale Offers Homeless One-Way Bus Tickets Home." *USA Today,* December 21. http://content.usatoday.com/communities/ondeadline/post/2011/12/ft-lauderdale-offers-its-homeless-one-way-bus-tickets-home/1#.UZacDlJ_CQE.

Wells, Ryan S., and Cassie M. Lynch. 2012. "Delayed College Entry and the Socioeconomic Gap: Examining the Roles of Student Plans, Family Income, Parental Education, and Parental Occupation." *The Journal of Higher Education,* 83(5):671–97.

7

Government Help

Shikha Bista

In many ways, the government's chief aim is to protect those it governs. It seeks to, in the most general sense, keep people from physically harming one another, make certain the economic playing field is fair, protect people from large-scale weather or invasion threats, etc. The degree to which the government actually accomplishes these feats, or even earnestly tries to, is the subject of much political chatter. Still, in the United States, we are taught about three branches of government—legislative, judicial, executive—all of which are supposed to provide a safety net to the people, including through the removal or punishment of problematic people. So, we have congress passing laws against pollution, the police responding to calls alleging abuse, judges sentencing thieves, the military assessing nuclear threats, the FDA testing the safety of medicines, etc.

The government tries, at least ostensibly, to help weak people in macro society. It has required there to be handicap parking spots, provided food assistance for the poor, and passed antidiscrimination legislation among many other things. That said, some, aligned with sociology's conflict perspective, believe that the government is actually only looking out for the powerful and that the whole apparatus that seeks to help the weak on the surface is only a guise meant to legitimate and solidify the position of the powerful in society. For example, some point to the disparate treatment of white- and blue-collar criminals as proof of this process. Even within this strain of thought, most critiques are placed in the macro level.

At the micro level, the government seems less involved. This may be the result of underreporting, an actual dearth of government activity in this sector, or both. Still, the government has crept into the world within social units, including some laws outlining proper behavior within the family. While much of this legislation began as moral legislation (rules regarding sexual behavior), nowadays laws meant to protect weak people are the most prevalent in this domain. So, we have child abuse and spousal abuse laws. The government has programs in place meant to help those who are relatively resource deprived—being physically weak or having a low social status—within social units. The two particular areas we will look at to exemplify the government's role in helping these people are school bullying and elder abuse.

Elder Abuse

The American population is greying. According to the Administration on Aging website, persons aged 65 years or older, who comprised 39.6 million in 2009 (the most recent year for which data is available), will include 72.1 million older persons in 2030, which is double the population represented in 2000 (Administration on Aging n.d.[a]). While 65 years or older represents the traditional cut-off age for older populations, a report released by the US Census Bureau (2011) draws our attention to the "oldest old," or what has been rendered the "fast-growing 90-and-older population." In 2010, persons aged 90 and over reached 1.9 million, which is said to be triple the number three decades ago. This reflected "4.7 percent of the older population (age 65 and older), as compared with only 2.8 percent in 1980" and is projected to increase to 10 percent by 2050 (US Census Bureau 2011).

The rapid growth of this population raises concern for their well-being, as there is now a larger number of older people who may become dependent on family members as well as long-term facilities for their daily needs. Those who are cognitively and physically impaired or lack adequate social support in the form of ongoing connections with others that make a person feel valued are susceptible to fraud, abuse, and exploitation. In particular, they may be more vulnerable to physical, psychological, and sexual abuse, caregiver and self-neglect, and financial exploitation. Further, these vulnerable adults are also less able to stand up to maltreatment and/or fight back if attacked or abused. Even if they are able, many seniors may not report the abuse for fear that reporting may lead to abuser retaliation or otherwise negatively affect their life. Disability can increase the isolation of older victims, who may already not ask for help or call the police due to shame and intimidation. There is a need for services and interventions designed to meet the specific needs of older victims of abuse and protect them from harm.

Of course, the government apparatus provides the salient forms of law enforcement, regulative checks, and preventative surveillance that are meant to protect the general population from each other and, to a lesser degree, themselves. So, murdering a person (elderly or otherwise) is a crime and is something that the police, courts, and regulatory agencies seek to minimize the occurrence of. The government has an ostensible interest in preserving the well-being of its citizenry. For the particular issues inherent in elder abuse, however, the government, in its various forms, has created some more specific measures that seek to help alleviate the problem. Many of these more specialized forms of government help are especially geared toward helping individuals who are at the mercy of others within their social units.

Several federal legislative initiatives such as the passage of Medicare, Medicaid, and the Older Americans Act in the 1960s are illustrative of the beginning of a shift toward increased awareness of, and attention to, the elder justice area. Since then, the Administration on Aging was established and charged with providing federal leadership in this area. More recently, the Elder Justice Act of 2009 (EJA), which is part of the Patient Protection and Affordable Care Act, took aim at developing and implementing strategies as well as providing federal resources to state and local programs that prevent, detect, treat, understand, and intervene in cases of elder abuse, neglect, and exploitation.

State and local governments are still, however, on the front line of addressing abuse in domestic, community, as well as long-term care facility settings. In each state, an Adult Protective Services (APS) program aims to identify, investigate, resolve, and prevent such abuse. As of today, fifty states along with the District of Columbia have implemented such programs. Each state's APS program varies in terms of definitions, types of abuse covered, the age at which the victim is covered, availability of legal remedies and criminal penalties for abusive behavior toward an older adult, reporting requirements, and investigative procedures. Institutional abuse is covered by state statutes, along with by Medicaid or Medicare statutes, which pursue prosecution of abuse occurring in federally funded facilities. All states have laws authorizing Long-Term Care Ombudsmen Programs, which are responsible for advocating on behalf of long-term facility residents who are abused. In addition, an increasing number of states have separate criminal statutes for elderly abuse, while in others, abusive behavior toward an older adult can be prosecuted only if it fits within the context of another crime, such as assault, battery, theft, or rape.

Despite the abundance of state statues and protective services, as well increasing interest in the legal recourse by APS workers, advocacy groups, government officials, and researchers, reported cases of or court data on elder abuse are few and far between. There is not a national data system that tracks elder abuse. This has resulted in a lack of national strategy to support and fund services to alleviate these situations. Many policy experts feel that APS programs would benefit from a national system for collecting and maintaining uniform data across states, as it would allow them to appropriately allocate funds, target efforts, as well as share best practices more strategically. In response to this, lawmakers are taking strides toward establishing a national foothold in fighting elder abuse. The role of the federal government under the Older Americans Act of 1965 (OAA) and the EJA in particular have led to national elder justice activities through the federal coordination of elder abuse prevention efforts to raise the visibility of the abuse of the elderly.

Still, according to the National Institute of Justice's research brief (Jackson and Hafemeister 2013), the issue is not of great enough concern for the government to address it in the same manner it has addressed child maltreatment, intimate partner violence, or violence against women. The brief contends that while child maltreatment and intimate partner violence were propelled onto the national stage by professional organizations such as the American Medical Association and grassroots organizations associated with the women's movement, there exists no powerful advocacy group that has taken up elderly justice with the same vigor and determination. Without a devoted advocacy group and with the absence of a "moral panic," legislators are more likely to channel limited resources and funding to issues that fall under the top priority of their constituents: "For every dollar of federal funding apportioned to family violence, ninety-seven cents is apportioned to child maltreatment, two cents is devoted to IPV [Intimate Partner Violence], and one cent is spent on elder abuse" (Jackson and Hafemeister 2013, 8). Needless to say, elder abuse remains underfunded compared to certain other forms of interpersonal or family violence: The relative lack of attention is further compounded by issues of "ageism"[1] that contribute to people's negative attitudes and apathy toward the elderly and their mistreatment (Nelson 2005).

Media activity, academic research, and government policy considerations are all experiencing an uptick of activity in this area (Falk, Baigis, and Kopac 2012). Although still largely "unrecognized, hidden, and underreported" (Falk et al. 2012; Kosberg 1998), there have been some high-profile abuse revelations involving the elderly. Some news reports have shed light on the plight of vulnerable older individuals across the United States. These individuals are abused, denied needed care, and/or financially exploited, often by those they depend on for care and basic necessities (see Ingles 2013; KTVU.com 2013). This abuse is usually perpetrated by those with whom these individuals are most intimately involved, such as family members, friends, or trusted others (Administration on Aging 2012; Gallo 2008). Around 90 percent of elder abuse is carried out by family members (Gallo 2008).

While intra-family abuse is being increasingly examined by authorities, abuse committed by people with legal or contractual obligation to care for the elderly in long-term residential facilities has also gained the attention of policy communities and researchers (Payne and Fletcher 2005). The federal government believes it has a responsibility to collaborate with and help states and communities develop the tools and resources needed to ensure the safety of their most vulnerable citizens through support, safety planning, legal advocacy, etc.

Federal Response to Elderly Abuse

The OAA was passed during the civil rights decade, when organizations and policymakers were petitioning Congress for the rights of older Americans. President Lyndon B. Johnson signed the OAA into law on July 14, 1965, in order to provide older adults with services and community support systems that would help them feel safe, healthy, and independent in their homes (National Care Planning Council n.d.). The initial emphasis of this legislation was mainly on "community planning and social services" by authorizing grants to states for enhancing research and developmental projects in these areas, as well as more broadly in the area of aging.

In 1974, Title XX of the Social Security Act was passed, which authorized states to use Social Service Block Grants to provide protective services for those eighteen and older of all income levels who were suffering from abuse. This stimulated the establishment of APS. By the 1980s, according to the National Association of Adult Protective Services (NAPSA n.d.), almost "all the states, in one way or another, noted that they had an office with responsibility to provide protective services to some segment of the population." In 1985, Senator Claude Pepper recommended Congress "act immediately to assist the states in preventing, identifying, and assisting our nation's elder abuse victims" (NAPSA n.d.). States have continued to provide APS services, adopting their own statutes that have resulted in state-specific definitions and provisions (NAPSA n.d.).

New provisions to the law have increasingly focused on improving the quality of services for victims of elder and vulnerable adult abuse and mistreatment (Administration on Aging n.d.[c]). The most recent version of act one of the OAA acknowledges the importance of "[f]reedom, independence, and the free exercise of individual initiative in planning and managing their own lives, full participation in the planning and operation of community based services and programs provided for their benefit, and protection against abuse, neglect, and exploitation" (NCPC n.d.).

The OAA established the Administration on Aging (AoA) under the Department of Health and Human Services, which is designed to administer and formulate programs for the elderly. The AoA administers grants to state and local agencies for elder abuse prevention activities (USGAO 2011). For example, the AoA has established the Prevention of Elder Abuse, Neglect, and Exploitation program through which it has strengthened the role of the federal government by offering or funding programs that: "[t]rain law enforcement officers, health care providers, and other professionals on how to recognize and respond to elder abuse; supports outreach and education campaigns to increase public awareness of elder abuse and how to prevent it; and supports the efforts of state and local elder abuse prevention coalitions and multidisciplinary teams" (Administration on Aging n.d.[e]).

Under the sponsorship of the US Administration on Aging, the National Center on Elder Abuse (NCEA) was established, which seeks to prevent elder mistreatment. The NCEA website provides relevant information, materials, and support, as well as technical assistance and training to states and community-based organizations (Administration on Aging n.d.[d]).

Amendments made to the OAA also specified that every state is required to have a Long-Term Care Ombudsman Program (1987). This program is designed to resolve complaints and advocate for residents (including through legal channels) of nursing homes, assisted-living facilities, and board and care homes. Further, the Ombudsman Program specified the long-term care facilities' duty to develop and implement appropriate written policies and procedures that prohibit mistreatment and abuse of residents along with ensuring that facilities "not employ individuals who have been found guilty of abusing, neglecting, or mistreating residents by a court of law or have had a finding entered into the state nurse aide registry concerning abuse, neglect, mistreatment of residents, or misappropriation of their property" (Hawes 2003).

The Elder Justice Act of 2009 authorized increased funding for the identification, prevention, or remediation of elder abuse in state and local agencies (Falk et al. 2012). It provides grant money to improve staffing and quality of care in long-term care facilities as well as increase the capacity of ombudsmen to report and resolve complaints of elder abuse. It also offers funds to states to boost the effectiveness of their APS departments. In conjunction with the Department of Justice, the EJA established "10 elder abuse, neglect, and exploitation forensic centers" that are designed to enhance the capacity of legal health professionals and law enforcement authorities in terms of collecting forensic evidence as well as to enhance the overall prosecution of crimes against the elderly (USGAO 2011, 7). Further, in order to accomplish its mission of promoting elderly justice, under the EJA, an Elder Justice Coordinating Council and Advisory Board was established and charged with coordinating federal activities and providing recommendation to Congress regarding multidisciplinary tactics and services for reducing elder abuse (Administration on Aging n.d.[b]).

States as the Primary Source of Protection of Older Adults from Abuse

Despite their being some action at the federal level, state laws are the primary source of government elder abuse protection; all fifty states have some form of APS program in place that offers the elderly and their families as well as other designated caregivers a network of social and health services (Center for Elders and Court n.d.). While each state may have its own general statement explaining the authority of APS (see example of North Dakota),[2] according to the National Center of Elder Abuse, APS is those "services provided to insure the safety and well-being of elders and adults with disabilities who are in danger of being mistreated or neglected, are unable to take care of themselves or protect themselves from harm, and have no one to assist them" (National Center on Elder Abuse n.d.).

Establishing a Formal Working Definition for Identifying Elder Abuse

The most commonly cited behaviors considered to be elder abuse have been highlighted by some leading federal agencies. This grouping offers a roadmap to others for detecting abusive situations as well as for making referrals of various cases to APS for individualized assessment or investigation.

According to the AOA, elder abuse is the "knowing, intentional, or negligent act by a caregiver or any other person that causes harm or a serious risk of harm to a vulnerable adult." Various types of mistreatments are defined. One commits elder abuse when subjecting a senior citizen to physical, emotional, or sexual mistreatment; by neglecting or abandoning him or her; or by exploiting a senior for financial gain. Further, even "self-neglect . . . whereby a senior citizen fails to perform essential self-care tasks" thereby "threatening his/her own safety . . . is also characterized as elder abuse." Because it does not include a perpetuator, there is some contestation over whether self-neglect should be considered a form of abuse. However, all APS programs are required to respond to allegations of self-neglect that may include court designation of a caregiver or a legal guardian to make decisions for individuals who are unable to take care of themselves.[3] States vary as to which parts of the above they include in their own APS definition.

Each state's APS system has its own notion of who to serve or an eligibility criterion for those considered an "elderly person" for this purpose. For instance, while 74 percent of the states report that they serve populations ages eighteen and over (i.e., provides services to at-risk adults or individuals over the age of eighteen who meet certain conditions defined in state statutes; see example of Alabama state law)[4] or focus on the victim's physical or cognitive vulnerability without regard to age, the rest of the states have variations, such as only serving those age sixty and above or other specific populations who must also hold the definition of "vulnerable," "dependent," or "elderly" before APS can take any action. For example, in the state of Washington, a "vulnerable adult" is defined as a person who is "(a) [s]ixty years of age or older who has the functional, mental, or physical inability to care for himself or herself; or (b) [f]ound incapacitated under chapter 11.88 RCW; or (c) [w]ho has a developmental disability defined under RCW 71A.10.020" (Washington State Legislature n.d.).

Along with this, each state's APS provides services for vulnerable adults who are in a "community setting," such as family homes; however, relatively few states have APS extend their services to individuals who reside in long-term care facilities (NAPSA 2012). For example, while Illinois provides protection to "eligible adults" who reside in "domestic living situations," Maine's APS program applies to residents of licensed nursing homes as well (Stiegel and Klem 2007). Additionally, in many states, licensing agencies investigate abuse in Medicaid-certified or state-licensed long-term-care facilities, which "typically include nursing homes, assisted-living facilities, and board and care homes" (USGAO 2011, 5).

Reporting Incidences

The primary responsibilities of each state's APS are to receive reports of alleged abuse, investigate whether the alleged abuse should be substantiated, and, if needed, arrange for necessary services to ensure victims' well-being. Many states' services provide a twenty-four-hour-a-day help hotline (a typical APS process for addressing alleged elder abuse can be found at http://ncea.aoa.gov/Stop_Abuse/Partners/APS/How_APS_Works.aspx).

When APS receives a report of suspected elder abuse that meets their eligibility criteria (if they do not meet eligibility, cases may be recommended to other services), an APS caseworker is assigned to investigate the case. The caseworker contacts the older adult to investigate the abuse and assess for any immediate risks. Once a victim is identified and a case is initiated, APS may then provide for various services such as counseling, money management, home medical services, and transportation. Substantiated cases that involve criminal activity against the adult are passed along to criminal courts or for police investigation. In these cases, many states' APS caseworkers may also be responsible for filing reports for their clients as well as advocating on behalf of the victims, as they may not have knowledge of their judicial rights (NAPSA 2012).

In the article "Elder Mistreatment and the Elder Justice Act" by Falk et al. (2012), one of the authors recounts the horrible injuries her ninety-three-year-old mother endured due to the negligence of a licensed practical nurse (LPN), who was designated by a hospice agency as her caretaker. Because none of the agencies responsible for her mother's care helped, she decided to report this incident. Below is an account of the steps she took as well as the role of APS in addressing her situation:

> I called the Area Office on Aging and was referred to the State Department of Aging 24-hour Elder Abuse hotline. The person covering the hotline took the relevant information from me and forwarded it to the director of our county's Adult Protective Services (APS) Unit. Within 24 hours, I heard from the APS director, who told me to file a report with the local police and get x-rays of mother's right arm and face. Both a police officer and an APS worker came to Mother's apartment and collected information for their respective reports. In February 2009, I filed a Statement of Complaint against the LPN

to the Professional Compliance Office of the Department of State. I asked for assurance that this LPN would be reprimanded and that appropriate action would be taken to ensure that nothing like this would happen to anyone else in the future.

Subsequently, I contacted the attorney in the Professional Compliance Office every few months for an update. In June 2011, I learned that the attorney wanted copies of the x-rays in addition to the x-ray reports that had been part of the original Statement of Complaint. The necessary Authorizations to Release Information were obtained and sent in August 2011 to a local investigator from the Bureau of Enforcement and Investigation of the Department of State (the same investigator who had conducted the initial investigation after my complaint was filed in 2009). When I spoke with him on November 4, 2011, he told me his report was complete and had been sent to the attorney at the Department of State Professional Compliance Office the week before. He said the attorney would review the new information and send the complete report to the Board of Nursing for review at their monthly meeting. I was to be notified when a determination was made. In March of 2012, the case against the LPN was closed. (Falk et al. 2012)

To encourage the use of APS in the case of abusive circumstance, many states have mandatory reporting requirements as well as mandated reporters (NAPSA 2012). (For example, Oregon provides categories of professionals and public officials who are mandated reporters; see https://apps.state.or.us/Forms/Served/de9373.pdf). Depending on the state, professionals and social service providers (e.g., police, attorneys, mental health providers, and nurses) who have regular contact with vulnerable and older adults are required by law to report suspected cases of abuse. In some states, financial professionals, such as bankers, are also being asked to make reports. For instance, Maryland enacted a law requiring financial institutions to report suspected financial abuse of older persons to APS or law enforcement within twenty-four hours of the suspicious activity (see http://mlis.state.md.us/2012rs/chapters_noln/Ch_324_sb0941T.pdf).

Because the issue of when to examine a person for possible mistreatment is somewhat complicated, especially when the victim may not self-report, the American Medical Association recommends adopting a systematic screening and assessment process for elder mistreatment in clinical settings in order to monitor symptoms as well as to privately interview vulnerable adults in the absence of visible symptoms (Actions of the AMA House of Delegates 2008). For example, the comprehensive geriatric assessment (CGA) is a useful multidisciplinary diagnostic tool for identifying elder mistreatment. It is used to collect information, such as their social, medical, personal, and family history, that can enable the assessor to gauge whether mistreatment has occurred (Tufts n.d.).

Civil Remedies and Criminal Codes

Mandated reporters or designated caregivers "can be held liable by both the civil and criminal legal systems for intentionally failing to make a report regarding their experiences with elder abuse" (Falk et al. 2012). With this, some states have enacted statutes specifying the penalties for failing to report child abuse or neglect. For example, California law states that:

> Failure to report physical abuse, abandonment, isolation, financial abuse, or neglect of an elder or dependent adult is a misdemeanor, punishable by not more than six (6) months in county jail or by a fine of not more than one thousand dollars ($1000), or by both a fine and imprisonment;
>
> AND
>
> Any mandated reporter who willfully fails to report physical abuse, abandonment, isolation, financial abuse, or neglect of an elder or dependent adult, where that abuse results in death or great bodily injury, is punishable by not more than one year in a county jail or by a fine of not more than five thousand dollars ($5000), or by both that fine and imprisonment. (Office of the Attorney General n.d.)

Institutional facilities, caretakers and mandated reporters may also be subject to lawsuits for negligence if they fail to provide reasonable standard care and there is an injury as a result (Falk et al. 2012). An illustration of such neglect with disciplinary action is provided below:

> In a New Work Case, the resident, a 91 year old woman confined to a nursing home suffered from strokes, organic brain syndrome, arteriosclerosis, and kidney disease. Her physician ordered heat lamp treatment for the patient's decubiti. Instead of the 60–75 watt usually used in such treatment, the licensed practical nurse on duty mistakenly used an infrared lamp of more than 100 watts. She placed the lamp 2 or 3 feet away from the patient's back and buttocks and left her unattended for 20 minutes. The patient rolled on to her back, exposing her upper legs to the lamp at distance of about a foot. When the burns were discovered, the physician was notified. He made no arrangements to examine the patient or to have her examined by another physician. Several hours later the supervisor, again, reached

the physician, who ordered the patient transferred to a hospital emergency room, although he knew or should have known that the hospital had no treatment for serious burns. The patient was then transferred again to hospital with a burn unit. The patient died 4 days later of bronchopneumonia resulting from the trauma of wounds. The commissioner of health found that the physician had failed to have the patient examined when he learned of the burns, failed to ensure that the patient received emergency first aid and subjected her to an extra transfer. The physician was found guilty of patient neglect and imposed a $1,000 civil penalty. (Fiesta 1996, 18)

In a similar case of neglect, but this time involving a family member, "the defendant was convicted of the involuntary manslaughter of her mother after her mother starved and froze to death in the home they shared." Because there was no contract between the alleged neglecter and the elder, the courts investigated the nature of the relationship between "alleged neglecter and the elder" (Stiegel, Klem, and Turner 2007). By establishing that the defendant was indeed the primary caregiver, in this case, "[t]he Virginia Supreme Court concluded the defendant had a legal duty to care for her mother and rejected the defendant's argument that she was a volunteer because evidence offered at trial demonstrated the defendant accepted sole responsibility for her mother and made it her full-time job to take care of her" (Stiegel et al. 2007, 6).

All states have general criminal statutes that can be applied in cases of elder abuse (USGAO 2011). (Visit WomensLaw.Org for information about state domestic violence laws, including criminal statutes and civil protection orders.) While some states have specified elder abuse as one more specific crime (e.g., California Penal Code 368; Nevada's Abuse, Neglect, Exploitation or Isolation of Older Persons and Vulnerable Persons), in others, elder abuse in itself may not be rendered a crime, and so abusive behavior toward an older adult can be prosecuted only if it fits within the definition of another crime such as theft, fraud, sexual assault, or battery (USGAO 2011). However, there may be increased penalties for certain crimes committed against the elderly in some states (e.g., Indiana and Florida). For more information about prosecution of elderly crime, see "Prosecuting Elder Abuse Cases: Basic Tools and Strategies" (Eukert, Kelitz, and Sanders n.d.).

School Bullying

Bullying often occurs when the individuals involved in the interaction possess a relative disparity of key resources. Perhaps bullying can only occur when the parties involved hold different amounts of physical strength, social connection, wealth, social status (including that related to race, sexuality, or gender), etc. Some say that psychological trauma, a key characteristic of bullying, is usually incurred only when the bullied individual is stuck in the situation with little opportunity for exit. Thus, these events are especially likely to occur inside of social units, such as schools, where permanently leaving is a difficult and, at times, calamitous enterprise. All other things being equal, two strong kids fighting on a playground would not be considered bullying and would not be likely to levy the same amount of psychological trauma. Likewise, if a weak kid is beaten up by an unknown stronger kid at a party in an area he was never planning to visit again, it would not be considered bullying or carry the same menacing effects. The full spectrum of ill effects manifests when this abuse is systematic, persistent, and hard to escape. Of course, it doesn't just have to be physical violence. It could be the "cool" kids teasing a "dorky" kid, rich kids tearing up money in front of a poor kid because they can, or straight kids mocking their homosexual classmates, among many other scenarios.

While the acts that constitute bullying have not suddenly manifested out of the ether, they may have grown especially pernicious over the last decade, or, more likely, we have grown to see them as more pernicious in the twenty-first century. We have seen one sensational bullying news story snowball into others—in the same way child kidnappings, crop circles, and Y2K dangers have done before—increasing awareness and sensitivity, leading to more cases, more reports, and more gas on the fire. Still, the structure of the social world inhabited by millennials may be especially conducive to bullying, thanks to the proliferation of technology and social media as well as society's distaste for disciplinary action. They know they are less likely to "receive a whooping" for their bad behavior and so do not have the same fear of punishment that earlier generations might have had. Regardless of why, we, as a nation, have taken an increasing interest in bullying, including crafting laws and government programs seeking to prevent its occurrence and to help those who have been negatively affected by it when it does occur.

Bullying hurts people in dynamic ways. The Illinois General Assembly has found that a safe and civil school environment is necessary for students to learn and achieve; that bullying is the cause of physical, psychological, and emotional harm to students; and that it interferes with their ability to learn and participate in school activities. Bullying has been linked to other forms of antisocial behavior, such as vandalism, shoplifting, skipping and dropping out of school, fighting, using drugs and alcohol, sexual harassment, and violence.

Of course, the government has long sought to protect people from being harmed by others, through both preventative and punitive means. Punching someone is assault, although when it happens among juveniles on a playground it rarely receives legal scrutiny. Similarly, discriminating against someone based on her race can be prosecuted as a civil rights violation; hurting this same person because of her race would qualify as a hate crime. Still, when these incidents happen within one school, in one community, they are also usually settled there, even if this settlement merely involves covering up the incident.

The school can hand out detentions, suspensions, warnings, or ask a kid to stare at the wall. It can also carry out preemptive programs that focus on proper ways to harness one's anger, or on diversity training, or on how "words *can* hurt." For the individuals involved, the school can provide counseling. This is still how most of the acts that are now considered bullying are handled, although the issue's prominence has led to recent legal changes, pressuring schools and communities to enact specific policies and practices aimed at thwarting bullying.

For the most part, the federal government has placed the onus on states and schools to enact bullying prevention strategies, using funding as both a carrot and a stick to steer the process. Schools receiving federal funding must prohibit bullying or risk losing their funding, but there is also federal grant money available to schools to apply toward bullying programs, which the feds advocate schools to implement. Additionally, the federal government has run several information campaigns and created a central website (www.stopbullying.gov) that shows different state laws and guidelines for states, schools, and people to use to learn more about how to handle bullying. Finally, if an act is a potential civil rights violation, the issue can be taken up in federal court.

As of the time of this writing, forty-nine of the fifty states had crafted antibullying legislation. These laws define certain behaviors as prohibited and provide schools with mechanisms for teaching students and staff about bullying as well as how to prevent it from occurring, how to report it, and how to hold the bullies accountable.

Although federal and state laws and recommendations exist, it is hard to determine whether they funnel down into anything tangible at the school or individual level. Schools are not as steadfast in implementing these changes as policymakers would like, and those that have made the changes may only be paying lip service to the law, not expecting the protocol to be effective. Even in cases where schools have strived to follow the law and/or independently created an antibullying environment in good faith, they may not actually be making any difference in helping those who are getting bullied or those who will likely be bullied in the future.

Increased Awareness of Bullying in the United States

School bullying has moved to the forefront of debates on school legislation (Long and Alexander 2010). Many argue that this increased concern is not reflective of a new problem, positing that bullying among children has existed for perhaps as long as there have been school systems (Carney and Merrell 2001). Further, because it is considered a commonplace human experience "that occurs across disparate cultures and educational settings" (Carney and Merrell 2001, 364), it is often assumed to be a normal process of growing up. The saying "kids will be kids" has long accompanied stories of bullying in schools. Today, the pervasiveness of bullying is less accepted as merely being a childhood "rite of passage" (Barone 1995), as government officials and members of the school community claim to be more attentive toward the negative effects of bullying that youths and local school systems face (McCallion and Feder 2013). The increased public attention and awareness toward this "age-old problem" (Hymel and Swearer 2009) is fueled by several trends.

One is youth violence that gets linked to bullying (e.g., McCallion and Feder 2013; Youth Suicide Prevention Program n.d.; the 1999 Columbine High School shooting[5]) as well as the heightened visibility of suicides among school-age children and adolescents that have been linked to repeated bullying (e.g., the 2010 suicide of Massachusetts high school freshman Phoebe Prince [Associated Press 2011]). These highly visible incidents, all of which have received national media attention, together with new and compelling research on the serious long-term consequences (Roland 2002; Gastic 2008) of bullying behavior on children's "academic, social, emotional, and physical health" (Mishna 2004, 234), together with research highlighting statistics on bullying patterns (see www.bullyingstatistics.org) have triggered the need for government and school systems to come up with more effective solutions to address and reduce the occurrences of bullying (Stuart-Cassel, Bell, and Springer 2011).

Social scientists and bullying experts have been unable to perform much longitudinal analysis on bullying behavior, as the concept has only recently shown up on research instruments (Fiori 2011). Some say "it is no more extreme, nor more prevalent, than it was a half century ago" (Bennette 2010). There is no definitive evidence that suggests increased awareness of bullying has grown as a consequence of more bullying (Fiori 2011). Instead, it may be that as more incidents of bullying-related violence/suicides are reported, and the circle of what society cares about continues to expand (Singer 2011), the public outcry has grown more adamant, and demands for legislative action more vigorous (Nash 2012).

Still, even while litigation over bullying may be at an "all-time high" (Long and Alexander 2010, 30), it appears to be overly simplistic to discuss this public outcry as merely a change in societal reaction (Nash 2012). Advances in communication technologies and the growth of social networking sites have been instrumental in drawing attention to issues of bullying, even while they have brought in a new complication. Acts of cyberbullying are said to be more "visible, pervasive and permanent" than earlier forms (Stuart-Cassel et al. 2011, 1). However, it is also more difficult to identify the perpetrators of cyberbullying, which encourages more cruel and abusive behavior. For instance, not only can inappropriate texts and images be sent to others within a matter of seconds via electronic media, but, unlike traditional face-to-face bullying, bullies can hide or keep their identities unknown in the cyber world by using fake accounts or pseudonyms (National Science Foundation n.d.). Further, this relatively new phenomenon imposes policing challenges, particularly for schools that question whether they can, or should, extend their legal authority in off-campus settings, which is where cyberbullying typically occurs (Willard 2007).

The exponential growth of systematic research on bullying has shed further light on such complexities as well as defined the bullying problem as a "multifaceted" phenomenon (Weaver et al. 2013, 157), requiring that it be met with stronger and more intricate policies. Research and innovation regarding bullying prevention and intervention are relatively new, so the laws concerning these behaviors are changing rapidly (Stuart-Cassel et al. 2011).

Federal Activities Related to Antibullying

The Departments of Education, Justice, and Health and Human Services have all carried out research and broadly disseminated information through a variety of media (USGAO 2012). On August 11, 2010, the US Department of Education, in conjunction with the US Department of Health and Human Services, organized the first Federal Partners in Bullying Prevention Summit (USDHS 2012a). The event engaged policymakers, government officials, and education practitioners in promoting antibullying efforts. It also highlighted the need for more comprehensive information about the existing status of state legislation in order to ensure that schools, districts, and states are fully cognizant of their responsibility and options to prevent bullying. In their efforts to expand on the goals of previous summits, the third annual conference was held in August of 2012 (US Department of Education 2012).

Also addressing the issue, the Obama Administration staged a White House conference on bullying prevention (2011)—the first of its kind. Opening the conference, President Obama underscored the need to "dispel the myth that bullying is just a harmless rite of passage or an inevitable part of growing up" (Lee 2011). Along with bringing issues of bullying to the forefront of American discourse, the conference addressed the need for all stakeholders (e.g., federal, state, and local governments, communities, and parents) to join forces in developing and implementing solutions.

Among other activities, the three federal departments, together with the White House, launched a federally sponsored central website (www.stopbullying.gov) in March of 2011. According to the US Department of Health and Human Services (2012b), "[t]he website provides a map with detailed information on state laws and policies, interactive webisodes and videos for young people, practical strategies for schools and communities to ensure safe environments, and suggestions on how parents can talk about this sensitive subject with their children. The site also explores the dangers of cyberbullying, and steps youngsters and parents can take to fight it."

The aim of this site is to consolidate all of the resources and content on bullying that are available on different federal and state government sites into one location, so as to present a more consistent and reliable federal message of support toward antibullying efforts to the public (USDHS 2012b). For example, it presents information on key policy components that are present in state laws across the United States in the document "Anti-Bullying Policies: Examples of Provisions in State Laws" (US Department of Education 2011). This document serves as a form of technical assistance for stakeholders looking to develop or revise antibullying legislation or policies while also attempting to ensure that policies are consistent with the identified best practices and policy prescriptions. An important policy component that the federal government compels the states to address is the investigation and response of bullying complaints.[6] A growing number of state bullying laws have, therefore, extended the role of law enforcement to manage bullying on school premises, by both requiring mandatory reporting of such acts by school personnel and requiring policies that contain clear processes on how to go about reporting such complaints to law enforcement or to establish sanctions (Stuart-Cassel et al. 2011).

Many school districts have outlined expectations for how schools are required to investigate bullying complaints. These may include procedures, such as creating a timeline for completing the investigation, or establishing the appeals process, and so on. Most of these schools also encourage or use their own staff to resolve bullying complaints "promptly" (Stuart-Cassel et al. 2011). Despite this, it has been found that many incidences may go unreported by the responsible administrators. For example, an article published in August of 2013 in EdSource. org reported the findings of a California State Audit of antibullying programs. It identified two incidents in the Sacramento City Unified School District where the administrator assigned to resolve a complaint of "bullying, harassment, intimidation or discrimination" was identified as the "same person named in the complaint for allegedly failing to take appropriate action to address the student incident" (Adams 2013). To avoid underreporting, some states, such as Missouri, have laws that include mandates that "schools impose sanctions on school staff who fail to comply with law enforcement reporting requirements" (*Mo. Rev. Stat.* §167.117.1) (Stuart-Cassel et al. 2011, 20). These stringent regulations are important because they impose legal expectations on schools and oblige school districts to comply with state law (Stuart-Cassel et al. 2011). Federal government efforts to collect and disseminate information regarding students' civil rights laws, as well as step-by-step procedures for filing complaints, are designed to help schools identify what procedures and investigative mechanisms they should use to determine when and how violations should be reported to law enforcement (USGAO 2012).

Legal Protection for Bullied Victims at the Federal Level

Legal recourse is also available at the federal level for some of those who are bullied: "In recent years, many state departments of education and local school districts have taken steps to reduce bullying in schools. The US Department of Education (Department) fully supports these efforts ... The movement to adopt anti-bullying policies reflects schools' appreciation of their important responsibility to maintain a safe learning environment for all students" (US Department of Education 2010a).

The federal government has become a strong advocate for policies and laws enacted at the state and school district levels. Legal protection under the federal government's jurisdiction, however, is limited to only those bullied individuals who belong to legally protected groups. Federal civil rights laws protect against discrimination or harassment based on sex, race, color, national origin, religion, or disability. Victims can only seek federal recourse when bullying leads to allegations of discrimination or harassment that are based on these characteristics. For example, federal agencies lack jurisdiction under civil rights statutes to pursue incidences of bullying, discrimination, or harassment based on characteristics such as sexual orientation, physical appearance, or socioeconomic status. Some states' civil rights laws extend beyond the protections afforded at the federal level. For example, California's "anti-discrimination laws" also protect individuals on the basis of citizenship, gender-related appearance, and behavior (USGAO 2012).

Existing Federal Legislation and Initiatives that Address Bullying

As bullying has become a heated national issue, several bills have been introduced to amend extant laws by specifically addressing bullying in schools. In 2011, the 112th Congress introduced several federal bills related to bullying. The Anti-Bullying and Harassment Act of 2011 (H.R. 975) amends the Safe and Drug-Free Schools and Communities Act (SDFSCA) (Govtrack.us 2011a). The SDFSCA was the federal government's main program aimed at preventing drug abuse and violence. It now includes protection against student bullying in public schools (Long and Alexander 2010). Similarly, The Safe Schools Improvement Act of 2011 (H.R. 1658/S.506) amends the Elementary and Secondary Education Act of 1965 to address and take action to prevent bullying and the harassment of students. The law requires that all schools receiving federal funding prohibit bullying and harassment, including conduct that is based on a student's actual or perceived race, color, national origin, sex, disability, religion, sexual orientation, or gender identity (Govtrack.us 2011b). The Student Non-Discrimination Act (2011) (H.R. 998/S. 555) expands on the Safe Schools Improvement Act, requiring school districts that receive federal funds to adopt codes of conduct specifically prohibiting bullying and harassment on the basis of actual or perceived sexual orientation or gender identity (Govtrack.us 2011c).

Prior to these amendments, many school safety and education policies did not view "bullying" as a standalone issue. The federal government often provides funding for research and demonstration programs that address school violence through major activities such as the No Child Left Behind initiative. This was reflected in its enactment of the Safe and Drug-Free Schools and Communities Act. While this federal legislation was enacted to provide federal support to promote school safety, it did not initially have an explicit focus on bullying or harassment among school children and in no way addressed the unique challenges faced by youth who are targets of bullying by their peers.

Today, federal legislative actions and programs can be used to secure funds and grants for antibullying initiatives (e.g., federal grant programs such as Secure our Schools and Academic Centers of Excellence fund antibullying initiatives to promote school safety)[7] as well as for collecting and reporting data and research on bullying (e.g., the School Crime Supplement to the National Crime Victimization Survey, Civil Rights Data Collection[8]) (McCallion, Gail, and Jody Feder. 2013). Requiring local education agencies to identify specific cases of bullying indicates a desire to create policies that speak to the rights of individual students to personal safety from student bullying. In the absence of a federal law providing direct protection for bullied victims, however, students may only seek recourse at lower levels of government or through national civil rights statutes.

Bullying as a Violation of Civil Rights Laws

On October 26, 2010, the Office for Civil Rights (OCR) sent state and local education officials a ten-page "Dear Colleague" guidance letter, signed by Assistant Secretary Russlyn Ali, outlining how federal civil rights laws can be applied to bullying. As part of the national commitment to thwart bullying, it was a reminder that "some student misconduct that falls under a school's anti-bullying policy also may trigger responsibilities under one or more of the federal antidiscrimination laws enforced by the Department's Office for Civil Rights (OCR)" (US Department of Education 2010a, 1).

The letter revisited key pieces of legislation enforced by the Department of Civil Rights that are related to discrimination and harassment in schools but that could also apply to incidences of bullying. It specifically pointed out that Title IV of the Civil Rights Act of 1964 prohibits discrimination on the basis of race, color, or national origin, Title IX of the Education Amendments of 1972 prohibits discrimination on the basis of sex, and Section 504 of the Rehabilitation Act of 1973 as well as Title II of the Americans with Disabilities Act of 1990 prohibit discrimination on the basis of a disability. Collectively, these pieces of legislation compel school administrators to be cautious of behavior that violates the civil rights of students while also demanding they respond "promptly and appropriately" (US Department of Education 2010a, 3) if a problem arises. The letter goes on to provide some "hypothetical examples" of behavior that may meet the threshold for violating each of these laws. Below is an illustration of a student suffering from harassment based on his disability:

> Several classmates repeatedly called a student with a learning disability "stupid," "idiot," and "retard" while in school and on the school bus. On one occasion, these students tackled him, hit him with a school binder, and threw his personal items into the garbage. The student complained to his teachers and guidance counselor that he was continually being taunted and teased. School officials offered him counseling services and a psychiatric evaluation, but did not discipline the offending students. As a result, the harassment continued. The student, who had been performing well academically, became angry, frustrated, and depressed, and often refused to go to school to avoid the harassment. (US Department of Education 2010a, 8–9)

According to the OCR, if this scenario were to actually occur, the school would be in violation of Section 504 of the Rehabilitation Act and Title II of the Americans with Disabilities Act, both for failing to recognize the behavior as disability harassment and for failing to investigate and take steps to remedy the situation. On the other hand, if the targeted student did not have a disability or other defining attribute that falls under the jurisdiction of civil rights, these laws would not have applied. The nature of the conduct, therefore, "must be assessed for civil rights implications" (US Department of Education 2010a, 3). The "label used to describe an incident (e.g., bullying, hazing, teasing)" (US Department of Education 2010a) is irrelevant, according to the OCR. A federally funded school is only obligated to respond under federal laws governing civil rights if the basis of the discriminatory or harassing behavior is race, color, national origin, sex, or disability. Practices like these, which require inequality to fit into established categories (e.g., racial), not only ignore abuse derived from inequalities yet to be established in the legal nomenclature but also serve to keep other types of abuse under the shroud of the social units within which they occur. These "off-book" abuses are less likely to show up in survey research, tallies of civil rights violations or hate crimes, or on activist websites. Repeated attacks by one student on another with no discernible racial or gender difference/motivation, and where both students are physically able to walk without the assistance of a wheelchair, face less legal, social, and scholarly scrutiny than their counterparts.

Although supporters have hailed the statement issued by the US Department of Education's OCR as a worthy attempt to address the need to protect certain groups from harassment and bullying, it has also been accompanied by strong criticism. Many bemoan that federal agencies, or the civil statutes related to harassment, lack the authority to pursue discrimination cases based solely on sexual orientation (StopBullying.gov n.d.[c]). For instance, Title IX outlaws discrimination based on sex[9] as well as sex/gender-based harassment[10] but claims that it does not have any jurisdiction over cases based solely on sexual orientation. An example of this is *Montgomery v. Independent School District No. 709* (Leagle 2000).

In Montgomery, a male student was reported to have been a victim of verbal and physical abuse by students who perceived him to be gay because he did not appear "masculine" enough. Because sexual orientation is not a protected characteristic under Title IX, the court dismissed the student's claim of sexual orientation discrimination. The court did find, however, that a discrimination claim based on a failure to conform to gender stereotypes was permissible under Title IX (USGAO 2012).

Although Title IX does not respond to harassment based solely on sexual orientation, in an attempt to curb bullying against LGBT youth, the federal government reminds federally funded educational institutions that protection under Title IX is afforded to "all students regardless of the actual or perceived sexual orientation or gender identity of the harasser or target" (United States Department of Education 2010a). This application of Title IX is not straightforward. As illustrated in *Montgomery v. Independent School District No. 709*, schools are only obliged to respond under Title IX if the sexual orientation harassment overlaps with sexual harassment or gender-based harassment (StopBullying.gov n.d.[c]).

Kenneth L. Marcus (2011), executive vice president and director of the Anti-Semitism Initiative at the Institute for Jewish & Community Research (IJCR), highlighted several other controversies dealing with the antibullying statement issued by the US Department of Education's OCR (2011). He argued that the federal government's attempt to provide "enhanced protections for gay students against bullying and harassment" by applying or reinterpreting existing antidiscrimination statutes has been vacuous (Marcus 2011, 53; see also Bader 2011). Marcus posited that if an individual is harassed for being both a lesbian and female, the OCR will investigate the sexism charges but disregard the sexual orientation issue. More specifically, Marcus claimed that while the document is not wrong in highlighting policies under civil rights that may apply to those forms of bullying that trigger antidiscrimination laws, it does not include any discussion on "non-discriminatory bullying"—that which may be the result of less-noticed resource disparities (Marcus 2011, 52). Ultimately, critics believe that the OCR's statement adds nothing new and is clearly geared toward protecting certain groups from "harassment in federally-funded educational programs and activities," which is a reminder that the federal government has severely limited jurisdiction over bullying (Marcus 2011, 52).

Terms such as *bullying, bullying and harassment,* or *bullying, harassment, or intimidation,* have been used interchangeably in many cases (an example of the definition of bullying in a state law that includes intimidation and harassment is included in the footnote) (Stuart-Cassel 2011, 60).[11] Despite this, it is important to make a "legal distinction" between bullying behavior and harassment because harassment can violate federal civil rights laws as a form of unlawful discrimination (Stuart-Cassel 2011, 17). The government's official antibullying site defines harassment as "[u]nwelcome conduct based on a protected class (race, national origin, color, sex, age, disability, religion) that is severe, pervasive, or persistent and creates a hostile environment" (StopBullying.gov n.d.[b]).

Again, while there can be overlaps in the definitions of bullying and harassment, StopBullying.gov has formally recognized that "not all bullying is harassment and not all harassment is bullying" (StopBullying.gov n.d.[a]). According to a report produced by the United States Government Accountability Office (USGAO) (2012, 3) that assessed federal and state bullying laws and regulations, "a single fight between two youths of roughly equal power is a form of aggression, but may not be bullying" (USGAO 2012). The USGAO report (2012) seems to recognize the influence of relative physical strength in interpersonal relationships. Others do as well.

Experts and federal agencies (see www.stopbullying.gov) have applied and endorsed the definition provided by Dr. Dan Olweus. Olweus is considered the pioneer of early research on bullying. He stated that bullying is different from other forms of aggressive behavior because it includes "intent to cause harm, repetition, and an imbalance of power"[12] (USGAO 2012, 3). He further claims that, compared to harassment, the nature of bullying is often covert or hidden, so it can occur without any "apparent provocation" or can be based on personal traits outside someone's sex, race, or other protected-group status under civil rights laws (USGAO 2012, 3). Thus, these events can transpire cloaked from social scientists who are studying inequality from the viewpoint of heavy macro variables. Students may be bullied based on the way they look, act, or speak. Because bullying in interpersonal relationships encompasses more "subtle behaviors" than those targeted by harassment statutes, these statutes do little to help the victim, from a legal perspective (Weaver et al. 2013).

Recognizing that there are limited legal options for bullied victims under federal harassment statutes, the federal government has endorsed the adoption of "anti-bullying policies that go beyond prohibiting bullying on the basis of traits expressly protected by the federal civil statutes" (US Department of Education 2010b, 1). While acknowledging the utility of recent efforts, the Department of Education feels that more effective antibullying policies are urgently needed at the state and school levels. In a letter to colleagues, Secretary of Education Arne Duncan (2010) stated: "Though laws are only a part of the cure for bullying, the adoption, publication, and enforcement of a clear and effective anti-bullying policy sends a message that all incidents of bullying must be addressed immediately and effectively, and that such behavior will not be tolerated" (U S. Department of Education 2010b).

The first line of legal defense in bullying prevention is, therefore, state antibullying legislation and the ensuing establishment of antibullying policies at the district level. In other words, disciplinary action and sanctions (for instance, in the form of suspensions and expulsions for students caught bullying) are taken care of mainly at the state and school district levels (Weaver et al. 2013). As the Secretary of the US Department of Education (2010b) stated, "Ultimately state officials will determine whether new or revised legislation and policies should be introduced to update, improve, or add bullying prevention provisions."

Formation and Implementation of State Antibullying Policies

In 1999, Georgia became the first state to pass antibullying legislation, which required schools to implement programs that explicitly addressed prevention. By 2012, forty-nine states had crafted various forms of antibullying legislation (see www.stopbullying.gov for a listing of states' laws and model policies designed to help schools adequately implement an antibullying strategy). States have formulated antibullying policies either through a series of amendments to extant educational or criminal codes, or introduced new laws addressing bullying-related behaviors in schools (Stuart-Cassel et al. 2011). In response to inconsistencies among these laws, and to requests for assistance regarding "creating or improving anti-bullying laws or policies in their states," the Department of Education (2011) released a guidance document titled *"Anti-Bullying Policies: Examples of Provisions in State Laws"* (Stop-Bullying.gov n.d.[d]). The document identified eleven key components that should be found in state antibullying laws:

- Purpose statement
- Statement of scope
- Specification of prohibited conduct
- Enumeration of specific characteristics
- Development and implementation of local education agency (LEA) policies
- Components of LEA policies
- Review of local policies
- Communication plan
- Training and preventative education
- Transparency and monitoring
- Statement of rights to other legal recourse

The guidance document (2011) offers full descriptions of each of these components, as well as specific examples from state laws and policies (see StopBullying.gov n.d.[d] for more details).

Stuart-Cassel et al. (2011) examined state bullying laws for the most commonly covered components in legislation. These were "requirements to develop district policies, statements of scope defining school jurisdiction over bullying acts, definitions of prohibited behavior, and disciplinary consequences" (15). They also found significant differences within each law's individual components. For instance, the study uncovered variations in how states defined bullying.

In general, bullying may be associated with "conflict or aggression, including physical harm, such as hitting, shoving into lockers; verbal name calling, taunts, or threats; relational attacks, such as spreading rumors or isolating victims from their peers; and the use of computers or cell phones to convey harmful words or images, also referred to as cyberbullying" (USGAO 2012, 4). With this,

> Some state laws focus on specific actions (e.g., physical, verbal, or written), some focus on the intent or motivation of the aggressor,

others focus on the degree and nature of harms that are inflicted on the victim, and many address multiple factors . . . Twenty-nine states define bullying in a way that encompasses relational aggression, while eight states clearly limit bullying behavior to physical or verbal acts . . . Thirty-six states now include specific statutes addressing cyberbullying or the use of electronic communications to inflict harm on victims. (Stuart-Cassel et al. 2011, 25–6)

Although definitions vary, the study also revealed that there are several terms and phrases that are common to many states' definitions. For example, the condition that bullying needs to be "sufficiently serious that it creates a hostile educational environment" is present in twenty-one state laws (Stuart-Cassel et al. 2011, 25). Further, most bullying laws conform to "research-based definitions" (e.g., the Olweus definition, discussed earlier) by including at least one of the three criteria: intention to harm, repetition, and power imbalance (USGAO 2012). The majority of states emphasize the intentional nature and the harms inflicted on targeted victims (e.g., West Virginia) (Stuart-Cassel et al. 2011). Only a small number of states (i.e., fourteen) refer to bullying as being "persistent, pervasive, or repeated over time" (e.g., Pennsylvania uses all three of these terms in its definition) (Stuart-Cassel et al. 2011, 25). On the other hand, no state explicitly requires that behavior involve "an imbalance of power to be legally defined as bullying," although some states incorporate this concept into their state model policies (Stuart-Cassel et al. 2011, 26). For instance, in the State Model Policy of New York, bullying is defined as "aggressive behavior that is intentional and involves an imbalance of power or strength. Usually, it is repeated over time" (Stuart-Cassel et al. 2011, 177).

Although it does not indicate this in its antibullying law's definition of bullying, Massachusetts recognizes the role played by a power differential in its prescribed professional development on bullying prevention: "The content of such professional development shall include, but not be limited to: . . . (iii) Information regarding the complex interaction and power differential that can take place between and among a perpetrator, victim and witnesses to the bullying" (Massachusetts Legislature n.d.).

Greene and Ross (2005) regard a "power differential criterion" as a critical element in differentiating bullying from other forms of aggressive behavior and conflict that occur among youth of "relatively equal prowess" (93). This is despite the complexities of establishing a legal standard or criteria for power imbalance "other than through membership in a class legally designated as needing protection" (Greene and

Ross 2005, 93). Along with specifying clear "legal expectations" and prohibited behavior, state policies are also expected to enumerate the specific characteristics that convey the coverage or legal protections for certain groups or classes of individuals. Seventeen states include language that names protected classes in their bullying definitions. Based on the analysis by Stuart-Cassel et al. (2011), the protected groups most commonly listed in state bullying laws are those covered under federal legislation, which include race, national origin, religion, sex or gender, and disability. Weaver et al. (2012) claimed that "to be effective, anti-bullying laws must go beyond harassment and be specific about the subtleness of bullying behaviors" (158) This is to say that laws must include a definition of bullying that is motivated by personal characteristics beyond those in antiharassment statutes.

Through these laws, several states have also extended civil rights laws beyond the protections afforded at the federal level by including personal characteristics such as sexual orientation, ethnicity, gender identity or expression, family status, physical appearance, weight, marital status, socioeconomic status, age, academic status, physical or mental ability and disability, and so on (USGAO 2012; Stuart-Cassel et al. 2011).

While states such as California and Vermont have identified the need to explicitly protect individuals listed in their enumeration of protected categories, Massachusetts law is not limited to bullying based on protected categories: "The [bullying] plan shall afford all students the same protection regardless of their status under the law."[13] According to Massachusetts officials, protected classes were intentionally absent from the state's law to ensure that all students are treated equally (USGAO 2012). There are differing perspectives on the benefit of explicitly enumerating classes to be specifically protected under bullying laws and policies. On the one hand, proponents who are in favor of this argue that enumeration will provide clear instructions to school officials about the need to protect the most vulnerable populations from bullying. For instance, studies have shown that there is a lower prevalence of bullying behavior toward LGBT students when bullying policies contain these explicit protections for vulnerable populations (Kosciw et.al 2010). On the other hand, some legal experts have also cautioned naming groups or limiting definitions of bullying to behavior motivated by certain listed characteristics. They argue that the "highly politicized nature of the enumeration discussion" leads to elongated discussions within state legislatures over which population should or should not be protected in laws, delaying their enactment (Stuart-Cassel et al. 2011, 29).

Conclusion

In the formation of antibullying statues at the state level, it is evident that state governments are expected to provide clear expectations and guidelines to assist school districts with the development and implementation of local policies to curtail bullying. For instance, along with adequately defining prohibited bullying behaviors (as was discussed earlier), state legislation needs to convey expectations of school policies regarding implementation procedures, such as reporting requirements, investigations, and procedures for implementing sanctions (e.g., disciplinary sanctions such as expulsion), school personnel training, and support provisions for bullied victims such as mental health services. In this sense, clear directions under the law are expected to close the gap between state mandates and actual enforcement at the school level. As Limber and Small stated: "Ultimately, the merit of any law passed to address bullying will depend upon the care with which the law is written (including its attention to the consistency with relevant social science research about bullying), and how effectively the law influences school policies and programs" (2003, 46).

According to Weaver et al. (2012), state lawmakers craft legislation that appears clear to them, with schools responding by attempting to create "firm policies" to adequately implement antibullying strategies, but the translation of existing laws and policies into actual practice within elementary and secondary school systems is considered to be rather "ambiguous" (Weaver et al. 2013, 167). Research highlighting the experiences of school districts in implementing bullying legislation reveals that legal requirements found in antibullying laws represent unfunded mandates, forcing schools to reallocate scarce resources to fund implementation. For instance, some antibullying statutes communicate responsibilities for school personnel in training and prevention; however, with scarce resources available, it places some administrators in constraining positions such as deciding whether they can afford to provide antibullying training and services (Dake et al. 2004). Evidence based on several studies, such as a study by Bradshaw et al. (2011) that examined teachers' perceptions of their school's prevention efforts, shows that school officials may struggle to adequately implement the teacher training provisions under the policy. Such studies have specified the need to fund these efforts.

By highlighting issues of implementation, such as resource constraints that may get in the way of translating existing laws into actual protection for schools, we are reminded of the various challenges and struggles schools face in complying with state laws and mandates.

Although still at a very nascent stage, studies have conducted extensive examinations of the effectiveness of having antibullying legislation as well as the effectiveness of school antibullying programs. For example, a study conducted by Srabstein, Berkman, and Pyntikova (2008) reviewed antibullying legislation from a public health standpoint; it looked at the degree to which such statutes have incorporated public health principles and policies. They identified the need for strengthening the implementation of prevention programs and laws by identifying and protecting against health risks associated with bullying, which can reduce its prevalence, and, therefore, improve public health. Other studies have also sought to measure the effectiveness of antibullying preventions beyond the public health perspective, and whether they have an impact on bullying behavior in schools (e.g., Merrell et al. 2008; Farrington and Ttofi 2009). Farrington and Ttofi (2009) conducted a meta-analysis of the effectiveness of antibullying programs in schools, as well as a systematic review of studies that examined the effects of having an antibullying program in place, by comparing intervention groups that received a program with those that did not. The study revealed that school-based antibullying programs are usually effective, and it identified program elements associated with a decrease in bullying victimization, such as "parent meetings, firm disciplinary methods, and improved playground supervision" (Farrington and Ttofi 2009, 43). In contrast to this, another meta-analysis of research across a twenty-five-year period, conducted by Merrel et al. (2008), found that although school bullying prevention programs appeared worthwhile in terms of "increasing awareness, knowledge, and self-perceived competency in dealing with bullying," there seemed to be less of a dramatic influence on "actual bullying and victimization behaviors" (41).

Similarly, in the fall of 2013, an article by Seokjin Jung and Byung Hyun Lee was published in the academic journal *Criminology*, with some alleged evidence running counter to the notion that antibullying programs were effective at lessening bullying. The media pounced on the study, and very liberal interpretations of the data were proliferated around the nation. However, the researchers were just performing a cross-sectional analysis of static survey data to establish correlations. Ultimately, studies regarding the efficacy of these new policies and school-based prevention programs have produced mixed results, with some studies revealing minimal meaningful impacts generated by intensive programs, and others suggesting that such programs can have a great impact. These results reveal a need for more effective research and for prevention measures that are explicitly designed to reduce bullying.

Notes

1. According to ALFA, "Ageism is a form of discrimination and prejudice, particularly experienced by seniors. Most seniors are mentally and physically active regardless of age with a great deal to contribute. However, societal norms marginalize seniors, treat them with disrespect, make them feel unwelcome and otherwise generalize as if they were all the same" (ALFA n.d.).

2. "'Adult protective services' means remedial, social, legal, health, mental health, and referral services provided for the prevention, correction, or discontinuance of abuse or neglect which are necessary and appropriate under the circumstances to protect an abused or neglected **vulnerable adult**, ensure that the least restrictive alternative is provided, prevent further abuse or neglect, and promote self-care and independent living" N.D. Cent. Code § 50-25.2-01(3).

3. "Help by family, friends, services providers, APS, or health care interventions can be offered but the person has to accept that help. APS can't remove a person from his or her home against their will or force them to accept help. Because of this, APS staff and law enforcement are sometimes stopped from providing help to people who need it. APS can intervene without the consent of the vulnerable adult only if all other avenues have been exhausted, the person is found incompetent by the courts, and a court order has been granted to appoint a legal guardian to make decisions on his or her behalf." http://www.americanbar.org/content/dam/aba/migrated/aging/Public-Documents/introduction.authcheckdam.pdf.

4. "Adult in need of protective services" is defined as "a person 18 years of age or older whose behavior indicates that he or she is mentally incapable of adequately caring for himself or herself and his other interests without serious consequences to himself or herself or others, or who, because of physical or mental impairment, is unable to protect himself or herself from abuse, neglect, exploitation, sexual abuse, or emotional abuse by others, and who has no guardian, relative, or other appropriate personable, willing, and available to assume the kind and degree of protection and supervision required under the circumstances." http://alisondb.legislature.state.al.us/acas/codeofalabama/1975/38-9-2.htm.

5. Research focusing on patterns of high-profile school shootings in the United States following incidences such as the 1999 Columbine High School shooting suggest that some of these shooters were repeat victims of "bullying and peer harassment, were unpopular, and they ultimately went on a shooting spree as a way of exacting revenge" (see Merrel et al. 2008; Vossekuil et al. 2002).

6. This is not to say that bullying complaints have not been filed at the federal level. However, the Department of Justice and Education only takes on cases for which it has jurisdiction. This includes resolving complaints concerning allegations of harassment/discrimination based on federally protected

classes such as race, class, disability, ethnicity, sex, and national origin. In fact, according to Justice officials, "the department is not statutorily required to investigate every complaint and thus evaluates complaints they receive to identify those that involve pressing matters or novel legal questions requiring government involvement" (USGAO Report 2012a). This is covered in the next section.

7. *"Secure our Schools Program (SOS)* funds can be used for anti-bullying initiatives, among other things. Grants under this program provide funding to state, local, or tribal governments working in partnership with public schools to improve school safety" (McCallion, Gail, and Jody Feder 2013, 21).

8. *School Crime Supplement to the National Crime Victimization Survey (SCS/NCVS)* is "co-designed by the US Department of Education and US Department of Justice. It is a national survey of students ages 12-18 in public and private K-12 schools. SCS/NCVS collects information about victimization, crime, and safety at school, including bullying. It is currently administered every two years." (McCallion, Gail, and Jody Feder 2013, 22).

9. *"Title IX of the Education Amendments of 1972 (Title IX)*, prohibits discrimination on the basis of sex, including sexual harassment, in education programs and activities. All public and private education institutions that receive any federal funds *must* comply with *Title IX*. *Title IX* protects students from harassment connected to any of the academic, educational, extracurricular, athletic, and other programs or activities of schools, regardless of the location. *Title IX* protects both male and female students from sexual harassment by any school employee, another student, or a non-employee third party" (US Department of Education 2008).

10. Title IX also "prohibits gender-based harassment, which may include acts of verbal, nonverbal, or physical aggression, intimidation, or hostility based on sex or sex-stereotyping" (US Department of Education 2010).

11. Example: "The 2010 Legislature passed Substitute House Bill 2801, a Washington State law which prohibits harassment, intimidation, and bullying. RCW 28A.300.285 defines harassment, intimidation or bullying as any intentionally written message or image—including those that are electronically transmitted—verbal, or physical act, including but not limited to one shown to be motivated by race, color, religion, ancestry, national origin, gender, sexual orientation, including gender expression or identity, mental or physical disability or other distinguishing characteristics" (OSPI n.d.).

12. According to stopbullying.gov, "bullying behaviors happen more than once or have the potential to happen more than once" (StopBullying.gov n.d.[b]).

13. Massachusetts General Laws, chapter 71 § 370, https://malegislature.gov/Laws/GeneralLaws/PartI/TitleXII/Chapter71/Section370/Print.

References

Action of the AMA House of Delegates 2008 Annual Meeting. 2008. "Report 7 of the Council on Science and Public Health." http://www.ama-assn.org//resources/doc/csaph/a08-csaph7-ft.pdf (accessed February 3, 2014).

Adams, Jane Meredith. 2013. "School Bullying Prevention Efforts Falling Short, Says Audit." http://edsource.org/today/2013/audit-says-school-bullying-prevention-efforts-falling-short/37495#.UpkrGMRDtsW (accessed December 20, 2013).

Administration on Aging. n.d.(a). "Aging Statistics." http://www.aoa.gov/AoARoot/(S(2ch3qw55k1qylo45dbihar2u))/Aging_Statistics/index.aspx (accessed February 3, 2013).

Administration on Aging. n.d.(b). "Elder Justice Coordinating Council." http://www.aoa.gov/AoA_programs/Elder_Rights/EJCC/Index.aspx (accessed February 3, 2014).

Administration on Aging. n.d.(c). "Older American Act." http://www.aoa.gov/AOA_programs/OAA/index.aspx (accessed February 3, 2014).

Administration on Aging. n.d.(d). "National Center on Elder Abuse (Title II)." http://www.aoa.gov/AoARoot/(S(pug3op55ghu3awnmncnq2l45))/AoA_Programs/Elder_Rights/NCEA/index.aspx (accessed February 3, 2014).

Administration on Aging. n.d.(e). "Prevention of Elder Abuse, Neglect, and Exploitation (Title VII-A3)." http://www.aoa.gov/AoA_programs/Elder_Rights/EA_Prevention/index.aspx (accessed February 3, 2014).

Administration on Aging. 2012. "What is Elder Abuse." http://www.aoa.gov/AoA_programs/Elder_Rights/EA_Prevention/whatIsEA.asp (accessed December 23, 2013).

ALFA. n.d. "Ageism." http://www.alfa.org/alfa/Ageism.asp (accessed December 23, 2013).

Associated Press. 2011. "Phoebe Prince School Bullying Lawsuit: Massachusetts Case Settled for $225,000." http://www.huffingtonpost.com/2011/12/28/phoebe-prince-bullying-la_n_1172755.html.

Bader, Hans. 2011. "Washington Invents an Anti-Bullying Law." Minding the Campus. http://www.mindingthecampus.com/originals/2011/03/_by_hans_bader_theres.html (accessed December 19, 2013).

Barone, F. J. 1995. "Bullying in School. It Doesn't Have to Happen." *NASSP Bulletin,* 79:104–7.

Bennette, Jessica. 2010. "Phoebe Prince: Should School Bullying Be a Crime?" *Newsweek.* http://www.newsweek.com/phoebe-prince-should-school-bullying-be-crime-73815 (accessed December 19, 2013).

Bradshaw, C. P., Tracy Evian Waasdorp, Lindsey M. O'Brennan, and Michaela Gulemetova. 2011. "Findings from the National Educational Association's Nationwide Study of Bullying: Teachers and Educational Support Professionals Perspectives." Washington, DC: NEA.

Carney, A. G., and K. W Merrell. 2001. "Bullying in Schools: Perspectives on Understanding and Preventing an International Problem." *School Psychology International,* 22(3):364–82.

Center for Elders and Court. n.d. "Elder Abuse Laws." http://www.eldersandcourts.org/Elder-Abuse/Elder-Abuse-Basics/Elder-Abuse-Laws.aspx (accessed December 23, 2013).

Dake, J. A., J. H. Price, S. K. Telljohann, and J. B. Funk. 2004. "Principals' Perceptions and Practices of School Bullying Prevention Activities." *Health Education & Behavior,* 31:372–87.

Eukert, K. Brenda, Susan Kelitz, and Deborah Sanders. n.d. "Prosecuting Elder Abuse Cases: Basic Tools and Strategies." National Center for State Courts. http://www.eldersandcourts.org/Elder-Abuse/Elder-Abuse Basics/~/media/Microsites/Files/cec/Prosecution%20Guide.ashx (accessed February 3, 2014).

Falk, N. L., Judith Baigis, and Catherine Kopac. 2012. "Elder Mistreatment and the Elder Justice Act." *OJIN: The Online Journal of Issues in Nursing,* 17(3). http://

nursingworld.org/MainMenuCategories/ANAMarketplace/ANAPeriodicals/ OJIN/TableofContents/Vol-17-2012/No3-Sept-2012/Articles-Previous-Topics/ Elder-Mistreatment-and-Elder-Justice-Act.html#Fulmernd (accessed December 23, 2013).

Farrington, D. P and Maria Ttofi. 2009. "School-Based Programs to Reduce Bullying and Victimization." *Campbell Systemic Reviews,* 6: 1–147. http:// osbha.org/files/School-Based%20Programs%20to%20Reduce%20Bullying%20 and%20Victimization,%20Farrington%20et%20al,.pdf (accessed September 19, 2014).

Fiesta, Janine. 1996. "Legal in Long-Term Care Part II." *Nursing Management,* 27(2):18–9.

Fiori, Lindsay. 2011. "Bullying—Increased Awareness, Cultural Changes Make It Seem on the Rise, But It's Not, Experts Say." *The Journal Times.* http://journaltimes.com/ news/local/bullying-increased-awareness-cultural-changes-make it/article_ de1770b2-2930-11e1-9b5e-001871e3ce6c.html (accessed December 19, 2013).

Gallo, Nancy R. 2008. *Elder Law.* New York: Cengage Learning.

Gastic, Billie. 2008. "School Truancy and the Disciplinary Problems of Bullying Victims." *Educational Review,* 60(4):391–404.

Kosciw, J. G., Emily A. Greytak, and Elizabeth M. Diaz. 2010. *The 2009 National School Climate Survey: Key Findings on the Experiences of Lesbian, Gay, Bisexual and Transgender Youth in Our Nation's Schools.* New York: GLSEN.

Govtrack.US. 2011a. "H.R. 975 (112th): Anti-Bullying and Harassment Act of 2011." 112th Congress. https://www.govtrack.us/congress/bills/112/hr975/ text (accessed December 19, 2013).

Govtrack.US. 2011b. "S. 506 (112th): Safe Schools Improvement Act of 2011." 112th Congress. https://www.govtrack.us/congress/bills/112/s506#summary (accessed December 19, 2013).

Govtrack.US. 2011c. "H.R. 998 (112th): Student Non-Discrimination Act of 2011." 112th Congress. https://www.govtrack.us/congress/bills/112/hr998 (accessed December 19, 2013).

Greene, Michael B., and Randy Ross. 2005. "The Nature, Scope, and Utility of Formal Laws and Regulations that Prohibit School-Based Bullying and Harassment." *Persistently Safe Schools.* http://www.njbullying.org/documents/ HamFish2005final.pdf (accessed September 19, 2014).

Hawes, Catherine. 2003. "Elder Abuse in Residential Long-Term Care Settings: What Is Known and What Information Is Needed?" In *Elder Mistreatment: Abuse, Neglect, and Exploitation in Aging America,* edited by Richard J. Bonnie and Robert B. Wallace, 446–500 Washington, D.C: The National Academic Press.

Hymel, Shelley, and Susan Swearer. 2009. "Bullying: An Age-old Problem That Needs New Solutions." Education.com, Feb 11. http://www.education.com/reference/ article/bullying-about-power-and-abuse-of-power (accessed December 19, 2013).

Ingles, Jacqueline. 2013. "Chuck Lyerly, 54, Is Accused of Severely Abusing a 93-Year-Old Woman He's Cared for Since 2010." *ABC Action News.* http://www. abcactionnews.com/dpp/news/region_pasco/Chuck-Lyerly-54-is-accused-of- severely-abusing-a-93-year-old-woman-hes-cared-for-since-2010 (accessed December 23, 2013).

Jackson, Shelly L., and Thomas L. Hafemeister. 2013. *Understanding Elder Abuse: New Directions for Developing Theories of Elder Abuse Occurring in Domestic Settings.* US Department of Justice. Washington, DC: National Institute of Justice. https://www.ncjrs.gov/pdffiles1/nij/241731.pdf (accessed September 19, 2014).

Jung, Seokjin and Byung Hyun Lee. 2013. "A Multilevel Examination of Peer Victimization and Bullying Preventions in Schools." *Journal of Criminology,* 2013:1–10.

Kosberg, Jordan I. 1998. "The Abuse of Elderly Men." *Journal of Elder Abuse & Neglect,* 9(3):69–88.

KTVU.com. 2013. "Millbrae Caretaker to Stand Trial on Assault, Elder Abuse Charges." http://www.ktvu.com/news/news/crime-law/millbrae-caretaker-stand-trial-assault-elder-abuse/nX28m (accessed December 23, 2013).

Leagle. 2000. "Montgomery v. Independent School Dist. No. 709." http://www.leagle.com/decision/20001190109FSupp2d1081_11071 (accessed December 19, 2013).

Lee, Jesse. 2011. "President Obama & the First Lady at the White House Conference on Bullying Prevention." The White House Blog. http://www.whitehouse.gov/blog/2011/03/10/president-obama-first-lady-white-house-conference-bullying-prevention (accessed December 19, 2013).

Limber, S. P., and Mark A. Small. 2003. "State Laws and Policies to Address Bullying in Schools." *School Psychology Review,* 32:445–55.

Long, Teresa, and Kristina Alexander. 2010. "Bullying: Dilemmas, Definitions, and Solutions." *Contemporary Issues in Education Research,* 3(2):29–34.

Marcus, Kenneth L. 2011. "Bullying as a Civil Rights Violation: The U. S Department's Approach to Harassment." *Engage,* 12(3):52–6.

Massachusetts Legislature. n.d. "General Law." https://malegislature.gov/Laws/GeneralLaws/PartI/TitleXII/Chapter71/Section37O (accessed December 19, 2013).

McCallion, Gail, and Jody Feder. 2013. Student Bullying: Overview of Research, Federal Initiatives, and Legal Issues. Congressional Research Service.

Merrell, K. W., Barbara A. Gueldner, Scott W. Ross, and Duane M. Isava. 2008. "How Effective are School Bullying Intervention Programs? Meta-Analysis of Intervention Research." *School Psychology Quarterly,* 23(1):26–42.

Mishna, F. 2004. "A Qualitative Study of Bullying from Multiple Perspectives." *Children and Schools,* 26, 234–47. doi:10.1001/jama.285.16.2094.

Nash, Lindsay. 2012. "New Jersey's Anti-Bullying Fix: A Solution or the Creation of an Even Greater First Amendment Problem?" *Brigham Young University Law Review,* 2012(3):1039–70.

National Adult Protective Services Association (NAPSA). n.d. "History: About Adult Protective Services from 1960 to 2000." http://www.napsa-now.org/about-napsa/history/history-of-adult-protective-services (accessed February 3, 2014).

National Adult Protective Services Association. 2012. "Adult Protective Services in 2012: Increasingly Vulnerable." http://www.napsa-now.org/wp-content/uploads/2012/06/BaselineSurveyFinal.pdf (accessed December 25, 2013).

National Care Planning Council (NCPC). n.d. "About the National Aging Network." http://www.longtermcarelink.net/eldercare/area_agencies_on_aging.htm (accessed February 3, 2014).

National Center on Elder Abuse. n.d. "Adult Protective Services" http://ncea.aoa.gov/Stop_Abuse/Partners/APS (accessed February 3, 2014).

National Science Foundation. n.d. "Recognizing a Cyberbully." http://www.nsf.gov/discoveries/disc_summ.jsp?cntn_id=122271.

Nelson, T. D. 2005. "Ageism: Prejudice Against Our Feared Future Self." *Journal of Social Issues,* 61(2):207–21.

Office of the Attorney General. n.d. "Your Legal Duty . . . Reporting Elder and Dependent Adult Abuse." http://oag.ca.gov/sites/all/files/pdfs/bmfea/yld_text.pdf (accessed February 3, 2014).

OSPI. n.d. "Bullying and Harrassment (HIB) Toolkit." State of Washington Office of Superintendent of Public Instruction. http://www.k12.wa.us/safetycenter/bullyingharassment/default.aspx.

Payne, Brian K., and Laura B. Fletcher. 2005. "Elder Abuse in Nursing Homes: Prevention and Resolution Strategies and Barriers." *Journal of Criminal Justice,* 33(2):119–25.

Roland, Erling. 2002. "Bullying, Depressive Symptoms and Suicidal Thoughts." *Educational Research,* 44(1):55–67.

Singer, Peter. 2011. *The Expanding Circle: Ethics, Evolution, and Moral Progress.* Princeton, NJ: Princeton University Press.

Srabstein, J., Benjamin E. Berkman, and Eugenia Pyntikova. 2008. "Antibullying Legislation: A Public Health Perspective." *Journal of Adolescent Health,* 42:11–20.

Stiegel, Lori, and Ellen Klem. 2007. "Threshold Eligibility for Adult Protective Services: Criteria, Provisions and Citations in Adult Protective Services, by State." American Bar Association Commission on Law and Aging. http://www.americanbar.org/content/dam/aba/migrated/aging/about/pdfs/Statutory_Provisions_for_Threshold_Eligibility_Criteria_for_APS.authcheck-dam.pdf (accessed February 3, 2014).

Stiegel, Lori, Ellen Klem, and Jenette Turner. 2007. *Neglect of Older Persons: An Introduction to Legal Issues Related to Caregiver Duty and Liability,* report by the National Center on Elder Abuse, American Bar Association Commission on Law and Aging. http://vajp.org/wp-content/uploads/2012/08/Neglect+of+Older+Persons.pdf (accessed September 19, 2014).

StopBullying.Gov. n.d.(a). http://www.stopbullying.gov/what-is-bullying/related-topics (accessed December 19, 2013).

Stopbullying.gov. n.d.(b). "Bullying Definition." http://www.stopbullying.gov/what-is-bullying/related-topics (accessed December 19, 2013).

StopBullying.gov. n.d.(c). "Federal Laws." http://www.stopbullying.gov/laws/federal/index.html (accessed December 19, 2013).

StopBullying.gov. n.d.(d). "Key Components in State Anti-Bullying Laws." http://www.stopbullying.gov/laws/key-components/index.html (accessed December 19, 2013).

Stuart-Cassel, Victoria, Ariana Bell, and J. Fred Springer. 2011. *Analysis of State Bullying Laws and Policies.* Washington, D.C.: US Department of Education.

Tufts.edu. n.d. "Comprehensive Geriatric Assessment." http://ocw.tufts.edu/data/42/499797.pdf (accessed February 3, 2014).

United States Census Bureau. 2011. "Census Bureau Releases Comprehensive Analysis of Fast-Growing 90-and-Older Population." http://www.census.gov/newsroom/releases/archives/aging_population/cb11-194.html (accessed February 3, 2014).

United States Department of Education. 2008. "Sexual Harassment: It's Not Academic." Office of Civil Rights. http://www2.ed.gov/about/offices/list/ocr/docs/ocrshpam.html#_rt3d (accessed December 19, 2013).

United States Department of Education. 2010a. "Dear Colleague Letter." Office of Civil Rights. http://www2.ed.gov/about/offices/list/ocr/letters/colleague-201010_pg3.html (accessed December 19, 2013).

United States Department of Education. 2010b. "Key Policy Letters from the Education Secretary and Deputy Secretary." http://www2.ed.gov/policy/gen/guid/secletter/101215.html (accessed December 19, 2013).

United States Department of Education. 2011. "U.S. Education Department Releases Analysis of State Bullying Laws and Policies" http://www.ed.gov/news/press-releases/us-education-department-releases-analysis-state-bullying-laws-and-policies (accessed December 19, 2013).

United States Department of Education. 2012. "U.S. Education Secretary to Address Third Annual Federal Partners in Bullying Prevention Summit." http://www.ed.gov/news/media-advisories/us-education-secretary-address-third-annual-federal-partners-bullying-preventi (accessed December 19, 2013).

United States Department of Health and Human Services (USDHS). 2012a. "Federal Partners in Bullying Prevention Summit." http://www.hhs.gov/secretary/about/speeches/sp20120806.html (accessed December 19, 2013).

United States Department of Health and Human Services. 2012b. "HHS and Education launch new Stop Bullying website." http://www.hhs.gov/news/press/2012pres/03/20120330b.html (accessed December 19, 2013).

United States Government Accountability Office (USGAO). 2011. *Elder Justice: Stronger Federal Leadership Could Enhance National Response to Elder Abuse.* http://www.gao.gov/assets/660/650074.pdf(accessed September 2014).

United States Government Accountability Office (USGAO). 2012. *School Bullying: Extent of Legal Protections for Vulnerable Groups Needs to Be More Fully Assessed.* http://www.gao.gov/assets/600/591202.pdf (accessed September 19, 2014).

Vossekuil, M., Fein, R., Reddy, M., Borum, R., and Modzeleski, W. 2002. *The Final Report and Findings of the Safe School Initiative: Implications for the Prevention of School Attacks in the United States.* Washington, D.C.: United States Secret Service and Department of Education.

Washington State Legislature. n.d. "Definitions." http://apps.leg.wa.gov/rcw/default.aspx?cite=74.34.020 (accessed February 3, 2014).

Weaver, Lori M., et al. 2013. "A Content Analysis of Protective Factors Within States' Antibullying Laws." *Journal of School Violence,* 12:156–73.

Willard, N. E. (2007). "The Authority and Responsibility of School Officials in Responding to Cyberbullying." *Journal of Adolescent Health,* 41:S64–5.

Youth Suicide Prevention Program. n.d. "Link Between Bullying and Suicide." http://www.yspp.org/for_youth/bullying_suicide.htm (accessed December 19, 2013).

8

Civil Society Help

Shelby Bierwagen

Individuals who are suffering, or susceptible to suffering, due to a relative lack of a key resource within a social unit can be helped by collectives operating in the civil sphere. For example, a motivated group of individuals can stage an intervention and provide resources to a person as a springboard for that person to leave an abusive relationship. These groups need not be formally recognized to be effective; however, there are many formal organizations that explicitly seek to address the needs of vulnerable populations. While these organizations may be more likely to serve those who are vulnerable in macro space, they also have policies and practices that position them to help those who are vulnerable in micro space (or in both spaces), even if those who are vulnerable in micro space are more hidden.

There are groups against school bullying (STOMP Out Bullying, see stompoutbullying.org) working to eradicate hunger (Feeding America, see feedingamerica.org), striving to help the homeless (National Alliance to End Homelessness, see http://www.endhomelessness.org/pages/aboutus), and endeavoring to protect the legal rights of women (Legal Momentum, see legalmomentum.org). The Reeve Foundation serves paralyzed individuals. It is "dedicated to curing spinal cord injury by funding innovative research, and improving the quality of life for people living with paralysis through grants, information and advocacy" (Reeve Foundation n.d.). Those with other forms of disability—and many others—might be served by the American Civil Liberties Union (ACLU), which "works to extend rights to segments of our population that have traditionally been denied their rights, including people of color; women; lesbians, gay men, bisexuals and transgender people; prisoners; and people with disabilities." The ACLU argues that "if the rights of society's most vulnerable members are denied, everybody's rights are imperiled" (American Civil Liberties Union n.d.).

Children's interests and security are championed by the Children's Defense Fund (CDF). The CDF is behind "policies and programs that lift children out of poverty; protect them from abuse and neglect; and ensure their access to health care, quality education and a moral and spiritual foundation. Supported by foundation and corporate grants and individual donations, CDF advocates nationwide on behalf of children to ensure children are always a priority" (Children's Defense Fund n.d.). The organization Prevent Child Abuse in America contends on its homepage that "innovative communities across the country are achieving great results in preventing abuse and neglect from ever occurring; we at Prevent Child Abuse America are committed to bringing this kind of ingenuity to communities everywhere" (Prevent Child Abuse n.d.). An organization called CEDARS strives to "help children who have been abused, neglected, and homeless achieve safety, stability, and enduring family relationships." It realizes the grim reality that many children face within their homes, within their social units: "Today's reality is harsh, and the challenges disturbing. All homes today are not safe for every child. Poverty, drug use, mental illness, criminal activity, and neglect place children at extreme risk" (CEDARS n.d.).

The older population also has groups specifically looking out for their interests. The American Association of Retired Persons addresses a wide swath of the needs of the older population in the United States: "Americans age 50 and older face choices and pressures unlike those of any other age group—choices few could have prepared for. As the charitable affiliate of AARP, AARP Foundation is working with struggling people 50 and over so they can regain their confidence as good providers and members of their communities. We focus on four priorities where immediate action and legal advocacy will have the greatest impact: hunger, income, housing and isolation" (American Association of Retired People n.d.).

These, of course, are just a few of many possible examples of nongovernmental groups that may be of help to relatively resource-poor individuals. In this chapter, we will focus on two particular types of civil organizations: religious and student collectives. In the United States, there are many Christian groups that offer services to needy individuals. Among other things, these groups provide spiritual counsel, refuge from abuse in the form of safe houses, food and other basic necessities, and financial counseling and assistance. Student groups primarily provide support to fellow students by helping them secure employment, insurance, low-rate loans, food through food banks, legal defense, help with transportation, assistance with stymieing the efforts of bullies, etc.

Help from Religious Organizations

There is an abundance of religious diversity in the world today, and it is hard to tally up the total number of different religions currently existing. Any line that could be drawn would be ambiguous and arbitrary. In some places, religion is strictly tied to the government. In others, there is some degree of separation. For our purposes, we will consider religious organizations as existing in the public sphere and as being those types of institutions that most people consider to be religious— regardless of whether they believe, participate, or care. This is an important part of civil society because religious organizations play such a big role in many people's lives. Furthermore, as religions have long sought to help people (even if many outsiders see some forms of supposed help as nefarious at best; e.g. the Crusades and saving souls through conversion), they are an ideal fit for this chapter.

Social scientists (e.g., Ellison, Gay, and Glass 1989) and cultural evolutionists (see Bulbulia 2004 for a review of this literature) alike note the utility in religion and religious organizations to help people get through their daily lives and prosper. Theology aside, the major function of religion, and the engine behind religion, may be its ability to set people at ease, give them a community, give them something to live for, etc.

While there are many religions in the United States, and they all offer help in some way (e.g., there are Jewish Community Centers; one pillar of Islam involves the practice of zakat—mandatory charitable giving by all Muslims who are financially able to do so), Christianity is the most popular, and so we will focus on the way Christian organizations help weak people without forgetting that other religious institutions and people and nonreligious institutions and people also do the same.

Christian organizations offer people refuge by welcoming them into their church, shelter, and even the homes of their members. Once there, they can also be offered food, clothes, shoulders to cry on, people to connect with, etc. But individuals can also have food delivered to their private home or pick it up at a soup kitchen or the end of a food drive. Likewise, needy people can get Christmas gifts through the church. Churches have clothing and toy drives to build up their supply; people know to take their extra clothes and Tickle Me Elmo dolls to churches when their children have outgrown them. There are men's groups, women's groups, teen fellowship, support groups for the grieving, and, of course, individual counseling. These assemblies offer spiritual nourishment but also help build more secular connections that can facilitate the completion of everyday tasks. There are church-run sports leagues and game nights. Sometimes, churches will even come together to pay the bills of a needy member.

While Christian organizations seek to serve the community in myriad ways, some types of help are particularly tailored toward, and useful for, weak people who are at the mercy of being in a social unit where they are relatively deficient in some key resource (e.g., physical strength, wealth, or status). In this section, we will highlight a few of these forms of help: spiritual/emotional guidance, the availability of shelters, the offering and facilitation of financial courses, and welfare programs.

So, someone with no strength who gets beat up by family members can turn to the church for a safe place to sleep. A woman without access to the family bank account can receive money from the church to pay for her needed medication that her husband refuses to buy. A person turned away from the rest of society can find refuge in the welcoming spiritual nourishment provided by the clergy.

Of course, this is not to say that people are not, at times, turned away or turned off by the church. Some even argue that the church does more harm than good. Still, we are just explicating the types of help churches generally offer to show another way in which weak people, as we define them, can get help.

Help from Christian Organizations

National surveys indicate that organized religion and the church is recognized as generally serving one civic purpose: poverty assistance. In telephone interviews conducted in 2010, when asked how the church can positively influence their community, participants mentioned addressing poverty and assisting the poor as the most common open-ended responses (Barna Group 2011). In online interviews, 19 percent cited "helping the poor or underprivileged people to have a better life" as the most common positive contribution made by Christianity to the United States, followed by evangelism and shaping/protecting morals (Barna Group 2010). While Americans strongly believe that the greatest responsibility for aiding the poor falls on the government (Simmons 2011), they believe that organized religion can do the best job of feeding the homeless and providing services to the needy (52 percent and 37 percent, respectively), as opposed to nonreligious groups or the government (Pew Research 2009).

With nearly one out of every ten Americans turning to religious groups to make ends meet[1] (Pew Research 2009), Christianity and the church serve as a component of civil society capable of aiding weak people. Additionally, social service providers are relying increasingly on churches to provide material, emotional, and spiritual support for victims in light of the financial difficulties facing public and nonprofit organizations (O'Neill et al. 2010). This chapter will discuss the general ways in which organized religion and the church can help weak people suffering from interpersonal resource deprivation, including the spiritual component of support, as well as examples of types of common programs and services offered via religious sources.

General Help

Because religion exists primarily for the spiritual needs of people, means of assistance aside from the spiritual are not always advertised publically. Searching a church's website will generally provide information about religious services and programs but falls short of describing ways to receive help aside from contact information of the office and clergy. Yet just because this information is not readily advertised does not mean it does not exist; absence of evidence is not evidence of absence. There are numerous ways in which organized religion in general, though specifically the church, can help weak people. This help often comes on a case-by-case basis, and the type of help that will be offered cannot be determined until the situation is assessed. Take, for example, a battered woman who lacks the strength to stand up to her husband who also hoards all of the family's money. She can walk into a church office and be given shelter to separate her from the abuser, assisted with filing a police report, and given food and hygiene items denied by her abuser. Alternatively, take a student who does not come from a high social status and does not have the luxury of not working during the school year. Members of the church could use their connections to help him find a job, provide him with a bus pass or carpool to reach his place of employment, or have the financial resources with which to partially fund his schooling through a scholarship. From supplies of foodstuffs and home items, to emergency financial funds, to personal relationships capable of providing other resources, the ways in which the church is able to help weak people is only limited by creativity, resources, and the known needs of the weak.

Emotional/Spiritual Support

In situations of abuse, it is rare that the perpetrator will allow the victim to discuss the situation with others and thus reveal the situation at hand.

This is presumed to hold true in cases of resource inequality perpetrated by those within social units. For this reason, victims of interpersonal abuse may not be allowed to be involved in religious organizations of any form. Victims of domestic violence are particularly vulnerable to this, as this abuse may be physically apparent, and members of the clergy are often deemed mandated reporters.

Still, for those in less controlling and less violent situations, attending religious services can cultivate emotional support via religiosity/spirituality.[2] Religious involvement has been shown to aid in maintaining good mental health and overall well-being (e.g., Strawbridge 2001; Meyers 2000; Mochon, Norton, and Ariely 2011). Aside from any claims regarding the results and outcomes of religious belief, the idea of a deity and the support that comes from fellow religious followers can provide relief. The mere presence of a deity can bring comfort in troubling times. In a study of HIV-positive individuals, Ironson and colleagues (2011) found that positive views of God were correlated with a slower disease progression more often than were other predictors of disease progression, such as depression, and other factors (e.g., initial disease status, age, gender). Further, connecting with the chosen deity through prayer or meditation may provide a sense of relief and comfort, helping one to know that he is not alone in the knowledge of his troubling circumstances. At a religious service, an individual can approach a member of the clergy or an experienced member of the congregation for prayer. This act of stating the troubles that resource inequality is bringing to an individual and then receiving support through the listening ear of the clergy and prayer for deliverance may be a powerful driver in lessening the emotional side effects, such as stress. In two separate studies, everyday stress and lab-induced stress were reduced when countered with prayer (Belding et al. 2010; Ferguson, Willemsen, and Casteñeto 2010). While spirituality alone does not intervene in instances of interpersonal resource inequality and deprivation, it can combat the emotional turmoil that accompanies this abuse. Religion and spirituality are a unique element provided by the church that other helping forms of civil society may not be able to provide.

Shelters

While generally not run by any single church or house of religion, faith-based city rescue missions and shelters provide many resources for struggling individuals. Often times referred to as homeless shelters, they are capable of serving populations other than simply the poor and homeless. The City Rescue Mission of Lansing, Michigan, is one example. Operating out of two locations near downtown, one functions primarily as a men's shelter and donation center, the other a women and children's shelter. In 2012, the Lansing shelter served 106,742 meals and provided 51,891 nights of shelter (City Rescue Mission 2013). Services provided by shelter employees and volunteers include daily chapel, Bible-based counseling, a biweekly health bus, public dining rooms, personal hygiene items, day and overnight shelter, clothing distribution, and a one-year, in-house rehabilitation program. Meals and shelter are available daily on a walk-in basis at specified times, requiring only a sign-in and some form of identification. The same procedure applies to the distribution of hygiene items, with products being available once every sixty days for each individual.[3] Clothing is provided as needed to overnight guests (City Rescue Mission 2013).

Services provided by shelters can be utilized by any individuals struggling to survive but may be particularly useful for those suffering at the hands of those they know personally. A night of shelter may mean the difference between a bed and the streets to someone suffering from physical abuse or who has been kicked out by a roommate for not being able to afford rent. Meals and hygiene items may only be attainable for an individual through these donations if someone within the household will not allow for access to these products—even when they are acquired through charitable means but end up in the home—or the money with which to purchase them. As a ready source of resources available free of charge to all individuals, shelters provide an easily accessible means of temporarily combating interpersonal resource inequalities.

Financial Courses

Programs such as Financial Peace University and the CAP Money Course founded by financial author and motivational speaker Dave Ramsey and Christians Against Poverty, respectively, both tackle issues of wealth in the family. Developed by Christian organizations and delivered through Christian churches, Financial Peace University is a nine-week course and the CAP Money Course three weeks. Both programs center on refocusing finances through budgeting, saving, paying down debt, and using cash instead of credit or debit cards whenever possible. According to the program's website, the average family participating in Financial Peace University pays off 5,300 dollars in debt and saves 2,700 dollars in the first ninety days (The Lampo Group n.d.[a]). In 2010, 7,000 people enrolled in the CAP Money Course (offered in the

United Kingdom, Australia, New Zealand, and Canada [Christians Against Poverty n.d.(a)], with 782 churches offering the course 268 times in January and February alone (Hutt 2011). Christians Against Poverty offers an additional Internet-based debt counseling service entitled CAP Money Plus to assist participants who still have difficulty with balancing a budget and paying off debt after completing the course (Christians Against Poverty n.d.[a]). An at-home study version of Financial Peace University can be purchased for an additional cost, though participation in the group courses is encouraged with either individuals or families participating (The Lampo Group n.d.[b]). Participation in the CAP Money Course is only offered in group settings through sponsoring churches, though families or individuals can enroll, with age-appropriate courses being offered for students and youth (Christians Against Poverty n.d.[b]).

Both programs hold the potential not only to combat financial resource inequality within social units but also to target the underlying issues. All steps of the programs are worked through together, with the understanding that both participants are to be in agreement on decisions regarding finances. While it cannot be guaranteed that the program will be 100 percent successful in this regard, any progress made can be of benefit to a victim of interpersonal resource abuse.

A couple or family may come into the program with one individual being in absolute control of the finances. One person may be forced to deposit all of her earnings into the controlling partner's bank account and have no access to these funds without permission. An unemployed individual may be given an allowance that is inadequate for subsistence. Any combination or variation of these situations in which an individual is taken advantage of financially may change as a result of the financial course. By working together on budgeting, saving, and paying down debt, both participants are, in theory, equal players in the financial situation of the social unit. It must be acknowledged that the perpetrators of this inequality may refuse to participate in these types of programs, or even if they do participate, the underlying control issues may not be completely resolved and financial transactions may still be closely monitored and limited.

However, even in the latter case, an individual may gain access to a joint bank account that had previously not existed, receive an increased allowance that closer meets his needs, or be able to keep a portion of her income that she previously never had access to. The additional accountability created via participating in the programs in group settings may serve as an additional agent to foster this internal change. While the entire truth regarding the financial situation within the social unit may not be exposed, any insight given to other participants serves as a tool for the victim. Pressure from other participants may push the perpetrator to make adjustments he had not intended upon, while having witnesses to the victim's situation gives both support and accountability for change. Additionally, emotional support from church members, more so than that from secular sources, may serve to reduce the negative impact on self-assessed health due to financial strain (Krause 2006). By addressing finances in cooperative terms, Financial Peace University and the CAP Money Course attempt to eliminate issues of financial inequality within family units by changing mindsets into treating money as a resource to be shared equally, regardless of its origin.

Welfare Program

The Church of Jesus Christ of Latter-day Saints also plays off of this idea of changing the way people think about financial issues through its extensive welfare system intended to teach self-reliance. Run almost entirely by volunteers, the system was originally established to help members of the Church but has extended its reach to those outside its membership. Centering on the idea of providing for oneself and storing up for the future, the Church owns canneries, farms, and factories throughout the United States, through which it can both provide needed items and teach individuals how to grow and store foodstuffs. Through the Church's Deseret Industries,[4] on-the-job training, and employment centers, it enable thousands to secure employment annually. While providing the means to secure food and employment are the two primary ways in which many individuals with a lack of resources are aided, additional assistance is given on a case-by-case basis. For example, a newly diagnosed diabetic was taught financial management skills, menu planning, and shopping for her new illness, and she was also given financial and food assistance during tough economic times (Church Welfare Program 2008). The Church's welfare system not only provides for struggling families but also teaches individuals how to provide for themselves in ways in which they were previously unable.

Conclusion

Despite allegations of pedophilia, corruption, sexism, or whatever current claim is running against a certain branch of organized religion,

56 percent of Americans have a "great deal" or "quite a lot" of confidence in organized religion/the church. Only the military[5] received higher public confidence scores (Simmons 2001). Even with this confidence, the effectiveness of the church is still in question. Two separate polls indicate that 21 percent of respondents could not perceive of any way that churches could positively contribute to their communities (Barna Group 2011), and 11 percent believe that Christianity has not made any positive contributions to the United States (Barna Group 2010). Despite what positive or negative trends emerge from public opinion, 78 percent of Americans identify as Christian[6] (Pew Forum 2008), 44 percent of which report that they believe God has called them "to be involved in the lives of the poor and suffering" (Gallup 2003).

Students Helping Students: Associated Student Organizations

We now turn to how students in America's schools help each other, focusing especially on how these collectives provide assistance to those in marginalized positions within their social groups.

Universities

Existing at many, if not most, universities and colleges are student-run associations and student-run governments that strive to serve the interests of the students. The Associated Students of Michigan State University (ASMSU) has the following mission statement: "The mission of the Associated Students of Michigan State University is to enhance our individual and collective student experiences through education, empowerment, and advocacy by dedication to the needs and interests of students. We are passionate about our purpose and the students we serve" (Michigan State University n.d.[a]).

Similarly, the mission statement from the Associated Students of Southern Oregon University states: "We've got your back. As the student government of Southern Oregon University, ASSOU fights for issues that matter to students, whether that's on campus, in the Rogue Valley community, or in the state of Oregon as a whole. As part of the Oregon Student Association, ASSOU is committed to making life better for students through social organizing, legislative advocacy, and voter registration" (Southern Oregon University n.d.[a]).

While not all services offered and purposes served by associated student organizations pertain to combating the ill effects of interpersonal resource inequality, a number can help in such situations, whether intentionally or inadvertently. The services offered by the ASMSU/

Council of Graduate Students at Michigan State University, the Associated Students of Southern Oregon University, the Associated Students of the University of Nevada/Graduate Student Association, and the Associated Students of the University of California, Santa Barbara, will be used as examples from both undergraduate and graduate student governments to illustrate some of the ways in which students help students adversely suffering from resource inequality in interpersonal situations. (For more information about these organizations than is provided in this chapter, see www.asmsu.edu, www.cogs.msu.edu, www.sou.edu/assou, www.nevadaasun.com, and www.as.ucsb.edu/our-services.)

Employment

As student-run entities, associated student organizations offer employment for students. At ASMSU, a brand new staff is hired every spring, providing part-time employment in marketing, graphic design, information technology, accounting, and many other fields. Employment with associated student organizations provides a work environment that is suited for students, one that understands that schedules will change as semesters and classes change and that part-time work is ideal. This opportunity may be uniquely beneficial to some students. Finding a suitable job that allows for a flexible schedule is more feasible for a student with personal connections and a high degree of cultural capital than it is for more disadvantageously positioned students; a student of high socioeconomic status may not find working to be a necessity, whereas his poorer counterparts cannot afford the luxury of not working.

For a student who needs to work due to his financial situation while in school and/or one who does not know anyone in a position of power in an employment situation, available employment elsewhere may not be compatible with the time demands of being a student. For these students, working a job designed for students may be the only option—an option that associated student organizations provide. Employment in and of itself may be liberating, aside from issues of status and financial inequality with other students. Furthermore, this employment may be especially liberating for students who are in families or relationships where they lack control of, or access to, finances. So, it is not just the kids from the poor families who may benefit, but also the kids from rich families who do not provide any financial support for the students. These jobs can help people buy groceries without being so demanding as to disallow them to finish their studies.

Not only does employment by an associated student organization provide for student-oriented employment, but it also helps to level the field between students with and without significant work experience. Students and the recently graduated often have difficulty finding employment due to a lack of experience. In recent national surveys on employers in the United States, a large majority requires or strongly prefers some form of experience (Holzer 1996, 1999; Regenstein, Meyer, and Hicks 1998). Even when prior experience is not ranked as one of the most important qualities in an applicant, qualities often rated as highly important, such as a positive attitude, reliability, and a strong work ethic (Regenstein et al. 1998), are difficult to fully present on a paper résumé or brief interview. The qualities that are hard to judge on paper are often measured by prior success in the workplace (60 percent of employers require references from previous employers, and 40 percent require prior work experience (Regenstein et al. 1998)). Internships are preferred by 91 percent of employers, yet only 50 percent of companies that offer such programs have hired an intern in the past six months (Millennial Branding 2012).

It is understandable that employers look for candidates with experience when hiring, as this may provide a quicker turnaround on training costs and productivity, yet without being hired, students have great difficulty gaining experience and are thus stuck in a catch-22. Some students are able to get around this dilemma due to status connections (e.g., family members in a company, grew up with head of hiring, or money to pay for special training programs). This status disconnect, between students with experience and those without, can be combated by the hiring practices of associated student organizations. Because only students are hired by associated student organizations, it is presumed that this lack of experience is understood, and through employment with the organization, students are able to gain experience.

Insurance

Some associated student organizations, such as the ASMSU/Counsel of Graduate Students, offer discounted health insurance plans available exclusively to their students and dependents. An uninsured, working-age individual lacking health insurance possesses a 40 percent higher death risk than insured counterparts do, with just under 45,000 deaths annually being attributed to a lack of insurance (Cecere 2009). For some students, this may be a critical service due to the fact that they have been denied health insurance through those closest to them. A student may be married to an individual who takes advantage of her employer-offered or individually bought health insurance plan and refuses to add a spouse or any dependents to the plan. Similarly, parents or guardians may drop a dependent from their health insurance plan once he graduates and moves on to college. In either case or in any variation of the two, individuals and their dependents are denied health insurance by those in their social units who are capable of offering said service.

This leaves the uninsured to either remain uninsured, attempt to utilize governmental health insurance programs that she may not qualify for, or buy health insurance from private companies. Private health insurance is often unaffordable by the majority of individuals unless offered through employers. In 2010, the average annual premium in the United States for health insurance in the private, individual market was $2,580 (National Association of Insurance Commissioners 2011). In 2012, the average annual premium for employer-based health insurance totaled $5,384, with a $4,266 employer contribution and a $1,118 employee contribution (National Association of Insurance Commissioners 2013). With private insurance costing more than twice the price of employer-based health insurance plans, the associated student organizations/university offer another option through their insurance programs. Because of the massive market at universities, these organizations are able to offer discounted group rates. While it is true that to qualify for these rates one must be enrolled at the university and pay costly tuition, the discounted rate is a less expensive option than private insurance for a student who has been denied health insurance by those within her social unit capable of providing it.

Loans

Many associated student organizations, including the ASMSU/Counsel of Graduate Students and the Associated Students of California, Santa Barbara, offer short-term loans with extremely low interest rates to students. During the first six weeks of a semester at Michigan State University, students may take up to a three-hundred-dollar interest-free loan per semester with no questions asked to be repaid within sixty days (Michigan State University n.d.[d]). At the University of California, Santa Barbara, the loans are also interest free and max out at four-hundred dollars per quarter (University of California Santa Barbara n.d.[c]). According to the National Credit Union Association, similar short-term loans from federal credit unions may charge an application fee, require borrowers to be a member of the credit union, and charge an annual percentage rate of up to 28 percent (National Credit Union Association n.d.). Loans of these magnitudes generally do not make much of a dent in tuition costs but may be substantial in terms of living expenses. Going into debt to pay for living expenses may be the only option for some students. In situations in which money is hoarded, especially that earned by the victim, either by a spouse or family members, a student may have no other means of obtaining the needed funds for subsistence. Loans dispersed through associated student organizations, though they do not address the underlying issue, can serve as an emancipating agent by giving the student the needed resource he has been deprived of.

Loans may also be needed by students due to issues of status in the workplace. At some universities, students are only allowed to work a certain number of hours, whether they are employed by the university or not. This is particularly the case for international students. At Michigan State University, domestic students employed by the university may only work twenty-nine hours per week while school is in session, and international students only twenty (Michigan State University n.d.[g]). At the University of California, Santa Barbara, domestic students may work a maximum of twenty hours on campus per week (University of California Santa Barbara n.d.[g]), and international students may only work twenty hours per week while school is in session, regardless of whether the employer is the university (University of California Santa Barbara n.d.[e]). This cap on work hours may not allow for a paycheck capable of providing for all of the student's needs. By obtaining a loan from an associated student organization, the discrepancy between income and expenses can be gaped until the student experiences a change in status (e.g., graduation, new employment, a removal of the work hour cap in between semesters, or a new visa agreement) that eliminates the need for loans to supplement her income.

Student-Run Food Banks

University-associated food banks are a common service provided to students and the community, with many being fully operated by students. Michigan State University, the University of Nevada, the University of California, Santa Barbara, and many other institutions operate these banks. The process for utilizing a food bank's resources varies by location. At Michigan State University, a student wishing to receive items from the food bank checks in with her student ID and completes a short interview. With these responses, volunteer workers determine the quantity and type of products that would be of use to the student. The volunteer collects these items, while the student has a choice of items from a "free-will pick up" selection (Michigan State University n.d.[c]). At the University of California, Santa Barbara, a photo ID and signed self-declaration of income is required at every visit (University of California Santa Barbara n.d.[b]).

Access to a student-run food bank holds potential benefit to individuals in many circumstances. For students who do not come from a high social status or simply do not have the monetary resources his peers hold, a food bank may be necessary to compensate for the disparity in financial resources to acquire needed foodstuffs and household items. A tight budget may leave a student forced to choose between paying for school-related and subsistence expenses. The student using a food bank is able to supplement her income with products and diminish the need for difficult budget choices and sacrifices. As with associated student loans, money may not be an issue within the family unit, but an individual may be denied access to these funds or food products by an overbearing and controlling spouse or family member. By utilizing a food bank, the student suffering from this type of abuse need not rely on resources denied within the social unit, but acquire these needed items for herself.

Student Legal Services

When conflicts arise that involve legal matters, receiving adequate counsel is often a costly endeavor. At Michigan State University and the University of California, Santa Barbara, the associated student organizations have set up ways in which to provide these services for free to students. At Michigan State University, Student Legal Services provide lawyers that both give advice and represent a student in court, while the Student Defenders do likewise for cases within the University Judicial System (e.g., academic dishonesty, alcohol in the dorms) when a licensed lawyer cannot be provided (Michigan State University n.d.[d]). While the Legal Resource Center at the University of California, Santa Barbara does not provide court representation, a licensed attorney is available to provide legal education, advice, and information on a number of issues common to college students, including criminal citations, family law, immigration, and landlord/contract disputes (University of California Santa Barbara n.d.[a]).

Campus Accessibility

Physical disabilities may leave an individual to be reliant on others in many aspects of their lives including hygienic tasks, household chores, and transportation. This reliance may be so strong that opportunities in the workforce are severely limited. A college education may broaden the spectrum of employment, yet entering a college campus may not be feasible due to these same mobility issues. The Associated Students of Southern Oregon University is just one example of a student group that recognizes this barrier to education, fighting to make its campus accessible and in accordance with the Americans with Disabilities Act (Southern Oregon University n.d.[b]). Disability advocacy groups addressing both physical and mental disabilities exist across the nation at nearly, if not all, colleges and universities, as well as the countless groups existing outside of higher education.

In May of 2013, the University of California at Berkeley reached a settlement with one such advocacy group, Disability Rights Advocates, to better provide textbooks and alternative media for visually challenged students and offer reminders of the process to request these materials (as this is an additional step nondisabled students do not need to complete) (New 2013). At the University of Cincinnati, a wheelchair-bound student created a group to raise money for motorized wheelchairs for students, organized events in which students and administration spend the day in wheelchairs on campus, and traveled with campus architects to identify areas that can be improved (Associated Press 2013).

Bike Shop

Run as a nonprofit, the Bike Shop offered by the associated student organization at the University of California, Santa Barbara, is a student-funded shop that both repairs bikes and teaches customers bike safety and repair. Students and staff can get their bikes repaired for free or at low cost by bringing in their ID and bike (University of California Santa Barbara n.d.[d]). While not operated by the associated student organization, Michigan State University offers a very similar service. Much of the work is done by volunteer students (Michigan State University n.d.[f]), with seven thousand bikes being repaired in one year (Michigan State University n.d.[b]). Intended for education and safety, the bike shops inadvertently work to shrink the resource discrepancy that exists in the university community due to issues of status. At some universities, not all students are allowed to have vehicles on campus. At Michigan State University, students living on campus may not register a vehicle until they reach sophomore status (Michigan State University n.d.[e]). This creates an inequality in transportation between freshmen and older students. Students at the University of California, Santa Barbara may only park on campus during nights and weekends or if they live more than two miles from campus, live in a main campus residence hall, or qualify for graduate employee parking (University of California Santa Barbara n.d.[f]). Even if a student is allowed a vehicle on campus, it may not be an option financially, whether due to the cost of parking or owning a vehicle in general, thus allowing for another transportation inequality based on financial resources. This can compromise the quality of a student's life, as well as education, when events, opportunities, and classes are not able to be taken advantage of because of the inability to drive to or on campus and other forms of transportation are inadequate for certain ends. By helping to provide students with reliable and safe transportation via bicycling, the bike shops provide one option to help bridge this transportation inequality. With a bike, mobility is quicker and more accessible than with other forms of transportation given the circumstances (e.g., walking, skateboarding, and public transportation). This may allow a student to enroll in a class, accept a job offer, or network in an organization that previously he was not able to attend because other forms transportation were not available in a timely manner or did not exist.

Campus Escorts

The Associated Students of the University of Nevada (ASUN) offer the Campus Escort Service. Available to all students, staff, faculty, and visitors, the Campus Escort Service offers free, safe rides after normal business hours from or to any location on campus or within two miles of the campus, so long as the campus is either the beginning or ending point. With a clear goal, the "ASUN Campus Escort Service will make its priorities safety and personal safety awareness for its community on or off campus" (University of Nevada, Reno n.d.). There is potential for the service to provide protection against acts of violence perpetrated by strangers, as well as against others within one's social unit. A victim of violence at the hands of a spouse, family member, or roommate could utilize this service to leave the situation without involving the authorities.

More than just protection, the escort service opens up opportunities for those who otherwise lack transportation. For whatever reason an individual may not have access to transportation after normal business hours (e.g., she cannot afford a vehicle, it is not safe to use public transportation after hours, or a roommate or family member forbids use of the shared vehicle at the needed time), the escort service provides another means of transportation.

This may allow an individual to hold a job that otherwise was inaccessible. If employment is not an issue, then perhaps night classes become an option. Social events often occur after normal business hours. The escort service may allow an individual the opportunity to connect and network with others outside of the social unit that had previously limited his mobility via transportation.

Safe School Ambassadors Program

Developed by the education and youth development nonprofit Community Matters,[7] the Safe School Ambassadors program has been implemented in nine hundred elementary, middle, and high schools in twenty-eight US states and two Canadian provinces since beginning in 2000. In a two-day training program, socially influential students, called "alpha" leaders,[8] along with several adults who volunteer as program mentors, are taught skills enabling them to identify multiple forms of mistreatment, resolve and diffuse these situations, and support isolated and excluded students. This may occur through interrupting the mistreatment as it is occurring, preventing mistreatment by discouraging peers from such behavior, or obtaining adult help in complex and dangerous situations. By identifying and training diverse student leaders in these skills, the "inside-out" approach uses these collective social networks and leaders to change the climate and social norms around bullying and mistreatment.

The Safe School Ambassadors program is research based, influenced by the work of Dr. Wendy Craig, Dr. Ron Slaby, and Dr. Dan Olweus, three prominent names in the bullying prevention literature. Incorporated into the design of the program are the ideas that bystander involvement is key in reducing bullying, students with high social capital are the most likely to intervene in a bullying situation, and students largely determine the social norms that allow for bullying (Craig, Pepler, and Blais 2007; Olweus 1993; OMNI Research Training, Inc. 2004; Slaby 2005).

The Safe School Ambassadors program claims it brings the following specific benefits to schools: increased academic performance; less bullying, intimidation, harassment, insults, and deliberate exclusion; increased tolerance, respect, and cultural competence; fewer discipline problems, suspensions, and expulsions; better coverage and fewer "blind spots" on your campus; breaking the "code of silence"; more students bonded to school; cost savings; reduced liability; increased opportunities for community service and service learning; compliance with legislative and other mandates (to see the complete explanations behind these benefit claims, visit the Community Matters website[9]). An evaluation of the effectiveness of the program conducted by academics from Texas State University and the University of Georgia found, as compared to demographically matched control schools without the program and Ambassadors, increased rates of bullying intervention among male Ambassadors, an improved school climate among friends of Ambassadors, increased rates of intervention by non-Ambassador peers, and an average drop of 33 percent in suspension rates after program implementation (while the control schools saw a 10 percent increase in suspension rates during the same time period) (White et al. 2011).

With student ambassadors averaging at least two intervention actions per week, more than 2,400 interventions are seen in a single school over one school year. These interventions lead to fewer instances of bullying, harassment, cyber-bullying, gang-related activities, and other types of mistreatment; increased attendance and academic performance due to fewer suspensions (resulting in absence); bullied students feeling more safe at school; improved relationships among students; and increased respect for diversity. Testimonials from schools that have implemented the program report fewer suspensions and expulsions, decreased administrative time spent on discipline, and, at one school, a 67 percent decrease in office referrals, 84 percent decrease in detentions, and 85 percent decrease in suspensions (Community Matters n.d.[b]).

Costing around 5,600 dollars per school to train forty students and six to eight adults, obtaining the funds for implementing the Safe School Ambassadors program is a concern for schools. The Community Matters website provides links to foundations and corporations known for funding such programs, as well as general localities that may offer support, such as police departments, health sources, and faith-based institutions. Links to several online databases for grant seekers are also provided. In addition to presenting contact information and potential sources of funding, Community Matters provides a Funding Toolkit with sample templates for grant proposals and a Suspension Cost and Loss Calculator[10] for calculating the potential return on investment requested by many funders seeking to underwrite school improvement programs.

Conclusion

Collectives of similarly positioned individuals have long sought to address the needs of their own. Labor unions, LGBT groups, and the NAACP are examples of groups that are primarily made up of the type of person that the group actively seeks to help. Students are no different. Student organizations provide assistance specifically tailored to the needs of students, some of whom are at the mercy of others within their social units for food, money, rides, and so on.

Notes

1. 9 percent of Americans turned to religious organizations for assistance, while 7 percent turned to nonreligious community organizations.
2. Turning to religion and its associated deity(s) for emotional support certainly can happen outside the walls of a religious building, such as in the home during personal reflection and prayer.
3. Those requesting hygiene items must also stay through the lunch meal.
4. Similar to Goodwill Industries.
5. 64 percent reported a "great deal" or "quite a lot" of confidence in the military.
6. The most populous religion in America, followed by unaffiliated at 16 percent.
7. Community Matters focuses on improving the "social-emotional climate" of schools and communities by providing programs and services to aid youth and adults in achieving this end (Community Matters n.d.[a]).
8. These students are identified through student and staff surveys.
9. http://community-matters.org/programs-and-services/about-ssa-how-schools-benefit.
10. Based on student suspensions that equal absenteeism, which lowers a school's attendance-based revenue.

References

American Association of Retired People. n.d. "AARP Foundation." http://www.aarp.org/aarp-foundation (accessed August 29, 2014).

American Civil Liberties Union. n.d. "About the ACLU." https://www.aclu.org/about-aclu-0 (accessed August 29, 2014).

Associated Press. 2013. "Ohio Student Fights to Make Campus More Accessible." *The Intelligence Wheeling News-Register,* December 29. http://www.theintelligencer.net/page/content.detail/id/432003/Ohio-student-fights-to-make-campus-more-accessible.html?isap=1&nav=536 (accessed January 28, 2014).

Associated Students of the University of Nevada. n.d. http://www.nevadaasun.com (accessed August 29, 2014).

Barna Group. 2010. "Americans Say Serving the Needy Is Christianity's Biggest Contribution to Society." *Barna Group,* October 25. https://www.barna.org/barna-update/faith-spirituality/440-americans-describe-christianity-contributions#.UuanLPso7ct (accessed December 23, 2013).

Barna Group. 2011. "Do Churches Contribute to Their Communities?" *Barna Group,* July 13. https://www.barna.org/congregations-articles/502-do-churches-contribute-to-their-communities (accessed December 23, 2013).

Belding, Jennifer N., Malcolm G. Howard, Anne M. Mcguire, Amanda C. Schwartz, and Janie H. Wilson. 2010. "Social Buffering by God: Prayer and Measures of Stress." *Journal of Religion and Health,* 49(2):179–87.

Bulbulia, Joseph. 2004. "The Cognitive and Evolutionary Psychology of Religion." *Biology and Philosophy,* 19(5):655–86.

Cecere, David. 2009. "New Study Finds 45,000 Deaths Annually Linked to Lack of Health Coverage." *Harvard Gazette,* September 17. http://news.harvard.edu/gazette/story/2009/09/new-study-finds-45000-deaths-annually-linked-to-lack-of-health-coverage (accessed December 23, 2013).

CEDARS. n.d. "Mission and History." http://www.cedars-kids.org/about (accessed August 29, 2014).

Children's Defense Fund. n.d. "About Us." http://www.childrensdefense.org/about-us/#sthash.I82xz0zQ.dpuf (accessed August 29, 2014).

Christians Against Poverty. n.d.(a). "CAP Money Course." https://capmoney.org (accessed December 6, 2013).

Christians Against Poverty. n.d.(b). "The CAP Money Course." https://capuk.org/i-want-help/cap-money-course/course (accessed December 6, 2013).

"Church Welfare Program Helps People Help Themselves During Tough Economic Times." 2008. *The Church of Jesus Christ of Latter-day Saints,* September 17. http://www.mormonnewsroom.org/article/church-welfare-program-helps-people-help-themselves-during-tough-economic-times (accessed December 6, 2013).

City Rescue Mission of Lansing. 2013. "About Us." http://www.bearescuer.com/about.htm (accessed December 23, 2013).

Community Matters. n.d.(a). "About." http://community-matters.org/about (accessed December 23, 2013).

Community Matters. n.d.(b). "Safe School Ambassadors Program Overview." http://community-matters.org/programs-and-services/safe-school-ambassadors (accessed December 23, 2013).

Craig, Wendy, Debra Pepler, and Julie Blais. 2007. "Responding to Bullying: What Works?" *School Psychology International,* 28(4):465–77.

Ellison, Christopher G., David A. Gay, and Thomas A. Glass. 1989. "Does Religious Commitment Contribute to Individual Life Satisfaction?" *Social Forces,* 68(1):100–23.

Ferguson, Jane K., Eleanor W. Willemsen, and Maylynn V. Castañeto. 2010. "Centering Prayer as a Healing Response to Everyday Stress: A Psychological and Spiritual Process." *Pastoral Psychology,* 59(3):305–29.

Gallup, George H. Jr. 2003. "How Are American Christians Living Their Faith? Part III." *Gallup,* September 30. http://www.gallup.com/poll/9364/How-American-Christians-Living-Their-Faith-Part-III.aspx (accessed December 23, 2013).

Holzer, Harry J. 1996, 1999. *What Employers Want: Job Prospects for Less-Educated Workers.* New York: Russell Sage Foundation.

Hutt, Brian. 2011. "Churches Helping People Get on Top of Their Finances in Austere Times." *Christian Today,* January 12. http://www.christiantoday.com/article/churches.helping.people.get.on.top.of.their.finances.in.austere.times/27345.htm (accessed December 6, 2013).

Ironson, Gail, Rick Stuetzle, Dale Ironson, Elizabeth Balbin, Heidemarie Kremer, Annie George, Neil Schneiderman, and Mary A. Fletcher. 2011. "View of God as Benevolent and Forgiving or Punishing and Judgmental Predicts HIV Disease Progression." *Journal of Behavioral Medicine,* 34(6):414–25.

Krause, Neal. 2006. "Exploring the Stress-Buffering Effects of Church-Based and Secular Social Support on Self-Rated Health in Late Life." *The Journals of Gerontology,* 61B(1):S35–43.

Lampo Group. n.d.(a). "Financial Peace University." Dave Ramsey. http://www.daveramsey.com/fpu (accessed December 6, 2013).

Lampo Group. n.d.(b). "Frequently Asked Questions." Dave Ramsey. http://www.daveramsey.com/fpu/faq (accessed December 6, 2013).

Michigan State University. n.d.(a). "About." Associated Students of Michigan State University. http://asmsu.msu.edu/about (accessed December 23, 2013).

Michigan State University. n.d.(b). "Data." Michigan State University MSU Bikes. http://bikes.msu.edu/about/data (accessed December 23, 2013).

Michigan State University. n.d.(c). "Distribution." MSU Student Food Bank. https://www.msu.edu/~foodbank/distribution.htm (accessed December 23, 2013).

Michigan State University. n.d.(d). "Services." Associated Students of Michigan State University. http://asmsu.msu.edu/services (accessed December 23, 2013).

Michigan State University. n.d.(e). "Student Permits." Michigan State University Police. http://police.msu.edu/permits.asp (accessed December 23, 2013).

Michigan State University. n.d.(f). "Volunteer." Michigan State University MSU Bikes. http://bikes.msu.edu/get-involved/volunteer (accessed December 23, 2013).

Michigan State University. n.d.(g). "Working on Campus—Questions and Answers." Michigan State University Human Resources. http://www.hr.msu.edu/hiring/studentemployment/undergrad/QnA.htm (accessed December 23, 2013).

Millennial Branding. 2012. "Experience, Inc. Study." http://millennialbranding.com/case-studies/experience-study (accessed December 23, 2013).

Mochon, D., M. I. Norton, and D. Ariely. 2011. Who Benefits from Religion? *Social Indicators Research,* 101(1):1–15. http://dx.doi.org/10.1007/s11205-010-9637-0.

Myers, D. G. (2000). The Funds, Friends, and Faith of Happy People. *American Psychologist,* 55(1):56–67. http://dx.doi.org/10.1037/0003-066X.55.1.56.

National Association of Insurance Commissioners. 2011. "Average per Person Monthly Premiums in the Individual Market." The Henry J. Kaiser Family Foundation. http://kff.org/other/state-indicator/individual-premiums (accessed December 23, 2013).

National Association of Insurance Commissioners. 2013. "Average Single Premium per Enrolled Employee for Employee-Based Health Insurance." The Henry J. Kaiser Family Foundation. http://kff.org/other/state-indicator/single-coverage (accessed December 23, 2013).

National Credit Union Association. n.d. "Short-Term Loans." MyCreditUnion. govhttp://www.mycreditunion.gov/what-credit-unions-can-do/Pages/Short-Term-Loans.aspx (accessed December 23, 2013).

New, Jake. 2013. "In Settlement with Disabilities Group, Berkeley Will Improve Access to Course Materials." *The Chronicle of Higher Education,* May 8. http://chronicle.com/blogs/wiredcampus/in-settlement-with-disabilities-group-berkeley-will-improve-access-to-course-materials/43727 (accessed January 28, 2014).

Olweus, Dan. 1993. *Bullying at School: What We Know and What We Can Do.* Cambridge, MA: Blackwell. http://www.purdue.edu/odos/soc356x/articles/7BullyingatSchool.pdf (accessed December 23, 2013).

OMNI Research Training, Inc. 2004. "Bullying and Its Prevention: Implications for the Safe School Ambassadors Program Prepared by OMNI Research and Training, Inc. for Community Matters." http://community-matters.org/research-and-results/literature-review (accessed December 23, 2013).

O'Neill, Erin Olson, Jodi Gabel, Stephanie Huckins, and Jeanette Harder. 2010. "Prevention of Child Abuse and Neglect through Church and Social Service Collaboration." *Social Work & Christianity,* 27(4):381–406.

Pew Forum. 2008. "Summary of Key Findings." Pew Research: Religion and Public Life Project. http://religions.pewforum.org/reports# (accessed December 23, 2013).

Pew Research. 2009. "Faith-Based Programs Still Popular, Less Visible." *Pew Research Center,* November 16. http://www.pewforum.org/2009/11/16/faith-based-programs-still-popular-less-visible (accessed December 23, 2013).

Prevent Child Abuse. n.d. "About." http://www.preventchildabuse.org/Pages/About.aspx (accessed August 29, 2014).

Reeve Foundation. n.d. "About Us." http://www.christopherreeve.org/site/c.ddJFKRNoFiG/b.4409743/k.C825/About_Us.htm (accessed August 29, 2014).

Regenstein, Marsha, Jack A. Meyer, and Jennifer Dickemper Hicks. 1998. "Job Prospects for Welfare Recipients: Employers Speak Out." *New Federalism: Issues and Options for States,* No. A-25. http://www.urban.org/publications/308016.html (accessed December 17, 2013).

Simmons, Wendy W. 2001. "Though Very Religious, Americans Most Likely to Say Government Is Responsible for the Poor." *Gallup,* January 30. http://www.gallup.com/poll/2065/Though-Very-Religious-Americans-Most-Likely-Say-Government-Resp.aspx (accessed December 23, 2013).

Slaby, Ronald G. (2005). "The role of bystanders in preventing bullying." *Health in Action,* 3(6).

Southern Oregon University. n.d.(a). Associated Students of Southern Oregon University. http://www.sou.edu/assou (accessed August 29, 2014).

Southern Oregon University. n.d.(b). "Issues." Associated Students of Southern Oregon University. http://www.sou.edu/assou/issues.html#ada (accessed January 28, 2014).

Strawbridge, William J., Sarah J. Shema, Richard D. Cohen, and George A. Kaplan. 2001. "Religious Attendance Increases Survival by Improving and Maintaining Good Health Behaviors, Mental Health, and Social Relationships." *Annals of Behavioral Medicine,* 23(1):68–74.

University of California Santa Barbara. n.d.(a). "About." Associated Students Legal Resource Center. http://legal.as.ucsb.edu/lrcservices (accessed December 23, 2013).

University of California Santa Barbara. n.d.(b). "About Us." Associated Students Food Bank. http://foodbank.as.ucsb.edu/eligibility (accessed January 28, 2013).

University of California Santa Barbara. n.d.(c). "Emergency Loans." The Associated Students of the University of California Santa Barbara. http://www.as.ucsb.edu/resources/emergency-loans (accessed December 23, 2013).

University of California Santa Barbara. n.d.(d). "Home." Associated Students Bike Shop. http://bikeshop.as.ucsb.edu (accessed December 23, 2013).

University of California Santa Barbara. n.d.(e). "F-1 Student Employment." Office of International Students and Scholars. http://oiss.sa.ucsb.edu/Students/F-1StudentEmployment.aspx (accessed December 23, 2013).

University of California Santa Barbara. n.d.(f). "Student "C" Permits." University of California Santa Barbara Transportation and Parking Services. http://www.tps.ucsb.edu/permStudent.aspx (accessed December 23, 2013).

University of California Santa Barbara. n.d.(g). "Student Employment." University of California Santa Barbara Library. http://www.library.ucsb.edu/human-resources/student-employment (accessed December 23, 2013).

University of Nevada, Reno. n.d. "Campus Escorts." http://www.unr.edu/campus-escort (accessed December 23, 2013).

White, Alexander, Katherine Raczynski, Chris Pack, and Aijun Wang. 2011. "Evaluation Report: The Safe School Ambassadors Program: A Student Led Approach to Reducing Mistreatment and Bullying in Schools." Community Matters. http://community-matters.org/research-and-results/literature-review (accessed December 23, 2013).

Conclusion

This book has dealt with a large, acute, yet mostly hidden problem of society: the everyday suffering of people. We tried to shift attention away from the tribulations people face as employees dominated by their employers, as college applicants at the mercy of the institutional process, as people being required to pay taxes they deem unjust and/or arbitrary, and as voters who feel their "options" are merely different shades of the same. We turned our attentions toward the tribulations that manifest within social units (that which people face as a spouse or a child, as a member of a school, as a resident of a long-term facility, etc.). Generally speaking, our quality of life can be divided into two parts: one depends on the "macro world," and involves mostly anonymous interactions, and the other involves the "micro world," and mostly consists of interactions with people we know well. Of course, micro- and macro-world suffering are intertwined. Often, the suffering caused by developments in the macro world (e.g., unemployment) generate suffering in the micro world (e.g., humiliation of the unemployed person within his family).

Happiness and Suffering Perspective

There are two perspectives in quality-of-life studies. One focuses on the level of happiness people experience. This is usually measured/reported in some sort of aggregate form, such as the "happiness index" of different nations or the average happiness levels of several categories of people. Another perspective focuses on people's sufferings. These two perspectives deal with somewhat opposite ends of the emotional spectrum. In the last few decades, several publications on happiness have drawn the attention of professionals as well as the public. One of the most authoritative writers on happiness, Martin Seligman, published several books: *Learned Optimism: How to Change Your Mind and Your Life* (1991), *Authentic Happiness: Using the New*

Positive Psychology to Realize Your Potential for Lasting Fulfillment (2002), *Flourish: A Visionary New Understanding of Happiness and Well-Being* (2011), and others. The collective *Handbook of Emotions* (2000 and 2008) mostly pays attention to "positive emotions." The very prestigious *International Survey of Values,* conducted over the last thirty years by the University of Michigan under the leadership of Ronald Inglehardt, also mostly ignores negative emotions, persistently seeking information about the level of happiness people experience in the different countries of the world. Sonia Liudmirsky's book *How of Happiness* (2012) has recently become particularly popular in this literature.

The Focus on Dependence

Unlike the "happiness approach," the "suffering approach" pays special attention to the dependence of human beings on each other, and considers people to be the primary cause of the sufferings of others—Sartre's "hell is other people" concept. Of course, this perspective does not deny that, in many cases, the dependence of one individual on others not only is necessary for the functioning of elementary forms of social life, such as marriage or friendship, but also brings material and psychological benefits to the dependent person.

People's dependence on others cannot be reduced to dependence based solely on wealth, race, and/or gender. The unequal possession of certain factors, such as a person's physical strength and health, access to information and intellect, sexual attraction, and networks of friends, divides people. Those with a lot of these resources are depended on by those who have less; those with less can be considered "weak" or "vulnerable" people.

Negative emotions bombard people in everyday life and come to the individual, whatever her position in the macro world. People's quality of life depends to a very great degree on how well they are able to avoid or lessen suffering.

Yearning for Power Over Others Yearning for Independence and Solitude

Meanwhile, most of social science disregards the important psychological feature of the propensity for one to yearn for power over others, and to derive pleasure from exercising this power once obtained, even if illicit means are used to acquire and apply the power. Exerting power and, in some cases, even the abuse of power can be the basis of one's identity, and highly related to one's self-esteem. It is probably those social scientists and the writers who described the human relations in concentration camps—Soviet, Nazi or Maoist—who plunged deeper than any others into the analysis of the psychology of people who used their power toward the exploitation and torture of others. The chiefs of the camps liked to recruit their aids from the prisoners (the notorious capos) exactly from these sort of people (see, among others, Cohen 1988; Kogon 2006; Suderland 2013; Todorov 1996).

While some people yearn to wield power over others, others (or the same people in a different context) try to minimize contact with others and even desire to be alone, or at least to be very selective in the choice of company. The desire to live alone is not only found among people on the autism spectrum or those struck by deep religious devotion. We observe this phenomenon among the most ordinary people. The urge to avoid contact is typical of many people who, being concerned about their self-esteem, try to avoid personal contact with those who can undermine it. The addiction to various devices—including opportunities to watch the world through the Internet or play innumerable games by oneself, as well as the opportunity to communicate with people without having direct, "face-to-face" contact through social networks—also explains the growing tendency to play alone.

Suffering in the Macro and Micro Worlds

The "suffering perspective" demands that researchers provide a clear distinction between the macro and micro worlds. We can talk about the macro factors that bring suffering to large cross-sections of the world's people: lack of freedom, political persecution, unemployment, hard working conditions, starvation, lack of access to material and cultural goods, low level of health services and education, and all sorts of discrimination based on real or perceived demographic characteristics. These forms of suffering can be partially attributed to the economic, political, social, and cultural structures in which people live their lives.

It is important to specify that those who happen to be the victims of suffering in the macro world are not individually chosen as targets by those who control the resources. Those doling out abuse in macro society do not know their victims personally; the oppressor and victim do not have emotional relations. For example, the CEO of a corporation does not usually order the firing of people whom she knows personally. It is probable that only high-level political opponents are known to their oppressors.

In the micro world, this dynamic works differently. Here, the suffering (besides the factors related to the dominant social structures) is generated by the members of formal and informal groups. These people are familiar to each other; the source and target of pain, humiliation, and discomfort will be known to both parties. The inequality in the distribution of resources among people who know each other has an additional negative impact on human relations; the abuse of power by people known to a victim is particularly bitter.

The idea of "victims" also acting as the perpetrators of various forms of abuses of power has escaped the attention of both scholars and public opinion. Social scholars' attention to the victims of victims has been minimal. The "victims" are often almost absolved for their pernicious behavior because they themselves suffer from the abuse of others. Meanwhile, various forms of abuse are being perpetrated by victims, who take revenge with Schadenfreude—not against those who abuse them but on other vulnerable people who lack the means to resist such abuse. The abuse of power perpetrated on victims provides them with an exemplar of behavior that may not have been known to them before. Hazing, as it happens in dormitories, schools, fraternity houses, military barracks, and prisons, is one of the rituals exhibiting this process.

No less important is social scientists' ignorance toward the role of fear in interpersonal relations, a powerful factor in the life of many social units (e.g., the family or school), which is generated mostly by an inequality in the distribution of resources. We detailed this phenomenon to a great degree in the special chapter on the resource of physical strength.

Of course, inequality in the distribution of resources can be considered the ultimate cause of the suffering found in the macro world too. This inequality, however, appears to be anonymous and rather abstract, and those who suffer from low income, inadequate medical services, or the impossibility of satisfying the requirements to enter a good college usually cannot credibly blame their suffering from these issues on their relatives or colleagues. Besides, ordinary people (or even scholars) rarely operate with the concept of resources when they discuss suffering derived from racism (to be a member of the dominant race or ethnic group in the specific situation is a sort of resource), from a lack of sexual partners, or from life in small cities where there are few opportunities for young people.

Individual Suffering and a Category of Sufferers

While human history is filled with people who have suffered in all strata of life, any society with minimal commiseration for the tribulations of others has paid special attention to those who are permanently suffering. In contemporary media (contemporary sociological literature mostly ignores this category), these people are termed *weak and vulnerable*. In this book, we tried to separate the sources of suffering into those that can be located in the macro world and those that can be located in the micro world. The weak and vulnerable people in each world can be very different, even if some people are weak and vulnerable in both. Of course, in some frames, all human beings can be regarded as weak and vulnerable, with, say, respect to death or even unrequited love. Contrary to the views described above—as well as contemporary media and the bulk of social scientists who do take on the issue—we do not equate weak people with the materially poor, or only with those who hold subordinate positions in a macro hierarchy. Still, whatever criterion of stratification is used, a higher proportion of those who belong to the lowest strata of the population are classified as weak people.

The Concept of Resources

In our attempts to describe the suffering of people, particularly suffering that arises in the micro world, we felt it was very important to reconsider the concept of resources and make it more inclusive. Until now, using a "resource perspective" to study a society was mostly limited to the concept of economic capital. With the appearance of the concept of social capital, and some of the works of Pierre Bourdieu and Amartya Sen, the concept of resources was greatly enlarged (though not enough, in our opinion). We have tried to convince our readers that along with economic, cultural, and political capital, the unequal distribution of many other resources—social status, intellect, education and information, physical strength, sexual attractiveness, place of residence, etc.—have a tremendous effect on people's everyday lives.

The Cause: The Scarcity of Resources

It is important to note that almost all resources are scarce. Food or shelter have been treated as scare resources by human society since its emergence because everyone needs them, and society is not set up in such a way that everyone gets to have them. Where demand outpaces supply, even in cases where demand is far from universal, scarcity arrives. Obviously, not everyone who wants to own artistic masterpieces, like paintings by Rembrandt or Picasso, can possess them. Not everyone can attend the performance of a star at Carnegie Hall either, as there are only so many seats, so much physical space, so many people allowed inside per the fire code, etc.

The relative deprivation of resources creates a problem for human life. For centuries, utopian thinkers dreamed of creating a society free of scarcity, where there was an abundance of resources for all. The famous slogan of the early Communists—"from each according to his ability, to each according to his need"—ignored the existence of scarcity and supposed that, with equal distribution, all human needs in a developed Communist society would be satisfied.

The drama of the scarcity of resources increases with the uneven distribution of resources. Those who have more of a certain resource at their disposal also have the opportunity to use other people— presumably those with less of it—in pursuing their interests. The concept of scarce resources is applicable to micro society in the same way that it is applicable to macro society. In both cases, an inequality in the distribution of resources generates social conflicts and abuses of power.

The Legal and Illegal Use of Resources

The exploitation of additional resources for egotistical interests can be legal or illegal (abuse of power). The owner of resources in a capitalist society has the right to use his resources—economic, cultural and political—to become even richer or to satisfy his various needs. He is often able to do this at a faster rate and to a higher degree than those without resources. An apparatchik in a totalitarian society uses his position in the hierarchy to access, at the expense of others, various limited resources such as closed good stores; the best educational, health or cultural institutions; or currency for travel abroad.

In social units, unequal distribution of resources among family members—money, free time, food—can also be "legal" (i.e., endorsed by the members of the family; how this endorsement is achieved is another issue). The character of personal relations changes radically when a husband establishes control over family money against the will of other family members, or when a superior orders her subordinates to perform domestic chores for her under the threat of an illegal punishment.

The Abuse of Power in Interrelations

The violation of people's rights in the macro world is the subject of a steady flow of social studies, whereas the abuse of power inside social units by those who have more resources than others has only gained modest attention in the last few decades. The "1 percent" is the symbolic group of people who "exploit" the numerical majority in the macro world, while, in the micro world, a significant part of the population participates in abusing its power over the majority in one way or another. In fact, millions of people who are themselves discriminated against in macro society abuse their power inside their families, schools, churches, hospitals, street gangs, etc. Only feminists have paid regular attention to this issue, focusing mostly on issues inside the family. This book has tried to cover this lacuna.

The Protection of Society

Contrary to more optimistic views, the abused people in social units are unable, as a rule, to protect themselves against the aggressive actions of others who possess a relative abundance of some key resource. Debates about the expedience and size of the help that weak and vulnerable people within social units should receive is now one of the fieriest debates in public life in America and other Western countries. The views vary. Libertarians see intervening in the lives of individuals as an infraction of people's privacy and, therefore, almost completely refuse to render aid to people suffering inside social units. Advocates of the active protection of weak and vulnerable people, on the other hand, reject the argument that uses the violation of privacy as a justification for society's indifference toward people's suffering, insisting that society should intervene in people's "private life."

The last few decades have seen a humanitarian tendency in American public opinion ("political correctness" is one of its manifestations). There has been a substantial increase in the movement that advocates assistance for people who are suffering in various social quarters, often invisibly (it is important to note that the level of assistance to such people in socialist countries with egalitarian tendencies, such as the USSR, East European socialist countries, or Cuba, was always relatively high).

Several forces participate in helping people who are suffering inside social units in the United States: the federal government, local governments, civil society, self-help organizations, and individuals. Coordinating the activities of all these forces is not an easy task. Take, for instance, the coordination of the activities of federal and local bodies in the fight against bullying, as seen in the government help chapter of this book. For the most part, the federal government has placed the onus on states and schools to enact bullying prevention strategies, using funding as both a carrot and a stick to steer the process. At the same time, federal civil rights laws protect against discrimination or harassment based on sex, race, color, national origin, religion, or disability. Only when bullying leads to allegations of discrimination or harassment based on these characteristics are victims able to seek federal resources. Spirited debates continue to take place, revolving around the application of law in the defense of civil rights for the protection of people against bullying.

Of the various forms of civil society helping suffering people in the United States, we chose to illustrate the role of religious organizations. While Americans strongly believe that the greatest responsibility for aiding the poor falls on the government, they also believe that organized religion can do the best job of feeding the homeless and providing services to the needy, including those who are weak in micro space.

The activities of Christian organizations illustrate this point. They offer people lodging by welcoming them into their churches, shelters, and even the homes of their members. Once there, they may also offer food, clothes, shoulders to cry on, people to connect with, and more. Someone can also have food delivered to their private home, or pick it up at a soup kitchen or at the end of a food drive. Likewise, needy people can get Christmas gifts through the church. Churches have clothing and toy drives to build up their supplies; people know to take their extra clothes and Tickle Me Elmo dolls to churches when their children have outgrown them. There are men's groups, women's groups, teen fellowships, support groups for the grieving, and, of course, individual counseling. These assemblies not only offer spiritual nourishment but also help build more secular connections that can facilitate the completion of everyday tasks. There are church-run sports leagues and game nights. Sometimes, churches will even come together to pay the bills of a needy member. So, someone with no strength who gets beaten up by family members can turn to the church for a safe place to sleep. A woman without access to the family bank account can receive money from the church to pay for the medication she needs but that her husband refuses to buy. A person turned away from the rest of society can find refuge in the welcoming spiritual nourishment provided by the clergy.

Other organizations, collectives of similarly positioned individuals, help their members to overcome the problems that emerge in their milieu resulting from an inequality in the distribution of resources. Labor unions, LGBT groups, and the NAACP are examples of groups that are primarily made up of the type of person that the group actively seeks to help. Students are no different. Student organizations provide assistance specifically tailored to the needs of students, some of whom are at the mercy of others within their social units for food, money, rides, etc.

Inequality in the distribution of resources inside social units, which creates a fertile environment for the abuse of power over the weak and vulnerable, is one of the most important social problems in contemporary society. This issue deserves the permanent attention of social science and the public.

References

Cohen, Elie A. 1988. *Human Behaviour in the Concentration Camp*. London: Free Association Books.

Kogon, Eugen. *The Theory and Practice of Hell: The German Concentration Camps and the System Behind Them*. New York: Farrar, Straus, and Giroux.

Levi, Primo. 1993. *Survival in Auschwitz*. New York: McMillan.

Neurath, Paul Martin. 2005. *The Society of Terror: Inside the Dachau and Buchenwald Concentration Camp*. Boulder, CO: Paradigm Publishers.

Shalamov, Varlam Tikhonovich. 1981. *Graphite*. New York: Norton.

Shalamov, Varlam Tokhonovich. 1980. *Kolyma Tales*. New York: Norton.

Solzhenitsyn, Aleksandr I. 1975. *The Gulap Archipelago, 1918–1956: An Experiment in Literary Investigation*. Books 1–3. New York: Perennial.

Suderland, Maja. 2013. *Inside Concentration Camps: Social Life at the Extremes*, trans. Jessica Spengler. Oxford, UK: Polity Press.

Todorov, Tzvetan. 1996. *Facing the Extreme: Moral Life in the Concentration Camps*. New York: Henry Holt.

Vladimov, Georgi. 1978. *Faithful Ruslan: The Story of a Guard Dog*. New York: Simon and Schuster.

Index